THE QUINTESSENTIAL ENGLISH ECCENTRIC:
ROBERT OAKESHOTT

THE QUINTESSENTIAL ENGLISH ECCENTRIC:
ROBERT OAKESHOTT

Hero of the Hungarian Revolution
Champion of African Development
and Employee Ownership

KEVIN SHILLINGTON

BROWN
DOG
BOOKS

Published under licence by Brown Dog Books and
The Self-Publishing Partnership Ltd,
10b Greenway Farm, Bath Rd, Wick, nr. Bath BS30 5RL

www.selfpublishingpartnership.co.uk

ISBN printed book: 978-1-83952-584-1
ISBN e-book: 978-1-83952-585-8

Cover design by Kevin Rylands
Internal design by Tim Jollands

Printed and bound in the UK

This book is printed on FSC® certified paper

MIX
Paper | Supporting
responsible forestry
FSC
www.fsc.org
FSC® C013604

Contents

'Write me as one that loves his fellow men'
(Leigh Hunt, "Abuo Ben Adhem", 1834)

Acknowledgments

I have acquired many debts in the writing of this biography, not least from Robert Oakeshott's family, friends and colleagues who have given so generously of their time and trust in interview, for which I am very grateful. Foremost among them are his sister-in-law Charlotte Oakeshott who entrusted me with Robert's letters, primarily to his mother, and his voluminous personal and business papers, and, besides personal memories and help through emails, provided the early contacts that set me off on the search for interviewees; his only surviving sibling, his sister Rose Gaunt, whose unique memories of her brother have been invaluable; and the late Charles Keen, the first of my interviewees, who not only helped to provide a framework for the story of Robert's life, but also recommended further contacts and willingly responded to my numerous email queries.

My sincere thanks to the many further interviewees who helped me to understand something of the personality and work of Robert Oakeshott, for he was so much more than the anecdotes of his humorous eccentricities that all remember so fondly. Many are directly acknowledged in the footnotes, but all contributed to my deeper understanding of the man and his work. Listed in the order in which the interview took place, I acknowledge and am grateful to: Tatiana Mallinson, Charlotte Oakeshott, Veronica Oakeshott, Anthony George Gater, John Jolliffe, Caroline Cox-Johnson, Mike Tiller, Katy Emck, Anne Charlton, David Wheatcroft, Lalage Wakefield, Neville Wakefield, David Erdal, Ann Tyler, Norman Watson, David Ellerman, Geraldine Norman, Graeme Nuttall, James Freeman, Mick Pearce, Patrick Burns, Isabella Tree, Jasper Gaunt, Ian Smith, Margaret Elliott, Nat Martin, Sara Flanders, Alison Kirton, Charles Burrell, Helena Gaunt, Neves Pereira, Cynthia Rickman, William Clarke, Jane Willoughby de Eresby, Roddy Bloomfield, Johnny Grimond, Anne Cotton, Éric de Rothschild, Aleksandra Mrčela, Quentin Seddon, Liz van Rensburg, John Pell, Lawrence Cockcroft, Eugenie Kostourkov, Jesse

Norman, Andrew Gunn, Mike Hawkes, Kit Bingham, Jacky Bodley, Mary Clemmy, Richard Gott, Laszlo Szesztay, Pippa Virdee, Marina Johnson, Ian Talbot, Isabel Oakeshott, Anstice Oakeshott, Gavin Rankin, and Thecla Mallinson.

My special thanks to Johnny Grimond, who, besides providing vivid memories of Robert, sent numerous photographs and lent me his papers containing, among other things, his correspondence with Robert; and to Sir Gavin Rankin for sending me copies of his father's Hungary-related papers and photographs. Thank you to Emi Claris for researching and translating documents concerning Robert and the Hungarian Revolution, and to Claudia Kovacs for her translated interview with an eyewitness to those events of 1956. Thank you all those who sent me photographs; those I have been able to use are acknowledged in the captions. Thanks, too, to the archivists of Tonbridge School, Kent, of Balliol College, Oxford and to Rosie Al-Mulla of the Peter Mackay Archive at the University of Stirling, all of whom kindly sent me copies of their records concerning Robert Oakeshott; the staff of the British Newspaper Archive for access to their copies of the *Sunderland Echo*, the *Financial Times*, *The Manchester Guardian* and *The Economist*; and Sally-Anne Shearn and Natasha MacMahon of the Borthwick Institute for Archives at the University of York for a day's most fruitful research in their recently acquired archives of the Joseph Rowntree Social Service Trust (now renamed the Joseph Rowntree Reform Trust).

I am particularly grateful to Johnny Grimond, David Erdal and Andrew Gunn for kindly reading an early draft of the completed manuscript. Their comments and valuable advice have been much appreciated, although responsibility for any errors of fact or interpretation remains mine alone.

My particular thanks, as ever, to Pip for her constant support and help through lockdowns and beyond.

Kevin Shillington,
October 2022

Preface

It was Tuesday 30 October 1956. The Hungarian Revolution had been raging for a week and the might of the Soviet Army was being pushed back from central Budapest. That morning Oxford student Robert Oakeshott lay on a bed of loaves of bread in the back of a food truck as it made its way clandestinely through numerous roadblocks to the heart of the revolution. With him was fellow student Ian Rankin, and between them they carried two suitcases containing two million doses of penicillin. They had no idea what they would find at their destination, but Robert felt a strong sense of duty to provide some moral support to his fellow students in Hungary.

As his friend Anne Charlton has observed of Robert Oakeshott's character, 'There are those who leave when there's a revolution, and those who go towards it. Robert was one of the latter.' And from the time of his decision at the age of twenty-four to hitch-hike into Budapest at the height of the student-led revolution, Robert indicated his intent to be a man who would leave his mark upon the world, a man who would dedicate his life to helping his fellow men, and women, in their efforts to make the world a better place.

His apprenticeship was six years as a journalist with the *Financial Times*, most of it working as a roving foreign correspondent; and when the moment came, he seized his chance to go to Africa, where he made a significant contribution to Zambia's emergence as an independent nation. Then to Botswana, where Patrick van Rensburg introduced him to an alternative view of education combined with the concept of cooperative production. This set Robert on the road to finding a 'third way' for economic enterprise – a cooperative model of industrial production through which he could help his fellow men achieve justice, fairness and industrial democracy in their place of work.

After a brave initial experience with a building cooperative and apprenticeship-training enterprise in Sunderland, in the North East of England, he founded Job Ownership Limited (JOL), which became his major life's work occupying, as it did, most of the rest of his formal working life, promoting the expansion of employee-owned businesses. By the time of his official retirement in 1998, he was recognised across Europe and in North America as a much-sought-after expert on the industrial democracy of employee ownership. The number of such businesses had expanded, thanks to Robert, to the extent that it was time to change his JOL thinktank into a membership organisation, the Employee Ownership Association (EOA).

The story of Robert's life is full of energy, initiative, humour, and love for his fellow human beings. He had a 'robust wit' and a great sense of fun. Described as 'perhaps the most convivial and worst-dressed man of his generation', his friends relished 'his intoxicating (and often intoxicated) discourse'.[1] He was a social reformer and philanthropist, who had the courage to challenge the status quo if he found it lacking in fairness and justice, and he played a leading role in the founding of several prominent charities. Although he received no public recognition from the British State, the fact of his full-length obituaries in all the leading broadsheets is an indication of the high esteem in which he was held within the wider British establishment. He did receive one award, however, which he valued highly: the 'Hero of Freedom' medal, presented to him by the Hungarian Government on the occasion of the fiftieth anniversary of the Revolution of 1956, where it all began.

* * *

I first heard of Robert Oakeshott while researching my biography of Patrick van Rensburg, and it quickly became clear that Oakeshott was a key figure in the success of the alternative education that van Rensburg was developing in Botswana in the 1960s. Historian Neil Parsons pointed me in the direction of the Robert Oakeshott Memorial Lecture of 2016 where I met Robert's twin brother Evelyn, who agreed to lend me Robert's

---

[1] Charles Keen, 'Robert Oakeshott obituary', *The Guardian*, 3 August 2011.

letters to his mother during his time in Botswana. He also remarked that their father had had a biography and, in his opinion, Robert deserved one too. The germ of an idea was sown. Unfortunately, Evelyn did not live to see my van Rensburg biography, but on returning the letters to his widow, Charlotte, the subject of a Robert Oakeshott biography arose again. The family had many more letters from Robert to his mother, and a few to his father, from his schooldays right up until his mother's death in 1976, as well as boxes of his business papers through to the early 2000s. And Charlotte assured me that I could borrow the lot.

Besides Robert's personal and business papers, I have had access to the archives of the Joseph Rowntree Social Service Trust, from whom Robert received regular grants. The archives, housed in the Borthwick Institute for Archives at the University of York, contain several voluminous files of correspondence between Robert and the trustees through the 1970s and 80s.

I have also drawn heavily on personal interviews with Robert's family, friends, and colleagues from all stages of his life. These have been particularly helpful in understanding Robert's personality. A common theme that shone through in many interviews, besides his powerful intellect and energy, was his humorous eccentricity, illustrated in numerous anecdotes; but also his great kindness, generosity, and love for his family and friends – a love that was returned in spades.

Although there has been much to write about the vast range of Robert's adult challenges and achievements, in writing this biography I have had to go back to the beginning of his life, and to his family background, to discover something of the making of this extraordinary man.

* * *

CHAPTER 1

Background and Childhood

Robert Oakeshott and his twin brother Evelyn were born into an upper-middle-class English family on 26 July 1933. Their mother, Noel Rose Oakeshott, was the daughter of Dr Robert Oswald Moon, a consultant cardiologist and Fellow of the Royal College of Physicians (FRCP) who, besides owning a house at a prestigious address in Marylebone, London W1, also leased as his family home the large Manor House of Copse Style, on a farm in the village of Aston Tirrold in South Oxfordshire. The twins' father, Walter Fraser Oakeshott, was at the time of their birth a master at Winchester College, one of the more prestigious public schools in England.[2] He was of similar class background to his wife, but without the wealth.

Walter's own father and grandfather had both been medical doctors, but both had died young. His grandfather, Dr John Oakeshott, had been killed in a street accident in Northumberland Avenue, Central London, in 1879 at the age of 41. He had had a substantial medical practice in the well-heeled North London suburb of Highgate but no financial capital, and he left his widow with seven daughters and two sons, and no source of income. His shocked friends and grateful patients rallied round. They arranged for a residential road connecting Highgate Cemetery, of Karl Marx fame, with Hampstead Heath to be named Oakeshott Avenue in his honour. More importantly, they also raised a trust fund to pay for the education of the youngest of the children, two teenage sons, both of whom

---

[2] The term 'public school' in England stems from their historic charitable origins. In fact, they were and still are the country's élite private schools, though they do offer scholarships to the wider public who cannot afford the fees, but who show a high level of academic attainment.

were determined to follow their father into the medical profession.[3]

The elder son, Walter, Robert's grandfather, graduated from St Bartholomew's Hospital as a gold medallist in 1889. Without the capital to purchase a medical practice in England, he accepted a salaried position as medical officer to a mining company in South Africa. This took him to Lydenburg in the mountainous eastern region of what was then the Afrikaner ('Boer') Republic of the Transvaal (today's Mpumalanga Province). Around the turn of the century, he married a local woman of Scottish-American descent named Kathleen Fraser. Dr Walter Oakeshott tended to patients on both sides in the Anglo-Boer War (1899–1902), and after the war their third child, the father of Robert Oakeshott, was born in 1903. He was named, after both parents, Walter Fraser Oakeshott.

In 1905, Dr Oakeshott caught pneumonia and died aged, like his father, just 41, leaving his widow Kathleen with three small children: a daughter Maggie and two sons, Jack and Walter, but no source of income.

Kathleen seems to have been aware that her late husband's family were of a class in England where private education was regarded as essential for a son to reach his full potential, preferably at one of the top public schools of England, followed by the University of Oxford or the University of Cambridge. She had no formal education herself, but she knew that to do the best for her children, she must travel to England and place herself in the hands of the Oakeshott family. They responded to her bold decision and provided her and the children with somewhere to live and modest financial support.

Two of her late husband's sisters, who had married well but had no children of their own, undertook to pay for the boys' education. Funds were limited, however, and from a young age Walter, the future father of Robert Oakeshott, knew that if he was to do well, it could only be by his own efforts and on academic merit. After prep school in Hastings, he won a scholarship to Tonbridge School in Kent where he thrived, developing a love for the Classics as well as for English Literature, English Language,

---

[3] Robert Oakeshott's ancestry and parentage are drawn largely from John Dancy's biography of Robert's father, *Walter Oakeshott. A Diversity of Gifts* (Michael Russell, Norwich, 1995).

and Medieval History. In his final year, in 1922 at the age of nineteen, Walter was head boy and won a Domus Exhibition to study Classics at Balliol College, Oxford.

Classics at Balliol was a four-year degree, divided into Mods (classical language and literature) for five terms and Greats (classical history with classical and modern philosophy) for seven terms. Walter had what he later described as a 'marvellous' time at Oxford. He enjoyed the academic work immensely and was well-prepared for the hard work that Mods and Greats entailed. He came down from Oxford in 1926 with a double first. Both his sons were to study Mods and Greats at Oxford, but the father had set the bar high for them to follow.

Like many Balliol men, Walter decided to pursue a career in education. His first teaching post was at Tooting Bec, a new state secondary school in Wandsworth, South London, where he taught Latin, English, and History. His social life at Oxford had centred on amateur dramatics with the Balliol Players, specialising in the Greek tragedies, and he and some of his Balliol friends now formed the Holywell Players so as to continue with their performances. And it was through the Holywell Players that Walter got to know Noel Moon, who joined the group as leader of the chorus.[4]

Noel, the eldest of four daughters and one son of Dr Robert Moon, was born in 1903, the same year as Walter Oakeshott. She was educated at Isabel Fry's Farmhouse School at Mayortorne Manor in Buckinghamshire. Fry was a Quaker, social activist and progressive educationist who believed in teaching through practical and physical work, as well as through book-learning in the classroom.[5] This was similar to the role that Robert was to develop in Botswana in the 1960s. Thus Noel, who took for granted the presence of servants in the home, learned the physical practicalities of milking a cow and other skills in dairy farming at school, alongside Latin, modern European languages, History, Literature, and Art, with additional tuition in classical Greek. She was thus able to go up to Oxford the same

---

[4] Dancy, *A Diversity of Gifts*, p 33.

[5] For Isabel Fry (1869-1958), see https://en.wikipedia.org/wiki/Isabel_Fry - [accessed, 16 March 2021].

year as Walter to study Classics as a 'home student', residing with DG Hogarth, the Keeper of Antiquities at the Ashmolean Museum. After Mods in 1924, she switched to a Diploma in Classical Archaeology, at which she thrived, coming top of her year in 1926 and winning a scholarship from the Gilchrist Educational Trust to study at the British School in Rome. By the end of 1926 she had published her first article on the 'Greek Vases of the Red-Figured Style'.[6] Thus she was at least the intellectual equal of Walter Oakeshott.

Through the Holywell Players, Noel and Walter saw each other regularly, and by the end of his first term at Tooting Bec in December 1926, Walter had proposed marriage and she had accepted. On the salary, however, of a junior member of staff at a state secondary school, living with his mother and sister Maggie at their flat in Prince of Wales Mansions, Battersea, Walter was in no position to support a wife, especially one used to living with servants, and her father withheld his approval.

Walter would clearly have to up his professional role and salary, and as a first step in that direction, after one year at Tooting Bec, he secured a post at the Merchant Taylors' School in the City of London. He was now within the private sector, at least, and on the first rung of the ladder towards the headmastership of a major public school. Noel, meanwhile, spent the first half of 1927 at the British School in Rome, and returned for further study at the Ashmolean and at the Hellenic Society in London. Her article, 'Some Early Italian Vase-Painters', published in the *Papers of the British School at Rome*, established her reputation as a highly-regarded specialist on the art and influence of the classical Greek vases of southern Italy.

At the end of that year, Noel's father finally relented and agreed to his daughter's marriage to Walter Oakeshott. The wedding took place on 11 April 1928 in the village church of Aston Tirrold. Balliol friend Hugh Keen was Walter's best man, and Noel's only brother, Penderel Moon, gave his sister a two-seater car.[7] After honeymooning on the Continent, they

---

[6] Published in the *Anglican Church Magazine*: Dancy, *A Diversity of Gifts*, p 34.

[7] Dancy, pp 44-46.

took up residence in the Prince of Wales Mansions flat in Battersea, which Walter's mother and sister had vacated to stay with relatives.

Walter had been acutely aware of his father-in-law's reluctance to accept him into the family, and he in turn felt uneasy within Noel's instinctively aristocratic social milieu. Walter was to develop a concern for the welfare of those at the other end of the social scale – something that would in due course be picked up and followed by his son Robert. He believed it was the right of everybody to understand something of economics, and while still at Bec's in Wandsworth he had begun lecturing in economics at the Working Men's College in Camden, North London. He later converted his Working Men's lectures into a book, *Commerce and Society: A Short History of Trade and its Effects on Civilization*, intended to promote the study of economics on the school curriculum.[8]

In 1931, after a brief spell in educational administration in Kent, during which Noel gave birth to their first child, Helena Kathleen, Walter returned to teaching, this time to the prestigious public school of Winchester College. Over the next seven years, he achieved an amazing range of scholarly work, in addition to teaching and supervising the removal of the College Library to a more suitable, though no less ancient building. He catalogued the library, discovered a manuscript copy of Malory's *Le Morte d'Arthur* in the Fellow's Library and wrote the first detailed description of it. He also began a study of the medieval 'Winchester Bible' that was in due course to become the peak of his scholarly and literary career, and in recognition of which he was later knighted.

The Great Depression of the early 1930s had impacted heavily on the working class, and unemployment had reached crisis levels. In 1936 William Temple, Archbishop of York, invited Walter to join a panel of enquiry to investigate the impact of unemployment on working-class communities. Walter obtained a year's sabbatical from Winchester College and threw himself into the task. He conducted most of the interviews with unemployed people in Merseyside and the North East, and he ended up writing three-quarters of the final report. It was published in 1938

---

[8] Published by Oxford University Press in 1936.

under the title *Men Without Work*.[9] Although the outbreak of war in 1939 temporarily solved the unemployment position for the duration, *Men Without Work* strongly influenced the Beveridge Report of 1942 that laid the foundations for the post-war welfare state.

It was during his time at Winchester, when Walter was heavily absorbed in his teaching and scholarly work, that Noel gave birth to the twin boys, in a nursing home in Wokingham, on 26 July 1933.

* * *

Walter registered the births as Walter Evelyn Fraser for the first-born (by twenty minutes) and Robert Noel Waddington for the second. Within the Oakeshott and Moon class and family milieu the eldest son was always regarded as the more important, and this was demonstrated through the names that Walter chose for his two sons. The elder was named after his own side of the family, the male having seniority over the female, and the younger boy after Noel's family, Robert for Noel's father and Waddington for her mother's maiden name. This lack of equality in terms of seniority was to be keenly felt by Robert. It did not affect his relationship with his brother; that was always very close; but it did with his father. At least throughout his youth and early adult life, Robert was to feel that his father regarded him as second fiddle to his twin brother, and in due course he was to rebel against it. On the other hand, judging by his letters to her, Robert was to develop a strong and close relationship with his responsive and supportive mother.

The twins appeared at first to be identical. Indeed, it is said that initially their father, Walter, could not tell them apart. The family gave them the nick-names Castor and Pollux, the 'Heavenly Twins' of Greek and Roman mythology who are represented in the constellation Gemini: Castor for Evelyn and Pollux for Robert. Castor was soon corrupted to Cargie or Cargs and within the family and among close friends it stuck with Evelyn for life. The nickname Pollux, on the other hand, did not survive, due to its

---

[9] *Men Without Work: A Report made to the Pilgrim Trust. With an Introduction by the Archbishop of Canterbury and a Preface by Lord Macmillan* (Cambridge University Press, 1938).

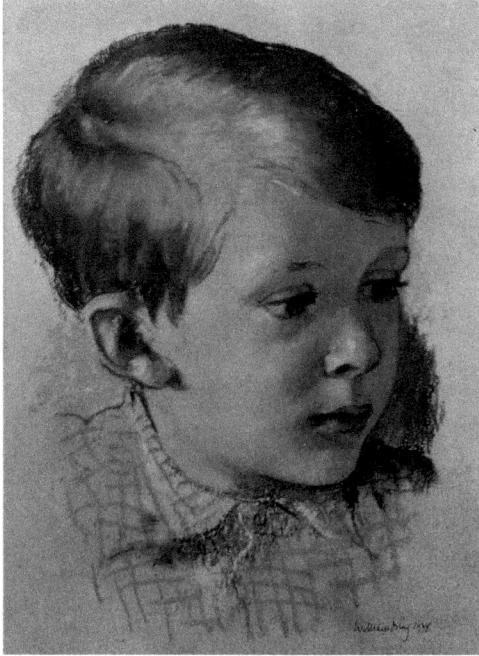

Robert aged five.
(By kind permission of the Oakeshott family)

obvious similarity to 'bollocks'.

It had been a long and difficult labour for Noel and, according to John Dancy, Walter's biographer, 'for their first few years [the twins] were a great drain on the health and energy of their mother'. During the initial months after the birth, Noel spent some time with her three small children at the Moon family home of Copse Style.[10] While Noel had been in labour, her own mother's health was failing, and ten weeks after the birth of the twins her mother, Ethel Waddington Moon, died. By staying at Copse Style during those months, Noel would have been able to see her mother during her final weeks and provide some moral support to her father. Soon,

---

[10] Dancy, *A Diversity of Gifts*, p 58.

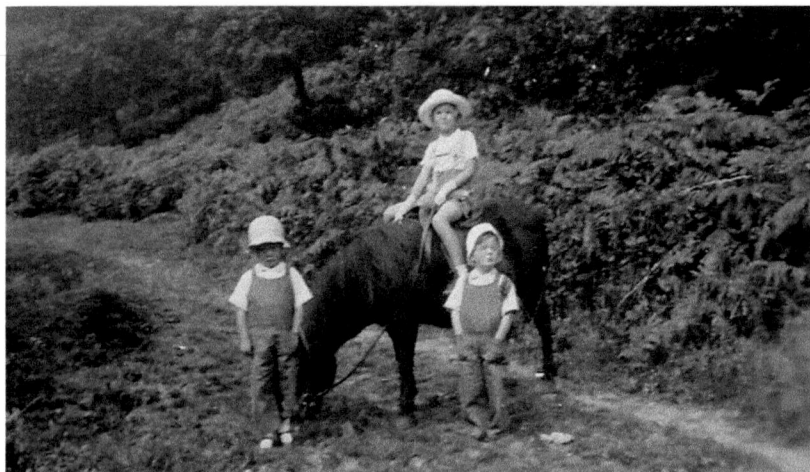

Evelyn, Helena and Robert, Holford, Somerset, 1937.
(By kind permission of William Clarke)

however, she settled back into the small house in Winchester where her time was fully occupied with looking after her three small children. Copse Style became a place to escape to with the children during holidays, to enjoy the countryside and the attention of several servants and her devoted father.

Within a few months of their birth, it became clear the twins were far from identical. They were socially inseparable, in ways that only twins can really understand, but during their early childhood years, the differences in character, physique and appearance became increasingly apparent. A family photograph shows them aged four, with Helena, six, on holiday in Somerset in the summer of 1937. Robert is clearly the shorter, with his dungarees overflowing his shoes. While Evelyn stands quietly, perhaps shyly, for the photograph, Robert, wearing glasses for poor eyesight, stands with both hands stuffed in pockets, looking up as if to say, 'Where's the next bit of fun?'

* * *

When Walter returned to Winchester from his sabbatical in 1938, with the twins now five years old, he was ready to go for a headmastership. And when the opportunity arose later that year, he secured the position of High Master of the Mercers' school of St Paul's in Hammersmith, West London, starting in January 1939.

With war pending and the expectation that London would be heavily bombed, most of Walter's first year at St Paul's was taken up with preparing to evacuate the entire school from Hammersmith to the countryside. The Mercers' Company, the premier livery company of the City of London and which owned St Paul's, acquired the use of part of the Easthampstead Park mansion of the Dowager Duchess and the Duke of Devonshire. It was in the village of Crowthorne, south-east Berkshire, close to Wellington College, whose governors agreed to share many of their facilities, and it

Robert, Rose, Evelyn and Helena with Grandfather Moon at Copse Style.
(By kind permission of William Clarke)

9

was 'within cycling distance [35 miles] of West London'.[11] It was a similar distance from the Moon family home in Aston Tirrold.

The boys, Robert and Evelyn, had initially attended an unregistered dame school in Aston Tirrold, run by a Miss Gordon. The spring of 1940, however, found them under the care of Miss Kathleen Collins and a Miss Amos at Little Thorpe in Aston Upthorpe, a little village conjoined to Aston Tirrold. This was their first experience of boarding away from home, and it was probably occasioned by their mother Noel's imminent expectation of the birth of her fourth child, a daughter, Rose Jocelyn, born at the end of May. Once her children had passed the baby stage, Noel tended to be a hands-off sort of mother, and on this occasion she left Rose from a very early age with a wet-nurse under the supervision of her father at Copse Style; and with the boys and Helena at Little Thorpe, she spent most of her time at Crowthorne where she helped with the running of the school's boarding houses.

Little Thorpe appears to have been a very small school, a personal arrangement, run for a select band of children. Besides the twins and Helena, their cousin Janet Mackay[12] was also there, as well as some other boys. And as the war news from the Continent grew ever grimmer, with the British Army retreating to Dunkirk, it is clear from Robert and Cargie's first letters home to their mother that they were happy at Little Thorpe. The boys were enjoying the little 'chicins' in the orchard, besides receiving a visit from 'arnt emly' (Noel's youngest sister Emilie, who was then living in London) and learning from Miss Collins the wonderful game of cricket. Robert wrote of 'having great fun' reading, while in a covering letter Miss Collins referred to Evelyn playing 'quite a good scale' on his 'Shepherd's pipe', with Robert 'getting on too' and always 'keen to excel'.[13]

It is believed that at some point that year or the next they may have attended a grammar school in Wallingford, not far away in the Thames

---

[11] Dancy, *A Diversity of Gifts*, p 94.

[12] The daughter of Noel's sister Margaret.

[13] *Oakeshott Letters*, Robert and Cargie to their mother, Little Thorpe, 17 May 1940, with covering letter from Kathleen Collins.

Valley, before transferring to their respective boarding prep schools at the age of eight.[14] The decision to separate the twins, fashionable in those days, would have been on the grounds they would be better able to develop their full potential as individuals. It is not clear what prep school Evelyn attended, but at some stage during those war years, he was to be found at what was called 'Hillside School', at Crownpits House in Godalming, near Guildford in Surrey. Robert, on the other hand, was sent to that part of Dulwich College Preparatory School which had been evacuated to North Wales.

Robert's destination was an old Victorian coaching inn, the Royal Oak, which is today an AA-recommended hotel in Betws-y-coed, the 'Gateway to Snowdonia National Park'. In those days it was rather run-down and neglected, which was perhaps why it was available for hire as a temporary school. It was certainly not prepared to receive a new cohort of pupils and Robert had to take with him not only his bedclothes and mattress, but the bedstead as well, sent in advance by train. Robert's first letter home says a lot: 'Dear Mummy we get a penny for every mouse and tuppence for every rat'.

Beyond that, the boys' only surviving letters home from their prep schools are those they each wrote describing the celebrations on Victory in Europe (VE) Day, 8 May 1945. Evelyn's, from Godalming, was smartly written with a full account of how they had heard the speeches of Prime Minister Churchill and the King on the wireless and had celebrated the day with 'lots of spam sandwiches and a great big hunk of corned beef', plenty of playtime and, in the evening, a huge public bonfire on Hascombe Hill, a few miles south of Godalming.

Robert's letter from North Wales described his celebrations in two long sentences – something that, properly punctuated, was to characterise his adult writing. His day was a slightly more modest affair, which was nevertheless 'super fun'. There were no spam sandwiches or corned beef, but, like Evelyn, they had plenty of playtime, heard the speech of 'Mr W.C. Churchill', gathered firewood and laid the foundation for their own bonfire in a nearby field. Then at 9.00 in the evening,

---

[14] Rose Gaunt, personal information.

… we heard the King after that we went to the field for the bonfire it was simply super some men came with thunder flashes the bonfire lasted till 11.15 then we came back and had baked potatoes and coco we read in bed till 12.15 a.m. then we were shut up.

That summer, the school returned to Dulwich in South London, and Robert remained there for one more academic year.

Meanwhile, in the summer of 1944 Walter, planning for after the war, had bought Bell House, a substantial old farmhouse in the village of Mersham, just north of Romney Marsh in Kent. It needed a lot of upgrading and repair work, but though smaller than Copse Style, it stood in a large garden with its own orchard. At only eight miles from the sea, and with great scope for country walks and cycling, the house was ideal for family holidays. Bell House was ready to receive its first family visitation for the Easter holidays of 1946.

One of Rose's earliest memories of Robert was possibly from this time when he would have been twelve, coming up to thirteen. She remembers him sitting in a room reading a newspaper from cover to cover. Already, at that age, he had become a compulsive reader, always with a book on the go, and through the reading of newspapers he kept himself well informed on a huge range of subjects. School holidays at Bell House tended to be the only time all six of the family were together. It was difficult for Rose to feel part of the others, being seven years younger than her nearest siblings and spending much of her time living with her grandfather at Copse Style. During the school holidays she would join the others for long walks on country lanes and footpaths, swimming in the murky water of a river and crossing the railway line by an old footbridge. On one occasion the boys dared her to sit on the edge of the bridge when the next train came through. Longing to gain acceptance into their world, Rose accepted the challenge and sat terrified on the parapet while the smoking steam train roared underneath. Years later, when he was up at Oxford, Robert was to acknowledge and regret he had not treated her better as a child, and they became firm friends.[15]

In 1946 Walter secured the Headmastership of Winchester College, a

---

[15] Rose Gaunt, interview, 7 October 2020.

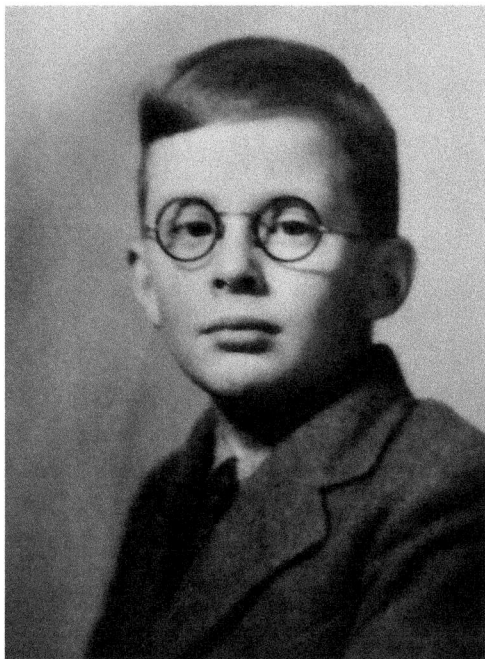

Robert in about 1945.
(By kind permission of the Oakeshott family)

position he would take up that September. By then the two boys, aged thirteen, were ready to go up to public school themselves, though they were still to be sent to separate institutions. Evelyn joined his father at Winchester College; Robert went to Walter's alma mater, Tonbridge School in Kent.

CHAPTER 2

Tonbridge School
1946–1951

It did not take Robert long to settle into life and work at Tonbridge. He was allocated to Ferox House – *ferox* meaning spirited or headstrong – and Robert did not disappoint in this regard. Through his letters home and those he wrote to the school magazine, *The Tonbridgian*, his school reports, and his contributions to the Debating Society over his five years at the school, one can discern the evolution of his complex adult personality.

His reports for his early years at the school revealed an emerging young man who, though full of energy, was not yet sure of his academic interests or confident of his intellectual ability. He showed plenty of enthusiasm, but his work tended towards the slapdash: 'unmethodical … very untidy … erratic', and 'punctuation did not appeal to him'. His English oscillated between the archaic and the colloquial; too often, what might have been good work 'degenerated into rhetoric as though his essay was a speech before a rather emotional debating society'. As for his French, something he would have found useful in his adult life: 'knowledge adequate; interest doubtful'. His Housemaster, Mr JM McNeil, remarked that he "trails his coat' a bit on occasions', a little too ready to challenge, though 'he certainly keeps the anti-classical faction on the alert'. But despite this criticism, 'his enthusiasm remains unabated'.[16]

In his letters home he experimented with both his style of handwriting and his mode of expression. When writing to his father, his handwriting

---

[16] *Oakeshott Papers*, Tonbridge School, reports: Michaelmas Term 1949, Lent 1948, Lent and Summer 1949. 'Trails his coat', an expression no longer in fashion, meaning to behave or speak in a manner deliberately designed to provoke a reaction, origin: 18th-century Dublin politicians.

tended to be neat and precise, while to his mother he wrote in a more flowing script that, when written at speed, becomes quite difficult to decipher. To his father, he would mention music, his progress in Latin or Greek, a play he had seen, or a book recently read. It was almost as if he were trying to live up to his father's expectations, an impossible task in his view; whereas to his mother, he would mention anything that came to mind. And if there was nothing much to report, he would write, '… our existence has tended to be Prosaic', or that the week had been 'an undulating succession of ups and downs'. At times he appeared to be striving for an upper-class manner of speech that was already going out of fashion. But he was still full of mischief; for instance, in what was probably his second year, he wrote to his mother,

> …Would you believe it I am going probably to the Vienna Art Exhibition [in London] on June 9th chiefly for the purpose of playing Bridge on the train and having a good time in town. Well, well I think that's all the news.[17]

* * *

Robert's time at Tonbridge coincided with the establishment and consolidation of the Cold War. By 1946, the wartime alliance of Britain, France and the United States with the communist Soviet Union – essential for the defeat of Nazi Germany – was already showing signs of strain. During 1947 it became clear the Soviet leader, Joseph Stalin, was intent on establishing communist control over those Eastern European countries which the Red Army had 'liberated' at the end of the Second World War. Robert, already a voracious reader, kept himself up to date on world affairs from the range of broadsheet newspapers available at Tonbridge. He absorbed the Western perspective on the Cold War and this was reflected in an early contribution to the school Debating Society.

The motion, 'That this House considers it preferable that our Country should ally with Russia rather than America', led to a lively debate. With the war with Germany less than two years in the past, most of those who spoke in the debate, for or against, did so in terms of military alliances,

---

[17] *Oakeshott Letters*, RO to his mother, undated, but probably early Summer term 1948.

past and present; or which side suited Britain now in terms of trade, for the country was in dire need of economic recovery. Robert, on the other hand, saw the issue through the spectrum of the evolving Cold War. His contribution was short and to the point. He simply 'advised against an alliance with communism'.[18] He does not appear to have explained his position. He may have felt it was self-evident: communism was the antithesis of the ideals of liberal democracy which he had grown up to believe were the basis of civilised life.

Later, when it looked as though Stalin was threatening an invasion of Marshal Josip Tito's Yugoslavia, Robert composed a poem entitled 'On Current Affairs' which included the lines,

> What boots it now that Rachel cries
> For children killed by Kremlin lies?
>
> …
>
> The western moon is on the wane
> Who knows if it will wax again
> But sure it is our lamps will fade
> If Stalin walks in this Belgrade.[19]

It began to become apparent while Robert was at Tonbridge that he felt somewhat overshadowed by his parents – both were academically and artistically brilliant, his father in particular, head boy of Tonbridge, a double first at Oxford and now Headmaster of Winchester. Feeling unable to match up to his father Robert decided, while still in his first year, that an essential characteristic of his personality at school was to be a rebellious wit. In a debate that proposed, 'That History in our Schools is a waste of time', he contributed a pithy one-liner, telling the House that he 'could not conceive that it was better to know the formula of M&B than the fundamentals of our history'.[20] The reference may have been to the algebraic

---

[18] *The Tonbridgian*, 1947, pp 203–4.

[19] *Oakeshott Letters*, from a poem composed at Tonbridge, enclosed in an undated letter home.

[20] *The Tonbridgian*, 1947, p 204.

formula $y = mx + b$, the bane of first year Mathematics, or, more probably, to the drug sulphapyridine, known as M&B 693. Whichever, it no doubt raised a laugh, as was intended. Oakeshott was establishing his style. On another occasion, he mocked the nonsense being spoken on the serious topic of war or peace by telling the House that he 'had had a bath, on which theme he elaborated at considerable length and with considerable irrelevance'.[21] But it was also here in the Debating Society that Robert honed his ability to argue any subject from any angle, a skill that later in life gave scope for much stimulating and amusing conversation.

He soon attracted around himself a small coterie of close friends at Ferox House, among them Loder Bevington, John Russell and Keith Payne, the latter two both mentioned in letters home to his mother. They enjoyed his amusing company, and this encouraged Robert to play to his audience, something he was to carry into his undergraduate years at Oxford. Many years later, in fact at the time of Robert's memorial in 2011, John Russell wrote that he and his other two friends still retained 'very fond and sometimes extremely funny memories of Rods and his exploits both at school and wherever in the holidays'.[22]

Although Robert shone within his circle of close friends, he seldom shone on the sporting field. His early enjoyment of cricket at Miss Collins' establishment was rewarded at Tonbridge by the presence in Ferox House, just one year ahead him, of that future great cricketing legend Colin Cowdrey who in his first year, at the age of thirteen, had played in the school's First XI and taken seventeen wickets over the two innings. Pride in the House hero Cowdrey fed into Robert's life-long love of cricket, although he himself never starred in the game. Physical sport was not his forte. He gained the basic athletics standards in various running events, including the mile and the 100 yards, but that was the pinnacle of his sporting achievement at school. In his third or fourth year he played 'rugger' in the 4th XV against local Judd School's 2nd XV. Tonbridge 'won handsomely', 29–8.

---

[21] *The Tonbridgian*, 1951, pp 281–2.

[22] From an email to Robert's niece Anstice Oakeshott, dated 1 December 2011.

... of which [he wrote to his mother] yours truly scored 3! In many ways it was a unique occasion for me. It is the first Away match I have played in at anything and I've no doubt it will be the last.

Nor was he keen on the Cadet Corps, describing hours of drill in the drill squad as 'hell on earth'.

Robert did, however, enjoy playing an improvised game for two players, probably of his own invention, called 'Prep-room Hockey'. It was played with cricket bats or golf clubs and a fives ball,[23] the object being to score against one of the two doors at opposites corners of the room. Apart from that, there were no rules. The hazards of the game were increased by the presence of a ping-pong table in the middle of the room. 'I play the game a lot,' Robert reported to his mother 'and apart from a few bruises and cuts am none the worse.'[24] He was to gain a lifelong reputation for playing and inventing wild and impromptu games, one of his favourites being 'Johnny, Johnny strike a light', an outdoor night-time game in which players hunt around in the dark, trying to catch the selected 'Johnny' who would light a match to indicate where he was or to further confuse the hunters.[25]

By the beginning of his fourth year at Tonbridge, he was firmly established as the great 'character' of Ferox House and seemed to think he could get away with anything.

In the Michaelmas term of 1949, he carelessly failed to turn up to a meeting about an upcoming Cadet Corps camp. Later, he discovered the meeting had allocated which platoons they would be in for the camp. All his friends in the house had been posted to a motor-bike platoon, while in his absence, he had been relegated to a 'rather awful platoon concerned with the RA [Royal Artillery]'. He went to the commanding officer and requested a transfer, which was promptly refused. Fresh from the rebuff, he complained at lunch about the unfairness of it all and said 'half-jokingly' to

---

[23] Similar to a cricket ball, in this version of the game.

[24] *Oakeshott Letters*, from undated letters to his mother.

[25] The game is described in Tim Heald, *Blue Blood Will Out* (MysteriousPress.com, 2013), p 5.

Mrs McNeil, the Housemaster's wife, that he would write to the Secretary of State for War, Mr Shinwell. Mrs McNeil 'related an occasion when she had written to the Chancellor of the Exchequer'. Thus encouraged, Robert promptly dashed off a letter of complaint to the Secretary of State for War. Manny Shinwell was an outspoken Scottish working-class politician in Clement Atlee's post-war Labour Government and was no doubt outraged to be troubled by such a groundless and trivial complaint emanating from one of those 'over-privileged bastions of private education' and he, or one of his senior civil servants, reported the matter to Robert's father, the Headmaster of Winchester College.

Walter Oakeshott's letter to his errant son does not appear to have survived, but Robert's response has. It is a revealing letter of self-analysis that explains much about both his character and his relationship with his father. Writing in neat and careful script Robert assured his father that he would 'certainly try to follow' what he called his 'advice', before adding,

> I am very sorry that you have had so much trouble over this but I think I can say *while not being over confident* that you will hear of it no more.[26]

Not only was his promise covered by a caveat, but he saw this as an opportunity to get certain things off his chest. After relating the circumstances leading up to the Shinwell letter, including Mrs McNeil's story of writing to the Chancellor of the Exchequer, he told his father he had sent off the letter without giving a second thought to its possible repercussions:

> … It was sent in a sort of reckless bravado I suppose. Partly also I sent it because I thought I should be admired by other boys for doing so – which was in fact the case. And this is I think at the root of the matter. It is as if I was quite a different person here from what I am at home. Here I always seem to be sort of acting a part and always trying to shine among the other boys while at home you as it were 'know me [for] who I am'. At home it would be useless to put on an act for you'd all see through it and I should just be thought ridiculous.
>
> Perhaps [he added] it is because at home I sort of feel in my bones that

---

[26] *Oakeshott Letters*, RO to his father, 11 October 1949 (my emphasis).

I play rather a 2nd fiddle to Cargie that here I try and get my own back by standing out among the others. That then is the reason I think behind the letter. I don't of course pretend it's an excuse which it isn't but I think it's the reason at the bottom.

He concluded the letter by informing his father that 'the Raquets [*sic*] is on Dec. 6 so I hope that you will be coming down then'. His father did not feel this was the time to reward his son with a visit, and he did not visit on Racquets Day.

* * *

It is notable that at the end of that term, Robert's teachers observed that he had 'turned an important corner'. According to his school reports, in his final two years he applied himself assiduously to his studies. His progress in both Latin and Greek was 'meteoric', and he was regularly top of his class in Latin and Greek unseens. No one in his Greek class showed a more 'alert & intelligent interest in the work', which he tackled 'with considerable power and enthusiasm'. He had not lost any of his sense of fun. He still loved to show off, having developed what his English and History master referred to as 'a very distinguished style, ... well adapted to evading the matter in hand'. Much of his work was still marked by 'amusing foolery', while his 'rhetorical prose would bludgeon any examiner into a state of insensibility'. What impressed them all, however, were his prodigious powers of energy and concentration. 'His energy', remarked the Head 'even if it is not yet organized, is very refreshing ... The torrent is now flowing very fast the right way, with no loss of turbulence or vigour. He has been a pleasure to teach, and the results are fine.'[27]

Robert's Housemaster, J M McNeil, was amazed that he could pack so much into his day. And because of this ability, he was able to ensure that his academic work did not dent his enjoyment of providing amusing companionship for his friends, nor did it interfere with his other interests.

---

[27] *Oakeshott Papers*, Tonbridge School, Michaelmas Term 1949, Lent Term 1950, and Summer Term 1950.

Indeed, McNeil observed that he treated time 'as a valuable and rational commodity', not to be wasted.[28]

Among other things, he took to the stage, and like his father, was active in founding a drama club. In May 1950 he wrote a satirical critique of the school's Dramatic Society for neglecting 'the Muse of Drama … Shakespeare or, if you prefer, Bacon', in favour of Drinkwater, Barrie and Shaw. And as if to show what a dramatic society *ought* to be doing, he and his friends formed *The Ferox Players*. But then, without a hint of irony, they chose to put on for their first production, Shaw's *The Devil's Disciple*. Robert took the lead role, of which *The Tonbridgian*'s drama critic observed,

> Oakeshott sustained the exacting rôle of the hero, DICK DUGEON [*sic*], with courage and intelligence, and his stage presence improved as the play proceeded. He did not always quite carry off the dash and swagger of this attractive Shavian rake and he will be a better actor when he can lose a

---

[28] *Oakeshott Papers*, Tonbridge School, Michaelmas Term 1950.

Robert (third from right) as Dick Dudgeon, in G B Shaw's 'The Devil's Disciple',
The Ferox Players, Tonbridge School, 1950.
(From the Oakeshott papers, by kind permission of the Oakeshott family)

certain nervous restlessness and learn the value of repose on the stage.[29]

At the end of the summer term of 1950 Robert turned seventeen, and he and his closest Ferox friends, Keith Payne, John Russell and Loder Bevington, decided to take a fortnight's summer holiday, hitch-hiking through France. Robert had been given some money by his 'Uncle Pendy' – (later Sir) Penderel Moon, Noel's only brother, who had served many years in the imperial Indian Civil Service in the Punjab, and in 1950 was under contract to the independent Government of India. His mother had suggested he spend the money on foreign travel. Payne's father had a boat in which he sailed them across the Channel from Tilbury to Ostend. From there they caught a train to Paris, and after a day in the French capital they set off on the road, hitch-hiking southwards. They managed to reach the south coast, where they bathed in the Mediterranean before heading back home. It certainly seems to have whetted Robert's appetite for foreign travel, something that was not readily taken for granted in the 1950s.

The following Michaelmas term – in his final year at Tonbridge – Robert's teachers had high hopes for his coming Oxford entrance examinations in January. He applied for a scholarship in Classics to Balliol College, his father's alma mater. His teachers felt he was 'coming on at a furious pace'. He was still writing 'some odd things at times', but there was 'a fine attack and vigour about his work'. His Latin master's advice for him in January was to 'remember that nobody expects him to be clever all the time'.

In the event 'his writing impressed the Balliol examiners'. His tendency to show off with irrelevant verbosity was in danger of suggesting that his brilliance was merely superficial, but this impression 'was corrected by his viva'.[30] He did not get a full scholarship, but won a Domus Exhibition, which would have particularly pleased him, as it put him on a level with his father.

During his final Lent term, after winning his place at Oxford, the Tonbridge Debating Society staged a mock political election. Interestingly,

[29] *The Tonbridgian*, September 1950, p 250.
[30] *Oakeshott Papers*, Tonbridge School, Lent Term 1951.

Robert, South of France, August 1950.
(John Russell-Rocca)

the timing of the debate lay between the general election of February 1950, narrowly won by Labour, and that of October 1951, narrowly won by the Conservatives. The Tonbridge 'election' debate covered the whole range of potential candidates: Liberal, Communist, Scottish Nationalist, Rationalist, Socialist, Anarchist and Conservative. Robert stood for the Rationalists. He dismissed Scottish Nationalism for being 'out of date by at least 350 years', which produced a laugh. As for Parliamentary Government, it was in his opinion 'becoming slightly ridiculous', and he supposed it was only 'being kept alive for the Festival of Britain';[31] another laugh. Rule by Rationalists, he claimed, would usher in a Golden Age of peace, freedom and universal toleration. 'Certainly, in such a state,' he told his audience, 'No one would be compelled to watch athletic functions'; more laughter.[32]

The debate was narrowly won by the Anarchist, who had likewise made sweeping promises of freedom and happiness for everyone. Oakeshott's Rationalist came a creditable second.

---

[31] The Festival of Britain, an entertainment and celebration of post-war recovery, ran on London's South Bank, from May to September 1951.

[32] *The Tonbridgian*, 1951, pp 10–11.

CHAPTER 3

National Service

1951–1953

In the summer after leaving Tonbridge, Robert decided to reward himself with a holiday on the Continent. This was long before cheap flights and regular holidays in southern Europe. The only means of travel available was by train or boat, or a combination of the two. His ultimate destination was unclear. He had no idea of relative distances or how long the journey would take. He allowed himself a month, setting off in the first week of August, just after his eighteenth birthday. Nothing was booked in advance; his only plan was to travel by the cheapest means possible. He had an unnamed companion for the early part of the journey, at least as far as Venice, which they reached by third class rail through France and northern Italy. From Venice he headed on alone for Trieste, then in dispute between Italy and the new Socialist Federal Republic of Yugoslavia.

Robert had a romantic vision of working his passage on a cargo vessel from Trieste to either Greece or Turkey. In the end he had to settle for the slow train through Yugoslavia, stopping off first in Ljubljana, the Slovenian city with which, much later, he was to become familiar. Once in Greece he found he could communicate satisfactorily through his knowledge of Ancient Greek. He spent about a week exploring the sites that were so familiar to him through his Classical studies, before crossing the Mediterranean aboard a 'cattle boat' to Benghazi. Libya at that time was still under post-war British military administration and, as ever, Robert's 'amazing luck' held up. He came across a retired Indian Army officer who arranged for him to be put up at the British Army base at Benina Airport, just outside Benghazi. Here he had free bed and lodging, with meals in the canteen. The British military establishment gave him access to several free transport possibilities. He was sorely tempted by a cargo flight to Tehran, which he very nearly accepted, thinking that from there he could reach Uncle Pendy in India, overland, in about a week. 'He would have been rather surprised to see one! [he confided to his mother] But then I thought about getting back & wiser councils, you will be glad to hear prevailed.'[33] In the end he settled for a boat to Genoa from where he caught the train to Boulogne and ferry across the Channel to Dover, leaving himself a couple of weeks before he was due to sign up for National Service.

* * *

National Service in the form of military conscription was introduced in Great Britain from 1947, initially for 18 months and from 1949 for two years. It was no coincidence that in 1947 India and Pakistan had gained their independence, which meant Britain no longer had access to the personnel and vast resources of the Indian Army, on which she had hitherto been able to call in times of need. Few, if any, in the British establishment foresaw at the time that most of the rest of the colonial empire would also be gone within little more than a decade. In the meantime, Britain had to defend her interests in her remaining colonial territories around the globe, to say nothing of contributing alongside America to other post-war commitments in Germany and the Far East. Thus, from 1949, all men aged 18 to 30 were eligible for two years' National Service call-up, with exceptions for blindness, mental disability, and the clergy. In addition, unofficially, and with much of the military need being in the defence of empire, Asian, African and Caribbean Britons were not called up, and the same applied to citizens of Northern Ireland.

Both Robert and Evelyn decided to postpone going up to Oxford and to complete their military service first, to get it out of the way. They might have hoped to serve together, but although they signed up for the same cavalry regiment, the 13th/18th Royal Hussars, they were assigned to different battalions and only met up at the very end of their two years' service.

---

[33] *Oakeshott Letters*, RO to his mother, Officers Quarters, Benina Airport, Nr Benghazi, 27 August 1951.

Robert duly reported for duty in mid-September 1951. The 'hell on earth' of hours of drilling that he had had to endure in the Cadet Corps at school was nothing compared to the induction and basic training course he had to undergo during his first six weeks at Catterick Camp in North Yorkshire. Life was one long 'hell on earth' of drilling, physical training, cleaning brasses, boots and webbing every day interspersed with regular 'fatigues':

> ... from the way one is treated, one would think one was doing a punishment. One is driven to it by Corporals who act as over-seers & the very worst jobs (scrubbing floors and cleaning quotas) are selected for those who like myself have the stik [*sic*] of P.O. (potential officer).[34]

Robert was never afraid of hard work in itself; he proved that by working far harder than most others throughout his life; but the monotony and apparent lack of purpose of early Catterick training really got him down. At the end of his six weeks of initial training, he wrote,

> ... One is expected to feel a new person after all this training. Needless to say, it is not the case. I don't feel I've changed one jot. I still find cleaning kit as intolerable & unrewarding as ever. I still am bad at it. One hopes that one is developing ones [*sic*] qualities of leadership but there is no tangible proof that one is.

Part of his training involved tank-driving. He found this exciting at first, but even there, monotony soon set in. And 'tank-driving' in a North Yorkshire winter, with snow and ice on the training tracks, meant mostly 'tank-cleaning' – 'a dirty, chilly and unrewarding pastime'. But in the new year of 1952 he got onto a wireless course which, 'though at first sight it seems less glamorous & exciting than tank driving, seems, in the long run decidedly preferable'. He felt the course would at least bring him up to 'the average starting point of those who have been scientists & electricians

---

[34] This and the following quotations are from Robert's undated letters from Catterick Camp to his mother in the autumn of 1951.

at school'.[35] He was then sent to Mons in Belgium for leadership training before being assigned for service overseas.

During Robert's two years of National Service (1951–53), Britain was struggling to retain control of her vast imperial possessions, and this meant maintaining military garrisons in no fewer than 35 countries around the world. Robert could have been sent to any one of them. The largest contingent was in West Germany, where Evelyn served part of his time. In the summer of 1952 Robert learned that he was being posted to Malaya for his second year of military service.

* * *

British rule in Malaya was being challenged by two pro-independence forces, the 'Malayan National Liberation Army', which ironically Britain had supported when it was formed to fight Japanese occupation during World War II, and the 'Malayan Communist Party'. Britain refused to recognise the conflict as a struggle to end her own occupation, preferring to refer to it as an 'Emergency', a law-and-order struggle against 'bandits'. Ironically, considering his later work in Africa, Robert was thus to be part of British military efforts to buttress colonial rule in the territory.

In August 1952 Robert sailed down the Solent aboard the troopship *Dilwara* with four weeks of shipboard travel ahead of him. Initially he was excited by the luxury of it all. He had the top bunk of a two-berth cabin, with its own basin and hot water – quite a change from the Nissen hut dormitories of Catterick Camp. Gin, whisky and cigarettes were incredibly cheap, and it was perhaps from this time that he developed a penchant for heavy drinking and heavy smoking, although he could not think he would 'ever be able to afford to travel so luxuriously at [his] own expense'. The food on board was not that good, with no fresh milk, but 'a four-course BREKKER! LUNCH & DINNER. And the whole place is swimming in butter'. Food – in quantity or quality – always loomed large in Robert's assessment of a person, place or occasion.

Official duties aboard ship were light, and Robert spent most of his

---

[35] RO to his mother, Catterick Camp, January 1952.

'all too abundant leisure time reading [*War and Peace*], playing games [of quoits], drinking, smoking and talking', there being 'one or two on board from Tons'. After just five days at sea, he concluded,

> Basically ... there can be no doubt that comfort & luxury are not substitutes for excitement & indeed interesting occupation. 4–5 weeks of this & especially the first 10 days to Port Said will be plenty for me.[36]

By the time they reached Port Said and the entrance to the Suez Canal, the political situation in Egypt was one of 'extreme delicacy', to put it mildly. Britain had retained control of the canal after World War II, its importance as a route to the Indian Empire being replaced from 1948 by its increasingly important role as a conduit for Middle Eastern oil. An Anglo-Egyptian Treaty forced on Egypt in 1936 had given Britain control of the canal until 1956, but the Egyptian Government had abrogated the treaty in 1951; and then on 3 August 1952, just three weeks before Robert's troop ship reached Port Said, Colonel Gamal Abdel Nasser's Free Officers' Movement staged a *coup d'état*, which left Britain's continued free access to the canal hanging in the balance. The troops aboard the *Dilwara* were placed under strict instructions not to talk with anybody on the bank as they passed through the canal at a speed of only eight knots, and 'to conduct [themselves] irreproachably & refrain from enciting [*sic*] the native population'.[37] Robert and the troops appear to have observed the stricture and the *Dilwara* passed through the canal without incident.

After brief stops at Aden and Colombo, the *Dilwara* docked at Singapore in the first week of September 1952. By then Robert was frantic to get off. He could not understand 'why anybody should regard a protracted cruise as an enjoyable holiday', and he could not understand why 'the Passenger Shipping Companies continue to flourish'.[38]

* * *

---

[36] RO to his mother, at Gibraltar, n.d. [9 August 1952].

[37] RO to his mother, at sea (c. Port Said), 15 August 1952.

[38] RO to his father, Majidee Barracks, Johor Bahru, 14 September 1952.

2nd Lieutenant Robert Oakeshott was stationed initially at Majidee Barracks in Johor Bahru, just across the Johor Strait from Singapore Island. He was part of 'A Squadron', in charge of A Troop – 100 men – though he was allowed a few weeks of settling in before his troop became operational. His leadership aim was two-fold, to ensure firstly that his troop was efficient and secondly that it was a happy unit. Whether he was a good troop leader, he confided to his father, 'remains to be seen'.[39]

There were, in Robert's experience, two sides to Army life, 'with the men & in the Mess'. He decidedly preferred the former. In the mess, he told his father,

> ... [is] what you might call good-chap-manship. If you can tell a mildly riské joke and are prepared to call everybody 'old fellow' then you are well on the way. Other almost essential things are ability to play golf, tennis & sail; partiality for drinking & a rather light head; good clothes and a nice bank balance. In these terms it may be that I shall have to regard myself as a failure 'in the mess'.[40]

Being in a cavalry regiment meant involvement in some form of motorised transport; but seeing that the Malayan conflict was primarily being conducted from the jungle, the work of Robert's troop was mostly providing armoured car escorts for food convoys between Singapore and Jemaluang, some 50 miles up country on the east coast. The convoys never came under attack while protected by the troop, though unprotected lorries often did. Robert's troop was occasionally ordered 'off-piste' into the jungle on foot in search of 'bandits' who had been raiding villages for food; but he never actually experienced the excitement of direct contact with 'the enemy', who knew the footpaths too well to fall into the trap of a poorly-laid British ambush. The only time Robert and any others in his troop fired their rifles at anything was at wild boar, which on two occasions they managed to kill, but found it very tough eating. To reassure his mother, he told her 'The chances of stopping a Bandit bullet on this job

---

[39] RO to his father, Johor Bahru, 14 September 1952.

[40] RO to his father, Johor Bahru, 14 September 1952.

are considerably less than those of being knocked down by a bus in Picadilli [*sic*]' – not very reassuring considering that his great-grandfather had been knocked down and killed by a horse-drawn vehicle in Northumberland Avenue, less than a mile from Piccadilly.

Soon after his troop became operational, Robert realised the military establishment were spinning false propaganda about their success against the guerrilla fighters. The 'Generals and political officers' were insisting that the 'bandits' were broken, whereas Robert learned from the police that at least one member of every rural family was 'in the jungle', while in Jemaluang alone, '66% [were] pro-communist and a greater proportion anti-British'. Even so, the main enemy so far as Robert was concerned was 'General Mosquito'.

> I would gladly swap some bandit activity with the continual bombardment of the mosquito.

Wearing pyjamas under his trousers, a silk scarf round his neck and insect repellent was 'all to no avail'.[41]

Nevertheless, when his mother asked for the justification for the British Army presence in Malaya, Robert took the standard establishment view that it was a fight against communism. With the Chinese Communist Party victorious in China since 1949, and Chinese military intervention in the Korean War in support of North Korea from 1950, it was readily assumed, and repeated by Robert, who had warned of the dangers of communism back in his school debates, that the withdrawal of Britain and her troops from Malaya would result in 'a Chinese Government in Kuala Lumpur within 48 hours'. That would not only mean servility for the Malayan people; but it would deprive Britain of access to Malaya's valuable resources of tin and rubber, so vital to her post-war economic recovery. And China's access to those same resources would strengthen communist China's own economy. There was no consideration that Malaya's tin and rubber might have better benefitted the country's own population, and then they might not have been quite so desperate to get rid of the British presence. But by 1952 Cold

---

[41] RO to his mother, Johor Bahru, 11 and 18 November 1952.

War fears were well-established, and like many in the West, Robert believed in the 'domino effect': if Malaya fell to the communist Chinese, Thailand and Burma would soon follow. That would threaten French Indochina[42] and make World War III almost certain. Robert acknowledged, as his mother suggested, that the British Army might not be achieving much in Malaya, but he believed it could be *preventing* a very great deal.[43]

Towards the end of his time in Malaya, the regular army routine was broken by a little sporting activity, and in May 1953 Robert achieved some success in athletics, winning both the mile and the two-mile on his squadron's sports day. He could not recall any previous occasion when he had ever won a race, although he admitted the competition was 'almost ZERO'. What thrilled him most was the chance he would now have of meeting up with his twin brother Evelyn who, in B Squadron, was stationed in Kuala Lumpur. He too had done well in his squadron's sports, and they would each represent their squadrons at the Regimental Sports Day near Kuala Lumpur in June. In the event, Evelyn won the quarter mile and Robert came second in the mile: 'not at all hot really', he commented modestly. What really pleased Robert, however, besides being with 'Cargs', was being up-county and thus avoiding being roped in for children's sports and fun fairs on Coronation Day, 2 June 1953.[44]

The two brothers met up again in Singapore, where they had a week together in July as they prepared for their return home and the end of their National Service. They sailed on the *Empire Trooper* and the two of them were appointed 'Ship's Education Officers' for the voyage. This entailed coaching 100 troopers for an examination at the end of the voyage, and keeping 50 children, aged five to thirteen, occupied for an hour and a half each afternoon. Perhaps it was from this latter experience that Robert later developed his penchant for throwing children's parties and inventing games for them.

---

[42] French Indochina: Vietnam, Laos and Cambodia, French colonial territories in Southeast Asia, 1887–1954.

[43] RO to his mother, 27 November 1952.

[44] RO to his mother, 30 May and 18 June 1953.

Robert seldom spoke about his National Service experience, describing it to his sister Rose as about as interesting 'as though you had to drive from London to Reading twice a day'.[45] His attitude to the service was reflected in the fact he never bothered to iron his uniform, a habit that remained with him all his life. Indeed, his commanding officer said he'd never seen an officer pass out in such a poor condition, though he had to admit Robert had shown great ingenuity.[46] For Robert, National Service was simply a duty that had to be completed, and he seems not to have kept up with any of the military people that he met, though he enjoyed telling amusing stories about his National Service experience and would imitate some of the idiotic officers of the mess, just to raise a laugh.

Their ship arrived in Southampton on 29 August 1953. Finally demobbed at the end of September, the brothers headed for their separate Oxford colleges: Cargs to Corpus Christi, Robert to Balliol.

---

[45] Rose Gaunt, interview, 7 October 2020.

[46] Caroline Cox-Johnson, interview, 6 November 2020.

CHAPTER 4

The Oxford Years
1953–1956

Going up to Oxford at the end of September 1953 marked a turning point in Robert's life. For the first time in his life, he felt really free: free from the strictures of boarding school and army discipline, and free from what he felt was the controlling presence of his father. His parents were still at Winchester during Robert's first year at Balliol; it was not until the following summer that they moved to Oxford, as Walter took up the appointment of Rector of Lincoln College. By then, Robert was well-established in his new liberated world.

Hitherto, Robert had had a slightly distant relationship with his father, by whom he felt controlled, both in his professional work and at home, through the subtle process of withholding his approval. Robert had followed in his father's footsteps, as far as he was able, even to the extent of winning a Domus Exhibition to study Classics at Balliol College. But he had found it impossible to live up to what he felt were his father's expectations. Now, at Balliol, he was able to give free reign to the rebellious spirit he had been nurturing since his early years at Tonbridge.

There can be little doubt that, certainly in the academic sphere, a strong influence on Robert during his Oxford years was Russell Meiggs (1902–1989), the dominant Balliol Classics don of the post-war decades, described in an obituary as 'one of the last and certainly one of the greatest of the old-style Oxford dons'.[47] He taught Ancient Greek and Roman History, but he was a master of the entire field of classical studies and 'managed

---

[47] Obituary, Russell Meiggs, *Proceedings of the American Philosophical Society*, Vol. 135, No. 3, 1991, pp 475-477 <https://www.ostia-antica.org/past/meiggs.htm> [accessed 1 June 2021].

to have an impact on virtually every undergraduate that passed through Balliol in his years there'. He challenged his students, demanding they go back to original sources and argue their tutorial essays from there. He could produce a cutting put-down of an essay that he felt failed to live up to his expectation of that student: 'What's the cash value of that?' or 'Nothing in that for Meiggs'.[48] It may have intimidated some youngsters straight from school, but he admired those who stood up to him and challenged his assessment. This would have appealed to the highly intelligent mind of Robert Oakeshott, who got to know him well, not least because Meiggs was the *praefectus* of Holywell Manor, the Balliol Hall of residence where Robert had his rooms during his freshman year. Robert would have appreciated Meiggs' legendary eccentricities and his 'jaunty disregard of conventional formalities'. In Robert's time, the Balliol rumour mill had it that Meiggs was of South American, even Inca origin.[49] With his long flowing grey hair (in those post-war years of short-back-and-sides) and his dark bushy eyebrows, Meiggs was easily recognisable, and even photographed by tourists, during his daily fifteen-minute walk between Holywell Manor in the east of the city and Balliol College on Broad Street in the city centre.

Meiggs' strict control of his undergraduate charges in the Manor did not deter Robert from staying out late at night. On one occasion he climbed out of a window and down a rope ladder after lock-up time.[50] He was also known for climbing railings to get back in and squeezing through tiny windows on the 'cat principle' that if the head got through, the body would surely follow.

At Balliol, Robert, or 'Rods' as family and close friends knew him, was able to fully develop his own eccentricities and his enormous sense of fun. He worked hard, with that unique capacity to cram into a matter of hours the amount of work that would take most others a day or more to work through; and he had a great social life. He drank liberally, as did many of his contemporaries at Oxford, including his brother Cargs, and overall he always retained his humour and pretty much his clarity of thought.

---

[48] Obituary, Russell Meiggs.

[49] *Oakeshott Letters*, RO to his mother, 'In the air to New York', 18 September 1960.

[50] Rose Gaunt, interview, 7 October 2020.

Robert relished his 'Oxford accent', that mode of speech so characteristic of the major public schools and the English upper class, especially in this period. It featured as part of his eccentricity. And to ensure this, he embellished his speech with affectations that he may have picked up in the officers' mess in Malaya, such as addressing friends and others as 'old fellow', and adding 'What!' at the end of statements, in the manner of P. G. Wodehouse's Bertie Wooster or Dorothy Sayers' Lord Peter Wimsey. He never softened his accent during his lifetime, leaving it to appear increasingly eccentric through the subsequent decades.

He found he already had quite a few friends at various colleges in Oxford, mostly through family connections, but he quickly built up a circle of close friends at Balliol, and it was with them that he did most of his socialising. Balliol at the time had about 300–350 undergraduates, all men, and by the end of his first year Robert had become a central figure of what became known as 'the Balliol gang'. Indeed, a number of undergraduates from other colleges gravitated towards Balliol, not just because 'Balliol had better dons',[51] but because the Balliol men had more fun.

There is a black and white photograph, undated, of Balliol men, possibly of Robert's year, with one row seated at the front and two rows standing behind, most dressed in sports jacket with college tie.[52] Noticeably the shortest man in the back row is Robert Oakeshott with thick mop of hair, wearing dark-coloured shirt with darker bow tie, and jacket undone, displaying what is clearly a colourful waistcoat. He has a wine glass raised to his lips, as though toasting the occasion. Standing next to him, and the only other man in the group holding a wineglass, is his great friend, the Irishman Antony Martin. Both men were notorious drinkers. And next to Antony stands Roddy Bloomfield, another of Robert's close friends in 'the Balliol gang'.

Other members of Robert's friendship group, though not necessarily all

[51] John Jolliffe (a Christchurch undergraduate contemporary of Robert's), interview, 28 October 2020.

[52] See following page – the photograph is reproduced inside the front cover of *Antony Martin. A Celebration of His Life, 1936–1997* (Privately published, 1997).

Balliol College, Oxford, back row from second left, Roddy Bloomfield,
Antony Martin and Robert Oakeshott.
(From Antony Martin. A Celebration of His Life, *privately published, 1997)*

Balliol undergraduates, included Francis Nichols, Maurice Keen and his younger brother Charles, John Jolliffe, Robin Blackhurst, Anthony Gater, Christopher Arnander, Rodney Leach (later Baron Leach of Fairfield), Tom Bingham (later Lord Chief Justice) and Peter Brooke (later Conservative Cabinet Minister). It is generally recognised that his closest friends were Antony Martin and Francis Nichols. And besides these, two of the brightest young women at or around Oxford in those years, Tatiana Orlov (later Mallinson) and Lady Jane Willoughby de Eresby, also became close friends of Robert and many within his group. Both were to remain lifelong friends and supporters of his later projects and charitable commitments.

The Indian scholar Ved Mehta, who went on to become a renowned literary figure and regular contributor to the *New Yorker*, arrived at Balliol just as Robert was entering his final year. By then Robert was well-established as one of the great characters of the college. Mehta would never have fitted into the camaraderie or ethos of the 'Balliol gang', but as an outsider, he was an acute observer of character. He saw Robert as 'one of the most engaging men at the college … quixotic, funny, serious, and a bundle of class contradictions'. Of his close-knit gang of public-school men from professional and upper-class backgrounds, Mehta observed:

> They had a sort of group personality, as if each were always in need of an audience. … They were known for strutting about – for constantly getting in and out of taxis, for hard-drinking, for exchanging jokes and criticisms in loud voices. Indeed, they conducted themselves as if they belonged to the governing class, and the place were part of their inheritance, … [They] seemed so confident of their class and position that some of them paid no attention to their dress. Robert was one of the scruffiest dressers in college … but his clothes did not disguise a very proper school voice or a rather ironic manner.[53]

---

[53] Ved Mehta, *Up at Oxford – Continents of Exile: 7* (Penguin Modern Classics, 2020), Chapter IV. This extract accessed 23/06/2021 from https://books.google.co.uk/books?id=OsryDwAAQBAJ&pg=PT92&lpg=PT92&dq=Robert+oakeshott+ved+mehta&source=bl&ots=A2VJlu2xMR&sig=ACfU3U0eX99TlBRadOhMfOBxjiRZ1kiwXg&hl=en&sa=X&vcd=2ahUKEwigpIq9s63xAhVPPcAKHQI3B3wQ6AEwBXoECAoQAw#v=onepage&q=Robert%20oakeshott%20ved%20mehta&f=false [accessed 7 November 2021].

Robert appears to have had a reasonable wardrobe when he first arrived at Oxford, but as his clothes suffered wear and tear, he paid no attention to replacing them. He was more interested in what people thought, and did not judge by appearances, applying this equally to the women whom he met. His brilliant intellect, liberally laced with humour leaning to the ridiculous, combined with consideration and kindness, was an attractive mix, for men as well as women. Tatiana Orlov who became a life-long friend, recalls her first meeting with Robert:

> We first met in 1955 at Oxford. Rodney Leach said, 'You must meet him'. We met outside New College, after Sunday Mass. There was Robert. He was very shy of girls, and his chuckle with head thrown back was partly to hide that. He had a bow tie, half undone and crooked, and he was pouring a glass of wine into the corner of his mouth. He was a complete contrast to Evelyn. He had no idea about appearances – that was completely secondary to him. His scruffiness was his signature image. We got on very well and very quickly became fast friends. He was so eccentric, his friends had something to do with perpetuating that. They found it amusing – the scrapes he got into, his shambolic presentation. Being with Robert was a mix of embarrassment and enjoyment. He became the central person in his group of friends at Oxford.[54]

It was while Robert was at Oxford that his sister Rose, younger by seven years, really got to know him. She was then nearing the end of her time at boarding school and during her short windows of opportunity, she would visit him and perhaps have tea in his room. This was how she first met Francis Nichols, and the legendary Russell Meiggs, and later Antony Martin. She recalls that on one Sunday morning Robert introduced her to the heady and refreshing mixture of Black Velvet[55] outside the Balliol Buttery. The two siblings found they had much in common; Robert sharing with his sister, 'you and I were the troublesome ones'. And for Rose, being with Robert in Oxford was a huge breath of freedom from the

---

[54] Tatiana Mallinson (née Orlov), interview, London, 2 October 2020.

[55] A cocktail of Guinness and champagne.

controlling expectations of her mother.[56]

He played 'rugger' during his first year, and he may have tried his hand at a few other sporting activities, though nothing at which he particularly shone. There was, however, one sporting event at which Robert did indeed shine: the Quadrangle Challenge. It has not been possible to trace the origin of this event, and it was the sort of activity that may well have been invented by Robert himself. The challenge was to race blindfold across the Balliol quadrangle, from touching the wall at one side, to being the first to touch the wall at the other. Robert had shown himself a capable though not exceptional runner at school and in his regimental sports day, but blindfold was something else. Robert's courage and determination to shine, in this latest eccentricity, was what gave him the advantage; for while everybody else's instinct told them to slow down when they thought they were nearing the other side, Robert ran flat out until he hit the wall face first – a guaranteed, messy-faced win for Oakeshott. His courage, combined with his desire to show off his eccentricity, was really exposed when he took on the challenge again the next year, with the same result.[57]

Aside from this brief and hilarious foray into physical activity, Robert much preferred intellectual activity, especially if it could be amusing. He loved debating, treating it as a form of extended conversation. He would occasionally speak at the Oxford Union, that prestigious forum for would-be prime ministers; but he much preferred something more personal and informal, and he 'led the launch, or relaunch of two debating societies, the Arnold and Brackenbury and the Asquith', the latter named after Herbert Henry Asquith, a Balliol Classics scholar (1869), and the last Liberal Prime Minister to hold a governing majority in the Commons (1908–1916). This left them free to debate whatever topic they fancied, and Robert had a huge range of interests and esoteric ideas. Both societies 'were also convivial clubs and very good fun'.[58] Just as at Tonbridge, he

---

[56] Rose Gaunt, interview, 7 October 2020.

[57] Anthony Gater, interview, 14 October 2020.

[58] Charles Keen, interview, 29 September 2020.

loved to follow a line of argument to its logical conclusion, especially if it led to the humorous or the ridiculous.

In his first term as a freshman, he was obliged to write weekly 'Freshman Essays', to be presented to the Master of Balliol, Sir David Lindsay Keir.[59] One of the early topics was 'Should Scientists as a Class be allowed to Govern?'. Rather than focus on the concept of democracy or the Platonic philosopher king, as one might expect of a classicist, Robert pointed out that contemporary scientists tended to suggest that 'in terms of recent discoveries a Utopian Age is not only possible but, as you might say, there for the taking'. This set him off on philosophical meanderings about the possibility of a future Utopia. He had recently read in *The Sunday Times* that the Swedes were getting bored with their 'most prosperous, just and well-organized society … [that] has been at peace for something like 150 years'.[60] In relating this to his mother, he recalled her recollection of the Dean of St Paul's – 'or was it Westminster?' – preaching about hell being 'infinitely boring', but did he, Robert queried, venture the corollary that 'heaven would be wildly exciting? … What if we do build a new Utopia & find something analogous to the Dean's conception of Hell?'. That life might be boring was anathema to Robert. He found his stimulation in a constant search for excitement.

* * *

He spent Christmas 1953 and New Year with the family, probably at Bell House. This would have been their last Christmas together in Bell House before it was sold in 1954. It was noted in the New Year's Honours List for 1954 that Walter Oakeshott's friend and Balliol contemporary, Dan Lascelles, had been knighted – KCMG – and more to the point, he was British Ambassador to Afghanistan. One can imagine Robert's eyes lighting up – he would go and pay him a visit during the summer vacation!

He talked it over with Francis Nichols who agreed it was perfectly

---

[59] Historian, son of a Scottish Presbyterian minister, fellow of University College, former Vice-Chancellor of Queens University Belfast and Master of Balliol 1949–1965.

[60] *Oakeshott Letters*, RO to his mother, 26 October 1953.

feasible and he would go with him. Francis bought a Land Rover, that most reliable of vehicles for long-distance, cross-country travel. The story told by Francis after the event was that the purpose of the trip was to deliver a Land Rover to the King of Afghanistan, Mohammed Zahir Shah, who was said to want one, but that when they got it there, he rejected it because he had wanted a long-wheelbase model. There is no mention of the King, or any of this, however, in Robert's contemporaneous letters home, from which it is clear they intended all along to drive the vehicle both ways. The purpose of the trip was adventure, pure and simple. This was years before the so-called 'hippy trail' of the 1960s and 1970s, and 'dropping in' on Sir Daniel Lascelles was their way of proving it could be done. Whether or not they succeeded, it would win them many plaudits among their friends.

Allowing themselves a month each way, they set off in the first week of July, with Ronnie Dworkin and Xanthe Wakefield hitching a ride with them as far as Salonika. They had originally intended to take the 'northern route' through Germany and Austria, but at Robert's prompting, they took a more southerly route via Geneva, where he had a luxurious and 'quite fabulous bath at the Station'. The glimpse of the Swiss Alps from the Simplon Pass into Italy made the route through Switzerland 'very well worthwhile'. From Milan, he was able to pick up on his travels of 1951, though he found the dead straight roads, like those of France, incredibly dull. Writing a decade before Britain's first motorway, Robert quipped:

> I think England must be the only country with deliberately & unnecessarily winding roads. How sensible![61]

Robert was charmed by the old-fashioned little villages of Yugoslavia and Bulgaria, where the donkey had yet to be supplemented by motorised transport – 'an ideal place for a holiday'. They reached Istanbul two weeks after leaving England and spent three days exploring the city. Robert insisted on calling it by its old Christian name, Constantinople, despite the official name-change in 1930. They found that as they travelled east from Western

---

[61] RO to his mother, Dubrovnik, 13 July 1954.

Europe the cost of living became progressively cheaper, apart from the cost of baths, which were 'progressively dearer in proportion as they became more necessary'. And the fewer Western Europeans one met, the more one tended to greet any that one did meet 'almost as blood brothers'. Perhaps, Robert speculated, 'in Afghanistan one will even find a bond with Persians' and wondered whether one would naturally find a strong bond 'with any warm-blooded mammal in a community of vegans?'.[62]

They crossed the Bosporus and were now truly 'in the East'. They headed south through Syria and Lebanon and on across the desert to Iraq where, Robert was delighted to report, in a British military base near Baghdad they had steak and two eggs for two shillings – a real luxury after a surfeit of dried fruit. From Baghdad they crossed into Iran – still Persia to Robert – where for several days 'one passes little but successive lines of latitude'.

Through the Afghan mountains on poor-quality dirt roads they were charmed by the incredibly hospitable villagers, always eager for them to stop and share a cup of tea. They finally reached Kabul on Tuesday 17 August, six weeks after leaving England. The original plan of a month each way was already overrunning, but the whole journey was such a tremendous experience that they appear to have lost some sense of time.

On contacting Sir Daniel Lascelles, who had been warned of their possible arrival, he invited them to stay at the Embassy. The contrast with the previous six weeks could not have been greater and they wallowed in the luxury of being waited on by Indian and Pakistani servants. They treated five days as guests of the ambassador as a well-deserved reward for the achievement of the journey.

It was 23 August when they finally bade farewell to their host. Aware now that they were way over schedule, they took a more direct route through Iran to eastern Turkey, thus by-passing Iraq, Syria and Lebanon. With Robert driving too fast to make up time, they came off the road in Iran as he tried to dodge an oncoming bus. Repair of the vehicle delayed them a week during which, besides trying to teach the local innkeeper how

---

[62] RO to his mother, Constantinople, 21 July 1954.

to play dominos, Robert composed a letter to his father, who would be installed as Rector of Lincoln College by the time they got back to Oxford. He knew he needed to prepare the ground for the worst scenario, that they might not make it back in time for the beginning of the new academic year. He admitted they had stayed too long in Kabul but excused it by the 'quite extraordinary hospitality' of his father's friend, Sir Daniel Lascelles. In Robert's style in writing to his father, he admitted that was no excuse, but it was '*the reason*' for their delay, and thus the driving too fast. He described the accident, spreading part of the blame to the bus driver who did not stop and assured his parents that neither he nor Francis had been hurt. The plan now, to make up time, was to drive as far as Istanbul and arrange for the vehicle to be shipped home, while they caught the Orient Express. In the event, they got home just in time for the start of term.

Robert now had a taste for foreign travel and was probably already planning his next adventure for the following summer vacation. By the time he completed his Mods exams at the end of the Hilary term – he got an upper second – he probably already had a destination in mind. He would go to America.

* * *

The Oakeshott and Moon families had a wide range of contacts in North America – relatives and friends – and Robert's journey to the United States was planned around a series of visitations which would take him across much of the continent. He was never shy about phoning people up and accepting, after suitably polite hesitation, their kind offer to come and stay. He, in his kindness and generosity, would not have hesitated to have anyone to stay with him, on the vaguest pretext, and he assumed the same of everybody else. He was such charming, amusing and interesting company that all his hosts seemed to welcome his virtually inviting himself.

To cross the Atlantic in the summer of 1955 was quite an undertaking, even by air. After a fairly standard twenty-two-hour delay at London Airport (Heathrow), Robert's flight finally departed on Saturday 16 July. They flew north to Glasgow's Prestwick Airport, where the plane refuelled for the transatlantic flight to Gander in Newfoundland, from where Robert

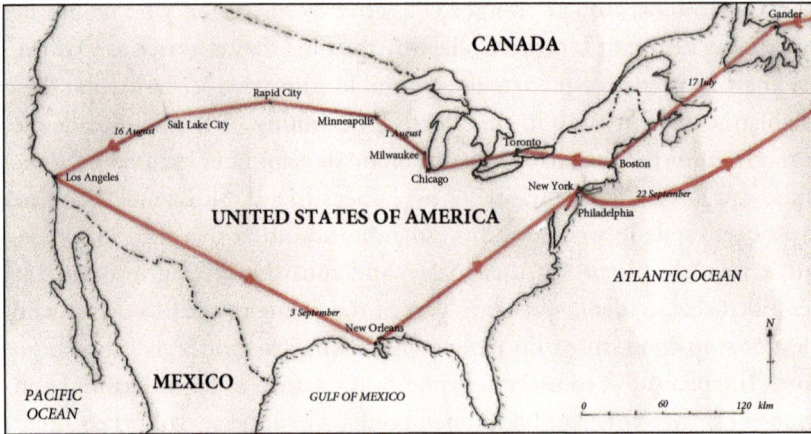

Robert's trip across America, July–September 1955 (by the author).

was able to fly on to Boston. He stayed for several days across the river in Cambridge with one of his father's Balliol friends, Professor William ('Bill') Coolidge of Massachusetts Institute of Technology.

What Robert first noticed about America, after the austerity of post-war Britain, was the abundance of goods in the shops and the 'in your face' advertising – on hoardings, aeroplane streamers, television and radio – most of it advertising what today would be called 'junk food'. Indeed, during his first few weeks in America and wearing the hat of English superiority, he was distinctly unimpressed by many of the people whom he met, aside from his hosts, who were all incredibly hospitable. The famed American bonhomie was much in evidence but, he wrote to his mother, it seemed to be regarded as 'a substitute for subtlety or reasoned argument. They laugh a great deal, but I have not yet heard a great joke which amused me'.[63]

After three nights in Toronto, he flew to Chicago where, at Anthony Gater's suggestion, he looked up an ex-girlfriend of his, a journalist, who invited him to stay with her parents in Milwaukee. 'There didn't seem

---

[63] RO to his mother, Toronto, Sunday 24 July 1955.

any good reason for not accepting so I went.' To introduce this eccentric Englishman to a bit of American culture, they took him to a major baseball game, which Robert rated 'very low (β triple minus) by any criteria'; but he was fascinated by what he saw as the 'overblown reaction' of the crowd, 'as if people would get excited about a billiard game'.[64]

In the train to Neenah 100 miles north of Milwaukee, however, his caustic view of America and Americans began to change: he fell in with 'the first not only progressive and intellectual American, but the first Democrat I have met over here', a freelance journalist, 'interesting and well read'. After staying with him a few days in Rapid City, he admitted to picking up a few words of American slang, though *not*, he stressed, 'CUTE', a word used for 'cats, china, animals, babies, new pairs of nylons & even young Curates'.[65] Overall, however, he was not impressed by the thoroughness of American education, believing too much effort was made to 'sugar the pill' with the result that 'in the outcome there is often no pill, or meat left'. History lessons in schools, for instance, might be entitled, 'who took the place of Film Stars in Ancient Rome?'.[66]

Ironically, Robert was heading south-west to Hollywood, where he appears to have been ever so slightly star-struck himself. He stayed three days with famed actress Jane Waddington Wyatt, her husband Edgar Ward and their two teenage sons.

Jane, a second cousin through Robert's maternal grandmother, was a star of the silver screen who rose to prominence in the 1930s and 40s, playing alongside the great male stars of the era: Ronald Colman, Gregory Peck, Cary Grant, Dana Andrews and Randolph Scott. At the time of Robert's visit, she was filming for the television series *Father Knows Best*, in which she played a devoted wife and mother and for which she won a series of Emmy Awards. She was, in Robert's words, 'great fun … rather like Mrs McNeil I thought – only more attractive looking (not that Mrs Mc is by any means plain)'. She worked a twelve-hour day for nine days

---

[64] RO to his mother, Neenah, Wisconsin, 1 August 1955.

[65] RO to his mother, Neenah, Wisconsin, 1 August 1955.

[66] RO to his mother, Salt Lake City, 15 August 1955.

a fortnight, but managed to spend a day with Robert, during which they visited Santa Barbara, 'a French Riviera-type resort'.[67]

Robert was pleased to note, in a country with a high divorce rate, the obvious success of Jane and Edgar's marriage.[68] Commenting from his own experience, he felt that 'bachelorhood' in America was generally frowned upon:

> ... to be single is to cut yourself off from great areas of social intercourse. Over here [when you order a single room] they give you a Double bed & expect you to bring along either a wife or a partner (on the continent they are more likely to give you a single bed and provide a partner).[69]

He spent a brief day and night in New Orleans before flying north to New York, where he stayed with 80-year-old 'Cousin Effie', another relative through Noel's mother. She was sprightly, active and good company. She took him to *Othello* the first night and to the opera and ballet on subsequent nights. She lived in East 50th Street, from where he enjoyed exploring Manhattan. He went down to Philadelphia for a weekend to visit a family called Smith, distant relatives of Francis Nichols. They had an extremely attractive daughter, 'young and beautiful!' he told his mother, 'All the ingredients for an agreeable weekend; I was very glad I went.' He sailed from New York on 22 September for the six-day journey to Southampton, sorry to be leaving Cousin Effie, 'a wonderfully kind person'.[70]

Despite mostly staying with friends, family contacts and relatives, Robert's great trip around North America would have set him back financially. He had probably drawn upon some money he had received from Uncle Pendy; but it was clear he would need to trim his sails somewhat on his next summer vacation, the last before his final year at Oxford.

---

[67] RO to his mother, New Orleans, 3 September 1955.

[68] They were to remain together from their marriage in 1935 until Edgar's death in 2000.

[69] RO to his mother, New Orleans, 3 September 1955.

[70] RO to his mother, New York, 13 September 1955.

CHAPTER 5

Eastern Europe
1956

Since his days at Tonbridge School, Robert had warned of the dangers of Stalin's communism, and there were many 'Westerners', Robert included, who believed that the death of Joseph Stalin in March 1953 opened the way for a thawing of the Cold War, and with it the prospect of a loosening of the Soviet Communist Party's grip on the countries of Central and Eastern Europe. The Yugoslav leader Marshal Josip Tito had already split with Stalin (in 1948) and was pursuing his own independent version of socialism, which included a certain level of worker control in state-owned enterprises, and accepting financial aid from the West. The split, however, may have prompted Stalin's crack-down on any independent tendency in the rest of the 'Eastern Bloc'. Now, with Stalin gone, anything might be possible.

Robert's opportunity for testing the tempo of the Eastern Bloc came at the fourth congress of the International Union of Students (IUS). Held in Prague in the last week of August 1956, it was billed as the 'IVth World Student Congress'. The IUS was a distinctly left-leaning, pro-communist organisation, expensively promoted by its mostly Eastern Bloc hosts as a showcase for the success of the 'People's Republics'. The British National Union of Students (NUS) was affiliated to the International Union and Robert, not known for any previous interest in NUS affairs, decided it would be interesting, and perhaps even fun, to attend the Prague Congress as part of a delegation representing the students of the University of Oxford. He was joined by his friends Peter Brooke and Jane Willoughby.

They travelled by train and on arrival it quickly became apparent that the 'Peoples' Democracies' were sparing no expense. Delegates were accommodated at the university, with hot and cold running water and 'excellent food (plenty of it, far better than at Balliol), free beer at meals and a hand-out of 120 crowns pocket money to boot'. With additional beer only three-quarters of a crown per pint, Robert quickly settled in. The congress itself was held in a vast hall, housing representatives from 80 nations ('I didn't know before this that there WERE that number'), each sitting at desks with headphones offering simultaneous translation in six languages.[71]

Robert was less impressed, however, by the general anti-colonial theme of the speeches in the plenary sessions which stretched across the first three days. The constitution of the NUS did not allow Robert and his colleagues to indulge in political speeches; the same did not apply to most of the other delegates, especially those from Africa, Asia and Latin America, all formerly, or still currently, colonised nations. Robert appears to have been expecting discussions with students from communist countries which would centre on concerns such as academic freedom, censorship of books, student travel and international exchange. As a result, he was taken aback by the almost universal hostility towards the 'colonial powers' expressed by so many of the student delegates for whom the main issue at stake was political independence. Indeed, it provoked Robert into privately expressing some racist hostility of his own. Writing to his mother about how the general atmosphere made the British and French delegates realise how much they had in common, he went on to write:

> By and large left wing and generally humanitarian principles to which it is easy enough to subscribe in the abstract, fail to survive intact when one is confronted with hordes of screaming & abusive blacks.[72]

The conference was, in Robert's view, 'a ludicrous parody of the assembly of the United Nations'; and by halfway through the second day Peter, Jane and Robert, tucked away in the back row of the hall, 'took to playing poker dice with kindred spirits among the French'. Somewhat to Robert's surprise, it was the delegation from Pakistan who smoothed things over by explaining

---

[71] *Oakeshott Letters.* Robert's record of the event is contained in a letter to his mother, dated 30 August 1956, and a three-page foolscap typed report, possibly prepared for the NUS.

[72] *Oakeshott Letters,* RO to his mother, 30 August 1956.

a few home truths to the delegates from the old imperial powers:

> ... that for the students of Africa and Asia, colonialism is not just another, personally remote, political issue but rather the urgent kernel of the whole business; that until independence is achieved and all the other indicators of second-class nationhood removed, it is emotionally impossible for them to participate calmly in discussion and debates about international student cooperation and more humdrum practical matters.[73]

This was an important lesson for Robert, who took the matter to heart, and thereafter, he and his friends made a conscious effort to speak to their critics and were pleased to find them 'reasonable and understanding about things' on an individual level, and 'even the Cypriots whom we asked to lunch were friendly enough there'.[74] The Cypriot War of Independence – 'Cyprus Emergency' in British parlance – was raging at the time.

By the end of the conference Robert had reached an understanding of the significance of political independence to colonised peoples and nations. Empathy, however, was one thing; the struggle to win the confidence of the students of these territories was quite another. He viewed the future of the post-colonial world through the prism of the Cold War, and the students as the key to its future. They were often the first generation of undergraduates in their country, and within as little as five years, or even sooner, 'unless they are in prison and possibly even then, will be leading the opposition parties in such places as ... French Equatorial Africa and Madagascar'.

> We cannot afford to allow the USSR and the Eastern countries a monopoly where contact with these men is concerned. We must try to win their confidence and to present them with an alternative to Communism which is progressive and attractive. This is why Britain gained more by sending observers to Prague than the Americans did by staying at home.[75]

In fact, the American response to the World Student Congress had been

---

[73] *Oakeshott Letters*, RO's typescript report on the Congress, p 2.

[74] *Oakeshott Letters*, RO to his mother, 30 August 1956.

[75] *Oakeshott Letters*, RO's typescript report on the Congress, p 2.

to promote an alternative 'International Student Conference', secretly funded by the CIA, whose inaugural meeting in Colombo overlapped with the one in Prague.

Robert, however, recognised the importance of real dialogue with the students of the colonised world, listening to and understanding their concerns and reasonable demands. Although he felt the Prague conference, spread over eight days, was far too long, he concluded that 'at least this observer would not have exchanged his ticket to Prague for one to Colombo'.[76] Meeting delegates from Africa and Asia made a deep impression upon him, and may have been the first step along the road towards his accepting, eight years later, an appointment to the planning department of an African country on the cusp of independence. At the same time, meeting with students from the communist Eastern Bloc states had sparked his interest in their fate and led directly to his resolve to go to Budapest when he heard of the student uprising there that October.

* * *

At the end of September 1956, Robert returned to Oxford to begin his fourth and final year of Greats. By this time he was living in a flat with a balcony that jutted out over the river in central Oxford. He used to greet dinner guests with the news that they would have to fish for their supper, though he usually had a backup of some food, even if it was not yet cooked.[77]

With his prodigious powers of concentration and work ethic, Robert was not going to allow his academic work to rule his life, as many did in their final year. And within weeks of the beginning of term his attention was drawn back to Eastern Europe as the struggle to break free from Soviet domination appeared to be gathering pace.

Two items dominated British news headlines during the early weeks of the new academic year: Nasser's nationalisation of the Suez Canal, with the possibility of British military action to reverse it, and the threat of a Soviet military attack on Warsaw to prevent the Polish Government from

[76] *Oakeshott Letters*, RO's typescript report on the Congress, p 3.

[77] Veronica Oakeshott, interview, 10 October 2020.

implementing anti-Stalinist reforms. The attack on Warsaw was averted in the third week of October by a deal between the Polish leader Władysław Gomułka and his Soviet counterpart Nikita Khrushchev. Significantly, the deal involved the promised withdrawal of Soviet troops from Poland. Hot on the heels of this agreement came news of major demonstrations in Hungary.

Inspired by the news of Gomułka's success, students from the Technical University in Budapest drew up a sixteen-point manifesto for reform and democratisation, headed by a demand for the immediate removal of Soviet troops from Hungarian soil. The manifesto was privately printed and circulated throughout the city on the morning of Tuesday 23 October. That afternoon, the students were joined by poets, intellectuals and workers, and with the support of students of the Military Academy, they staged a huge demonstration demanding 'Russians out!' and the restoration of Imre Nagy, the reforming Communist Prime Minister who the previous year had been dismissed by the Stalinists of the Hungarian Communist Party (officially, the 'Hungarian Workers' Party'). Soviet symbols were attacked: a large red star on top of a trade union building was pulled down and wherever a Hungarian flag was displayed, the red star in the centre was cut out. By 6 pm some 200,000 demonstrators had assembled in Parliament Square. Imre Nagy came out onto a balcony of the Parliament Building and appealed for them to disperse. All might have ended peaceably, until at 8 pm the hard-line Communist Party leader Ernő Gerő made a radio broadcast in which he condemned the demonstrators as 'bourgeois reactionaries'.[78] Infuriated by the reaction to their peaceful demands, the demonstrators split into two groups.

A crowd of several thousand workers and others converged on the massive bronze statue of Joseph Stalin that had stood so prominently in central Budapest since 1951. They tried unsuccessfully to pull it down with steel rope, before some industrial workers arrived with oxy-acetylene torches and cut it off at the boots.[79] The crowd hauled it away and hacked

---

[78] Rupert Colley, *The Hungarian Revolution, 1956* (Rupertcolley.com, 2016), p 62.

[79] In 2006, the fiftieth anniversary of the Revolution, a Memento Park of communist era statues was opened on the outskirts of Budapest, with the bronze boots of Stalin prominently erected on a plinth.

it into pieces for souvenirs over the next couple of days.

Meanwhile, news spread that a student delegation that had entered the State Radio building were being held there by the secret security police, the dreaded AVH.[80] The crowd outside, demanding their release, tried to force their way into the building. The AVH, positioned in upper-story windows, lobbed tear-gas cannisters and then fired live bullets into the crowd, killing several civilians and injuring many others.[81] In doing so, they turned a peaceful demonstration into a violent confrontation. The crowd reacted by seizing two unmarked vans containing AVH personnel. They beat up or killed the men inside and took their weapons.

This was the state of the situation that Robert would have read about next morning in *The Manchester Guardian*, filed from Budapest at 2 am. It was the only British paper to make it their main front-page story.[82] The idea that he should go to Budapest and help the students in their struggle probably did not consolidate in Robert's mind until the following day, when news came through of a serious escalation of violence in Budapest. AVH snipers had opened fire on a huge crowd that had come to Parliament Square to protest about the shooting of the night before. With hundreds left dead or wounded, the massacre fanned the flames of revolt into a full-scale revolution, and several units from the Hungarian Army tore the red stars from their uniforms and sided with the revolutionaries. The hard-line Stalinists of the Hungarian Communist Party, acting in accord with the Kremlin and hoping to contain the situation, agreed to the appointment of Imre Nagy as Prime Minister, but then called for Soviet tanks to come into Budapest from their Hungarian bases to help 'restore order'.

By now the demonstrators had become 'freedom fighters' and took on the Soviet tanks armed merely with rifles – taken from or willingly supplied

---

[80] Államvédelmi Hatóság – 'State Protection Authority'. For the past decade the AVH, often recruited from Hungarian former Nazi thugs, had acted with impunity, terrorising the Hungarian population, with secret surveillance cameras in homes, a network of informers, often recruited through threat of torture, and the constant fear of the knock on the door in the night, leading to detention, torture and often death or disappearance.

[81] Colley, *Revolution*, pp 66–67.

[82] *The Manchester Guardian*, Wednesday 24 October 1956, p 1.

by the army, police and factory armouries – and 'Molotov cocktails', a glass bottle with spring lid, filled with petrol, with a piece of cloth attached and the lid closed. Once lit, the holder had only a few seconds before the bottle exploded. It could be simply thrown, or, more effectively with the tanks, lobbed into the turret, or inserted into the petrol tank. The Soviet tanks appeared to be driven by young inexperienced Russian crews and without clear direction. Many got stuck down narrow streets where they could not manoeuvre and were vulnerable to attack, by rifle fire from upper windows, or from Molotov-cocktail wielding youths, many of them in their early teens. The other targets of the revolutionaries were the AVH. They were attacked, hunted down and lynched, many of them strung up by their feet on lamp-posts and trees.

Factory and other workers reacted by coming out on general strike, and the revolution quickly spread to major towns and cities throughout Hungary; indeed, the southern city of Pécs seems to have started ahead of Budapest. There was no central organisation or leadership. Each town or region set up its own revolutionary committee, with locally-elected leaders, many of them barely in their twenties. Showing extraordinary maturity, these committees attended to local needs and did whatever they could to help in the cause of the revolution.[83]

On Thursday 25 October, as he read in Oxford of the escalation of the revolution in Hungary, Robert made up his mind to go and help. He was in his final year. By the time he left Balliol the following summer, he would be 24. In deciding to go to the heart of the revolution that October, Robert was, perhaps subconsciously, laying down a marker for his future life after Oxford. Hitherto, he had enjoyed a fantastic social life, part of which involved philosophising and conversing, with great humour and much alcohol, on any subject under the sun. He would continue with all of that, but from now on he would prove himself a man of action. Where other people only talked, Robert talked *and acted*. If there was a problem, he would find a solution. It was to be an attractive characteristic of his

---

[83] United Nations (UN), *Report of the Special Commission on the Problem of Hungary*, Supplement 18 (A/3592) (New York, 1957), pp 21–22.

personality that people were to remark upon for the rest of his active life, until he was laid low by illness in his seventies.

Initially, it was not exactly clear what Robert could do to help, besides offering moral support to his fellow students in Hungary: perhaps in some non-combatant role, such as helping the wounded, but one thing that would justify the trip would be to carry as many doses as possible of that wonder-drug, the antibiotic, penicillin, as it was clear that Budapest's hospitals were struggling to cope with the mounting casualties. Robert put the idea to a meeting in the Balliol Common Room. It evoked great excitement and Robert and his friends started a fund to pay for the medicines. Within a day they had raised £20, a fair sum by the standards of the day. Francis Nichols' sister Anne organised volunteers to address envelopes to extend the appeal beyond the college, and contributions began to come in not merely from Balliol students and other colleges, but from an extensive array of parents and friends. A group travelled over to Cambridge and got more support there. This was all very promising for Robert, but how would he get to Budapest?

Robert's renowned initiative came into play, and he had the bright idea of becoming an instant journalist. He telephoned the office of the editor of *The Observer*, David Astor, justifying his direct approach on the grounds that Astor was a fellow Balliol man and Robert was a great friend of Astor's niece, Lady Jane Willoughby. Robert loved to use his aristocratic connections. He left a message with Astor's secretary, offering to write about the Hungarian Revolution if *The Observer* would provide him with two airline tickets. Astor was already about to send his own, experienced, Hungarian-born correspondent, Lajos Lederer, but his interest was piqued by the cheek of this Balliol undergraduate. Why Robert needed *two* tickets was unstated, but a little while later Astor's secretary phoned back to say the paper was sending him two return tickets to Vienna and 'Mr Astor looked forward to reading whatever Oakeshott wrote'.[84]

The plane tickets came through on the morning of Friday 26 October and Robert had to decide who would go with him. Initially 'everybody' wanted to go; but then it dawned on many that they would never get

---

[84] Ved Mehta, *Up at Oxford. Continents of Exile:7* (Penguin, 2020), e-book, Chapter IV.

permission to be absent from college during term time, especially in their final year, and to leave without permission could invite serious disciplinary measures, something that did not deter Robert. Once the tickets were there and the decision had to be made, only five came forward, all of them among the original contributors to the Balliol Relief Fund. They drew lots, and the second ticket went to Ian Rankin (later, 4th Baronet Rankin). Rankin was from Christ Church College. He was not a member of the Balliol gang, or even a particular friend to Robert. He was, however, very keen to provide medical and logistical aid to the Hungarian students and was an early contributor to the Balliol Relief Fund.

The two young men were driven to London Airport by Rodney Leach and other members of the gang that afternoon. It was only when he got to the airport that Robert telephoned the Balliol Porter's Lodge to report that he was going to Budapest on a mercy mission. He was taking 2 million doses of penicillin, to help the students of Hungary, and he would be away for a few days. The university police were known in student parlance as 'bulldogs' and according to Anthony Gater, 'The Bulldog barked!'[85] but, as Robert had intended, it was too late to prevent his departure. Leaving them at the airport, Robert's friends returned to Oxford to inform the Oakeshott and Rankin parents of what their sons were doing.[86] As Ian's son, Sir Gavin Rankin, has pointed out, both Ian and Robert were mature young men who had done their National Service and understood something of the dangers of entering a war zone.[87] Nevertheless, Robert's sister Rose recalls her parents and herself spending a very anxious week, terrified that Robert had gone too far this time, and that he would be killed.[88]

[85] Anthony Gater, interview, 14 October 2020.

[86] Ved Mehta, *Up at Oxford*, Chapter IV; and *News Chronicle*, Monday 29 October 1956, p 1, from 'News Chronicle Reporter' [Ian Rankin from Vienna]. I am grateful to Sir Gavin Rankin for copies of his father's reports in the *News Chronicle*.

[87] Gavin Rankin, interview, 22 June 2021.

[88] Rose Gaunt, interview, 7 October 2020.

CHAPTER 6

Into the Heart
of the Revolution
1956

The departure of their plane was delayed until 4 am on Saturday morning, 27 October, and Robert and Ian flew into Vienna along with *The Observer*'s Lajos Lederer. While Lederer went to search out the latest news from Hungary and find transport to the Austrian border, Robert visited Tatiana Orlov, who happened to be spending some post-Oxford time in the city, staying in a vast old house that took in paying guests. It was run by Caroline 'Lilly' Schomburg and was known as the 'Palais Schomburg'. Indeed, through Tatiana and her contacts, it became an informal social centre at this time for English people wishing to meet Austrians.

Tatiana remembers that Vienna was in a state of hysteria.[89] Austria had only recently declared itself a neutral state, a precarious neutrality situated geographically between two military alliances, the American-dominated NATO and the Soviet-dominated Warsaw Pact; and the Viennese feared that the Soviet reaction to the Hungarian Revolution would put their neutrality to the test.

That Saturday afternoon Robert and Ian got a lift with Lederer as far as the Austrian border with Hungary. They witnessed chaotic scenes of vehicles carrying medical and food aid arriving at the border from across Western Europe, most of it Red Cross though, conspicuously, nothing from America, as noted ashamedly by a reporter from the CIA-funded

---

[89] Tatiana Mallinson, interview, 2 October 2020.

Radio Free Europe.[90] It was not clear who was in control on the Hungarian side: the official border guards or the local revolutionary committee. It was clear, however, at least for the moment, that it was not (yet) under the control of the Soviets. The news from Budapest was that the brutal fighting of the past five days was still going on, though the Hungarian 'freedom fighters', who had been joined by sympathetic members of the Hungarian Army, appeared to be getting the better of the Soviet tanks and armoured personnel carriers. According to that day's *Manchester Guardian*, up to 10,000 people – Soviets, AVH and revolutionaries – had been killed in the city. Although that figure was not later confirmed, casualties were undoubtedly heavy on both sides.[91]

The two Oxford students returned to Vienna for the moment, though it is not clear what they did on the Sunday. They appear to have parted company from Lederer, who made his own way into Budapest. According to Ian Rankin's contemporaneous report, he and Robert got a lift back to the border on Monday 29 October.[92] They crossed into Hungary in pouring rain and got as far as Sopron, just three miles in from the border on one of the main roads to Budapest. Sopron, a town of 30,000 inhabitants, had elected its own revolutionary committee who, with remarkable calmness and efficiency, and with the support of the whole community, were doing their best to cope with a huge logistical problem. Local Hungarian vehicles were driving to the frontier, loading up with food and medical aid, bringing it as far as Sopron, off-loading and going back for more. This needed to be loaded into whatever other vehicles could be found in Sopron and taken into Budapest where, because of the general strike as well as the fighting, food was becoming as important as medical aid.

Robert decided to stay in Sopron for another day to see what he could do to help with the logistical problems while Ian went back to Vienna,

[90] Fritz Hier, 'A Hungarian Diary', p 3, Austria/Hungary border, Sunday 28 October (https://digitalarchive.wilsoncenter.org/collection/104/radio-free-europe-and-radio-liberty) [accessed 22 June 2021].

[91] *The Manchester Guardian*, Saturday 27 October 1956, p 1.

[92] *News Chronicle*, Tuesday 30 October 1956, p 1: 'We cross the border with Oxford's penicillin', by Ian Rankin.

both to see how he could help at that end, and to file a report to the *News Chronicle*, a liberal London daily newspaper with whom he appears to have had an arrangement. Ian's report was front-page news the next morning under the heading: 'Two Oxford men (with Penicillin) fly on mercy mission'. The report included a head-and-shoulders photograph of Robert in his National Service uniform. Readers were invited to contribute to the British Red Cross, the Committee of Hungarian Exiles in London and to the Treasurer (Maurice Keen) of the original Balliol Relief Fund, which by now had grown to become the 'Oxford University Hungarian Relief Fund'.[93]

Meanwhile in Sopron, Robert came across three young Hungarian mothers who could speak English. All were members of the local revolutionary committee:

> To hear them talking about the revolution, their revolution, was a profoundly moving experience.

It was stressed by all whom Robert met in Sopron that this was,

> ... a revolution of all the people, young and old, male and female, intellectuals, factory workers, peasants – 'everybody', as I was constantly told, was behind it.[94]

Robert spoke to a large crowd, with the aid of an interpreter, praising their efforts, especially that of the youth, and explained that he was a student from Oxford University who was there to give them moral support. They were especially pleased to hear that he and his friend had brought a large supply of medicines for Budapest. One of the young women from the committee arranged transport for them both for the next day, Tuesday 30 October. By then Ian had re-joined Robert and they made a 'somewhat clandestine journey from Sopron to Budapest ... in the back of a food

---

[93] *News Chronicle*, Monday 29 October 1956, p 1.

[94] *Oakeshott Papers*, RO's personal account of the Hungarian Revolution, typescript (8 or 9 November 1956), prepared for publication by *The Observer*.

*Budapest, 30 October–2 November 1956, during the brief hiatus
between the initial Russian withdrawal and their final assault.
(Ian Rankin, by kind permission of Sir Gavin Rankin)*

lorry, lying on loaves of bread'.[95] It was a five-hour journey with numerous roadblocks along the way, and one never knew for sure who might be manning them, friend or foe.

As they arrived in Budapest that Tuesday afternoon, the fighting was more or less at a standstill. Imre Nagy had broken free from control by the Stalinist hardliners, most of whom were in hiding or, like Ernő Gerő, had left the country. Nagy, now able to form a new government, brought in members of several re-emerged political parties with the promise of free, multi-party elections. Two days previously, on Sunday 28 October, with the Soviet armed forces showing signs of withdrawing from the capital, Nagy had declared a ceasefire. On Monday 29 October he had announced the abolition of the AVH, and on Tuesday 30 October he announced his cross-party cabinet. This included Hungarian Army Colonel Pál Maléter, who had defected to the revolutionary cause. He was promoted to General and appointed Minister of Defence. The revolutionary fighters felt they now had a voice in government, and the student leaders liaised closely with Maléter.

By the time Robert and Ian arrived in Budapest, most of the Soviet armed forces had withdrawn to a point a few miles to the north-east of Budapest. Some small-scale fighting continued, most of it hunting down and mopping up any remaining AVH resistance.[96] Crowds were out on the streets viewing the devastation – burnt-out tanks much in evidence, badly-damaged buildings, power lines down, bodies still lying in the streets, and broken glass everywhere. There was no celebration, no hysteria, just quiet relief that the fighting was over for the moment: that this initial stage of the revolution had prevailed. But there were no illusions about the struggle ahead, and no trust that the Soviets would not be back. For the moment, the task ahead was to clear up the rubble and broken glass and get life back to some sense of normality. It was generally accepted that people would return to work the next Monday, 5 November.

---

[95] RO's personal account.

[96] *News Chronicle*, Friday 2 November 1956, p 1: 'They are doomed men in Budapest these hated AVH', by Ian Rankin, Budapest, Thursday.

Neither Robert nor Ian mentioned in their writings where they stayed in Budapest, but once they had delivered their load of penicillin, they each explored the city and its revolution in their own way.[97] Robert contacted one of the student leaders who arranged for him to make speeches, as he had in Sopron. Standing on a soap box at street corners, and in the face of such a humbling testament to the courage of the youth of Hungary, Robert felt a strong responsibility to explain his presence. Speaking in his classic upper-class English voice, with the aid of an interpreter and to the sound of desultory gunfire, he spoke as a fellow student, praising the brave students of Hungary who had stood up against communist oppression and started the revolution, assuring them they had the moral support of the students of Oxford who were raising money for the cause, and the eyes of the world were upon them.[98]

It would have been a student leader who arranged for Robert to interview the Minister of Defence, General Pál Maléter, sitting in his office, probably in Killian Barracks in the heart of Budapest:

> 'Do you want to know', Maléter asked, 'how your fellow-students and even schoolchildren have been disabling Russian tanks?'

He produced a soda-water bottle from under his desk and proceeded to demonstrate, though without fuel, how the students and even young schoolchildren had used them on the Russian tanks, often climbing on top to lob them into the gun turret.[99]

Robert had a further meeting with a group of young revolutionary leaders on Thursday 1 November. He was impressed by their calm maturity:

> I got the impression that the staggering events of the last ten days had given the Hungarian people, and particularly their youth, a marvellous inner strength and faith in themselves. They were justifiably proud in [*sic*] what they had achieved, but there was no complacency. They had no

---

[97] Lajos Lederer stayed at the prestigious old Hotel Gellért, but he would have been on *Observer* expenses, not available to Oakeshott and Rankin.

[98] Tatiana Mallinson, interview, 7 October 2020.

[99] *Oakeshott Papers*, RO's personal account, November 1956, pp 2–3.

illusions as to the further sacrifices they might have to make.

They were behaving calmly and with a full sense of responsibility. There had been virtually no looting. They greeted us with tremendous warmth and wonderful affection. But they were in complete control of their emotions. ...

One thing was certain; they would not yield one inch of the ground they had gained. They would fight for what they had done – if need be until they were all dead.[100]

When Robert asked what people like him, especially students in Britain, could do to help, they told him they wanted 'only moral support. But they couldn't have too much of that.' They needed to know that people in the West understood what they had achieved and wholeheartedly supported their aspirations. But if fighting broke out again, 'they would welcome other kinds of support'.[101]

It is now known that after prevaricating for a few days, the Soviet leader Nikita Khrushchev decided on the night of Wednesday 31 October that the Soviet Military Command in Hungary would crush the revolution. On Thursday 1 November there were signs of new Soviet troops entering the country. Prime Minister Nagy lodged a formal protest with the Soviet Ambassador to Hungary, Yuri Andropov.[102] That evening, Nagy broadcast to the nation a 'Declaration of Neutrality', appealing to neighbouring nations to respect a 'free, independent, democratic and neutral Hungary'.[103] In doing so, he was withdrawing Hungary from the Warsaw Pact. As he understood it, he was negotiating the withdrawal of all Soviet troops from Hungarian soil. All his efforts, however, were in vain.

It is clear from Robert's account that he was no longer in Budapest when the Soviet High Command launched its revenge attack on the city in the early hours of Sunday 4 November. He probably left with Ian on

---

[100] RO's personal account.

[101] RO's personal account.

[102] Later Head of the KGB, and later still, briefly until his death in 1984, one of the last of the old-style Soviet leaders before Gorbachev, *glasnost* and *perestroika*.

[103] United Nations, *The Problem of Hungary*, p 25.

the afternoon of Friday 2 November. Quite apart from the renewed Soviet threat, they had done all they could in Budapest and they both needed to get back to Oxford, for they had already been absent without leave for one full academic week. Large numbers of Hungarians were already boarding any vehicles they could find to try to get out of Budapest, and it was clearly time for the two Oxford undergraduates to leave while they still could.

It is known that Robert drove out in a car apparently borrowed from the British Legation. There were a lot of children sheltering in the British Embassy and they tried to join Robert's car, thinking he was an international rescue party, but they had to be turned away. According to Jane Willoughby, Robert was very upset by that incident.[104] Ian Rankin wrote of their journey out, travelling with three journalists as passengers:

> Budapest [was] ringed by innumerable nationalist check points, consisting of three or four armed youths in each case. At one of these points, we failed to stop and were fired upon by a trigger-happy teenager. One bullet, a dum-dum, missed one of the passengers by three inches and tore a hole the size of a cricket-ball in the rear door. We stopped but were later allowed to proceed.[105]

That evening they arrived safely in Vienna, from where Ian was able to phone through a report to *The Observer* that appeared in that Sunday's paper under the heading 'Students led Hungarian Revolt'.[106] It is not clear whether or where Robert's report, written on 8 or 9 November, was published.

On returning to their respective Oxford colleges at the weekend, the two young men were welcomed by the students as returning heroes. Having been humbled by the mature courage and example of the Hungarian students, Robert modestly played down any heroism of his own. When talking of his personal experience, he tended to make light of it, and he

---

[104] Jane Willoughby, interview, 6 April 2021.

[105] Sir Ian Rankin, personal papers, longhand draft clearly prepared for publication. With thanks to Sir Gavin Rankin for sending copies of his father's Hungary-related papers.

[106] *The Observer*, 4 November 1956, p 7.

spread the story that he had only decided to go to Hungary because he had an essay on Roman history due for Russell Meiggs that Saturday and he could not think of anything worth writing on the subject.[107]

He and Ian were probably summoned before the Masters of their respective colleges on the Monday morning, but Ian's reports to the *News Chronicle* had kept everyone aware of the nature of their 'mercy mission', and it was clear that they had the admiration of many of the dons.[108] In any case, news had by then come through of the scale of the brutal Soviet attack on Budapest at dawn on the Sunday morning. Everybody was just thankful that Oakeshott and Rankin had come out alive, and they probably got no more than a verbal ticking-off.

* * *

Robert and Ian were not the only students to visit Budapest during the revolution. There were a number from Cambridge and at least one other group from Oxford. The latter consisted of first-year student Christopher Lord, Michael Korda, nephew of the Hungarian-born film producer Alexander Korda, Roger Cooper, and Russel Taylor. They drove to Budapest in an old VW Beetle, carrying several million doses of penicillin, although they did not arrive until Saturday 3 November, on the eve of the Soviet attack. They spent the next several days holed up in the basement of the Astoria Hotel – the 'war hotel' for foreign journalists – whilst it was being bombarded by Russian tanks. They eventually left Hungary on 11 November. Christopher Lord later went back to Hungary and was arrested, but that is another story.[109]

Nevertheless, Robert appears to have been the one who started the whole ball rolling. On the fiftieth anniversary of the Revolution, his heroism was to be officially recognised by the Hungarian State when he

---

[107] Mehta, *Up at Oxford*, Chapter IV.

[108] *News Chronicle*, 29 October 1956, p 1.

[109] *Radio Free Europe*, transcript of broadcast, 1 November 1956; and 'Molotov Cocktails from Oxford', interview with Christopher Lord, 2 November 2006 - https://24.hu/fn/gazdasag/2006/11/02/oxfordi_molotov_koktel/ [accessed 18 April 2021]. I am grateful to Emi Claris for translating both documents.

was awarded the 'Hero of Freedom' medal at the Hungarian Embassy in London.[110] Christopher Lord received the same award. Ian Rankin's absence from those awards may have been because, through his articles in the *News Chronicle*, he was perceived by the Hungarians to be a journalist doing his professional job, rather than a student on a heroic mercy mission. It was not only the Hungarians who regarded Robert as a hero; he was also widely regarded as such in Britain, at least in the months following his return from Hungary. He was invited to speak at several venues, at the University and elsewhere, including at least one secondary school, and he had an article published in the *Times Higher Educational Supplement*. The latter was a thoughtful assessment of the revolution, its origins and aims, and the central role played by students.[111] It may have been the quality of the writing of this article that attracted the attention of Gordon Newton, the editor of the *Financial Times*. And thus opened a promising career for Robert.

* * *

Aftermath: the crushing of the Revolution
Late on Saturday night 3 November 1956, Pál Maléter, together with his Minister of State, his Chief of Staff and an army colonel had been invited to a Hungarian Soviet command post, ostensibly to discuss the withdrawal of Soviet troops. They were arrested by the NKGB (the Soviet secret police) and spirited out of the country to Romania.

By dawn on Sunday 4 November 1956, Russian tanks[112] had seized control of all the bridges in Budapest and the main roads in and out of the city. Within hours they had complete control of central Budapest, crushing

---

[110] *MTI_2006_Oakeshott,* 'Honours awarded in London to British public figures on the anniversary of 1956, November 15, 2006, London Embassy': with translation from the Hungarian by Emi Claris.

[111] *Times Higher Educational Supplement*, Friday 16 November 1956.

[112] Although part of the Soviet Armed Forces, the tanks were the classic Russian T-54 and the light T-34, operated almost exclusively by Russian crews. Some 1,500 tanks and several thousand other Soviet military personnel were deployed across Hungary to crush the Revolution.

all the main resistance points by firing indiscriminately left and right along the main thoroughfares of the city. It was a clear revenge attack for the humiliation of their loss of 26 tanks and many more armoured personnel carriers during their earlier intervention. That night they parked many of their tanks under floodlight in the main boulevard of Andrássy Street; but they came under such sustained rifle, grenade and Molotov Cocktail attack that on subsequent nights the tanks left the city at dusk and returned at dawn each morning.

By the end of Monday 5 November, most of the major buildings of central Budapest had been severely damaged or reduced to rubble. The Parliament Building was one of the few prominent structures to remain unscathed. Young revolutionaries kept up small-scale guerrilla resistance, at least for the rest of that week, fighting on a matter of principle rather than expectation of success.

In Sopron, so familiar to Robert Oakeshott, four Russian tanks entered the town on the afternoon of Sunday 4 November. The resistance of some lightly-armed students and other youths was quickly crushed. That first day of the Russian assault some 5,000 refugees crossed the border and the Austrians set up refugee camps to house and process them.

After his final broadcast at dawn on 4 November, Nagy fled to the Yugoslav Embassy. He was later tricked into leaving this sanctuary, was kidnapped by the NKGB and taken to Romania. In April 1958 Nagy, Maléter and the journalist Miklós Gimes were submitted to a staged trial on a charge of treason, and executed.

Having initially worked with Nagy in the first week of the Revolution, János Kádár, from the Titoist wing of the Hungarian Communist Party, left Budapest for Moscow on 1 November 1956. As the Russian tanks moved into Budapest on 4 November, Kádár was declared the head of the 'restored' communist government. He remained at the head of the Hungarian Government, initially as Prime Minister and then as Secretary General of the Hungarian Communist Party, until 1988.

In Britain, after Ian Rankin returned from Budapest, his mother, Lady Jane Rankin, set up a charity, 'Aid to Hungary (from Britain)' to provide medical and logistical aid to the Hungarian refugees in the Austrian border camps. Among the charity's Council members were David Astor of *The Observer* and Lady Jane Willoughby, who was to spend some time working at the refugee camps, as did Tatiana Orlov. Ian Rankin returned to Austria in December, on special assignment for the *News Chronicle*, investigating 'the organisation of relief and medical aid to Hungary'.[113] He did not get into Hungary on this occasion; the borders had been closed; but he witnessed many refugees still clandestinely crossing the frontier into Austria. He also commented upon the activities of Hungarian people-traffickers profiteering from their countrymen's desperation.[114]

[113] *Sir Ian Rankin's Hungary papers 1956*: Sylvain Mangeot, Foreign Editor, *News Chronicle*, 'To Whom it May Concern', 11 December 1956.

[114] *Rankin Hungary papers*, Ian Rankin to his parents, 'Austria, not so far from a beautiful mobile kitchen', Saturday [22 December 1956].

CHAPTER 7

Sunderland Echo

1957–1958

It must have taken Robert a while to wind down from the drama and excitement of his Hungarian trip. But now he was in his final year at Balliol, and turning his attention to academic work, he won prizes in Latin and Greek poetry. He certainly had the exceptional intellect required for a first-class degree, like his father, but in the event, he gained an upper second, rather than a first. For Robert, as for his brother Cargs, who also gained an upper second, four years at Oxford had always been about much more than academic achievement, and the wider education about life, values and friendship gained at Oxford was irreplaceable.

The circle of friends that Robert accumulated at Oxford was to remain with him for life. Once he had judged you, in his terms, a 'very good egg', a 'good egg', or even a 'moderate egg', you were admitted to his trusted circle, and he would hold to that friendship through thick and thin. 'Bad eggs' did not feature. If he delegated a task to a good egg, he did so with total trust that the task would be carried out conscientiously. He would support you in any undertaking of your own and would assume the same support in return. And if there were ever any doubt about the latter, his charm, generosity of spirit and enjoyable company were almost guaranteed to win you over.

But what was he to do to earn a living in the world beyond Balliol? There does not appear to have been any clear plan. Besides visiting friends and relatives in that summer of 1957, he used personal contacts in search of a variety of jobs. He informed his mother in early September, for instance, that through some contact in the Foreign Office, he had met 'the Sultan' in Whitehall, with a view to possible employment. Which Sultan and what employment was not mentioned – his mother obviously knew – but in any case, in the meantime something more interesting had come up.

At some stage over the summer, he had been contacted by the *Financial Times (FT)*: the Editor, Gordon Newton, would like to speak with him. An interview was arranged for Monday 9 September 1957. Newton had been Features Editor and Leader Writer for some years at the *FT* before taking over as Editor in 1950. He saw the future of the paper as growing beyond financial and business news, with its bald figures of assets and returns. He broadened its coverage to include international political news and coverage of the arts. He was rewarded with increased sales, reaching 100,000 by 1953. He strengthened the paper, against all predictions, by hiring high-flying graduates straight from Oxford and Cambridge. Among his early protégés was the future editor of *The Times*, William Rees-Mogg.[115]

Newton would have noted Robert's escapade to Hungary and the clarity and quality of his article for the *Times Higher Education*, so it is not surprising that Oakeshott was one of the young Oxford graduates he approached in the summer of 1957. Robert always did well at interview, and sure enough he was offered a job on the editorial side of the *Financial Times*,[116] starting in April 1958, on condition that he spend at least three months working for a regional newspaper in the meantime. The main reason for that condition may have been at the insistence of the National Union of Journalists, but it was to prove a fruitful apprenticeship for Robert.

By the beginning of September 1957, Robert had already committed himself to teaching History for a term at a secondary school. A letter to his mother suggests the school may have been in Dorking.[117] A letter from a Mrs Sullivan, who presumably worked at the school, recalled one occasion when Robert had 'overslept in the train and had to take first period in [his] dinner jacket'. It was clear to Mrs Sullivan that Robert's time at the school 'would be temporary',[118] which indeed it was. Immediately after

---

[115] https://en.wikipedia.org/wiki/Gordon_Newton [accessed 6 June 2021].

[116] *Balliol Archives*, OakeshottRNW+3, RO to the Master, n.d. (c. early March 1958).

[117] *Oakeshott Letters*, RO to his mother, Sunderland, 8 March 1958.

[118] RO to his mother, Sunderland, 22 February 1958.

celebrating the 1958 New Year with the family, he travelled north to take up a short-term appointment as a journalist on the *Sunderland Echo*.

* * *

Robert learned invaluable life lessons during his three months in Sunderland. Not only did the sub-editor's blue pencil teach him much about the skills of rapid and accurate journalistic writing on a wide range of hitherto unknown topics;[119] he was also introduced to the realities of working-class life. For somebody of his background, the latter was an education. He lived in digs, where he was well-fed with a hearty breakfast and an early evening meal – 'tea' – of egg and chips, or a chop and chips, served with bread and butter and plenty of strong tea. 'Dinner', he learned, was a midday meal, whatever its size, and his was usually a sandwich bought near his place of work.

On the journalist front, his colleagues were 'friendly & cigarette lending', but he was initially left wondering how long he could maintain an interest in the 'utterly miscellaneous character' of local news, and how long it would be before the novelty wore off. In his first week, he reported briefly on 'a local skiffle group (a kind of jazz)', and the launching of a ship, 'sans ceremony or champagne'.[120] But then he delved deeper in his reports and became utterly charmed by the character and spirit of the working-class people whom he met.

He began by investigating the Farringdon school boycott. A group of 60 angry mothers from a new estate in the suburb of Farringdon were withholding their five- and six-year-old children from school. They had initially been offered places at the new-build infant school on the estate, but just before the start of term in January 1958, they were informed by the Local Education Authority that their part of Farringdon had been re-zoned and they would have to send their infants by bus to more distant schools, out of their district and across the main Durham-Sunderland

---

[119] RO to his mother, 12 January 1958.
[120] RO to his mother, 17 January 1958.

Road.[121] The infant school on their estate had been filled by children from the other end of Farringdon and the mothers 'smelt foul play'. 'People here have a nose for injustice', Robert informed his mother, and what on the surface might have seemed a trivial matter was 'not uninstructive about the character of Sunderland dwellers'.[122] Thanks to the publicity Robert managed to obtain for them in the pages of the *Echo*, the mothers got a hearing at a meeting of Sunderland Town Council. Their case was referred to the Education Committee[123] and, thanks to more support from Robert and the *Echo*, the matter seems to have been settled satisfactorily.[124]

The editor was aware that Robert was at the *Echo* for just a few months to learn the ropes, before transferring to the *Financial Times*, and he was prepared to give him a variety of assignments. Thus, in February Robert was assigned to some court reporting and on one occasion sent to Durham to cover the Assizes. Anticipating a morning of dull routine, Robert seated himself in the Press Box, close to the corner of the bench:

> Imagine my delight, therefore, when bringing up the rear of a column of eminent dignitaries (Judge, High Sheriff, Ld. Lieutenant & what not) I found Tom B.[125]

When the dignitaries finally sat down, Robert found he and his great Balliol friend Tom Bingham were 'within easy whispering range'. They had high hopes of dinner at the Judge's table, but that fell through, and they ended up sharing a humble but most enjoyable meal at Robert's digs.

By this time Robert was thoroughly enjoying his work, particularly his conversations with a wide range of working-class Sunderlanders, such as some of the women from the local over-sixties 'Darby and Joan Club', or the 'weather-beaten old salt', forced to retire from the sea by an accident

---

[121] *Sunderland Echo*, 6 January 1958, p 9.

[122] RO to his mother, 7 January 1958.

[123] *Sunderland Echo*, 16 and 17 January 1958.

[124] *Sunderland Echo*, 22 and 23 January 1958; and *Oakeshott Letters*, RO to his mother, 26 January 1958.

[125] RO to his mother, 2 February 1958.

that led to the loss of an arm: 'his yarn was as good as anything in Conrad'. He had learned to appreciate the 'all human interest' coverage of the *Echo* – 'how sorry I shall be to leave them'.[126]

In the short time Robert had been with the *Echo* he had earned the respect of the editor and by mid-February he was being allowed to pursue topics on his own initiative. Thus, he spoke with the Sunderland Moral Welfare Officer and learned from her the fate of 'unwanted' children, often born to unmarried teenagers – the stigma of illegitimacy being still strong in the 1950s. There was 'a waiting list of people eager to adopt infants up to three years old', with a preference for girls, but school-age boys were almost impossible to place. Robert wrote a piece highlighting the case of an eleven-year-old boy who wanted just three things: 'the affection of a mother, the security of a home – and a father who would take him to football matches on Saturdays'. It was written with such compassion that the editor agreed to publish it under Robert's own name – a rare privilege for journalists at the *Echo*.[127]

As ever, Robert felt the looming shadow of his father, especially as some of Walter Oakeshott's research for the 1938 Report, *Men Without Work*, had been conducted among the unemployed of the North East. The editor of the *Echo* must have been aware of the family connection, because he asked him to do a piece on Sunderland's unemployed and agreed to give him 'a pretty free hand'.

Levels of unemployment in the late 1950s were very much lower than they had been in the 1930s, but Robert recognised that in times of almost full employment 'no one pays much attention to the unemployed', which, in his view, was 'a good enough reason to join the slender dole queue and meet some of Sunderland's workless men'.[128]

Throughout his life Robert was a great listener; he encouraged people to express their opinions and frustrations; he could at times lay down 'the law' as he saw it; but one could be sure that his version of 'the law' was

---

[126] RO to his mother, 17 and 26 January, 22 February 1958.

[127] *Sunderland Echo*, 28 February 1958, p 8.

[128] *Sunderland Echo*, 7 March 1958, p 19.

well-researched and well-informed.[129] Listening to the unemployed men of Sunderland as they left the Employment Exchange with their weekly benefit, however, was a humbling experience. He found their stories, 'strong, even harrowing stuff'.[130]

> It would be folly to underestimate the bitterness of these men. It was directed against a variety of targets. The Conservatives: 'Conserve,' said one, 'that means keep. Conservatives, the party of them that keep. How can we be Conservatives? We haven't got anything to keep.'[131]

This sort of response gave Robert 'a clearer idea of why there [was] only one Tory seat in County Durham'.[132] The greatest daily problem faced by these men was how to fill their time between visits to the Employment Exchange to draw their weekly payment.

> 'I go for walks,' said one. 'I hang about the streets,' said another. 'I try to kill time and then I go to bed early to put myself out of my misery,' said a third.

There was no unemployed men's club, such as had existed in the 1930s, and training courses were few and hard to come by.

There appeared to be complacency in official circles because the national level of unemployment was only 2 per cent. But as Robert pointed out in his perceptive article, being down and out under low levels of unemployment was so much harder to bear because you were on your own, without even the camaraderie of large numbers of your mates in the same position. When he asked how they would respond if there was a 'Sunderland Training Centre', with a range of courses freely available, they all agreed they would take full advantage of it; but perhaps even more importantly,

> … if only there was somebody to whom they could look as being really concerned about their situation; then it seemed to me their morale would go up a hundredfold. They seemed to brighten up enormously even talking to me.

---

[129] John Jolliffe, interview, 28 October 2020.

[130] RO to his mother, 22 February 1958.

[131] *Sunderland Echo*, 7 March 1958, p 19.

[132] *Balliol Archives*, OakeshottRNW+4, RO to the Master, n.d. (c. early March 1958).

The nearly full-page article 'By Robert Oakeshott' was headlined:

UNEMPLOYED WOULD WELCOME TRAINING CENTRE IN SUNDERLAND.[133]

Although Robert was soon to move on to higher-status employment at the *Financial Times*, he valued what he had learned at the *Echo*. He felt he had 'profited from this spell in the North East',[134] and his concern for the Sunderland unemployed was genuine. The memory of his time in their company remained with him and when, after some years of working in Africa, he returned to the United Kingdom with a determination to set up a workers' cooperative with multiple apprenticeships, it was to Sunderland that he took his idea.[135]

* * *

In March 1958, in anticipation of working at the *Financial Times*, Robert wrote to Toynbee Hall in the East End of London asking if they had any accommodation available. Toynbee Hall was a not-for-profit organisation dedicated to the eradication of poverty and offered itself as 'a place for future leaders to live and work as volunteers in London's East End, bringing them face to face with poverty, and giving them the opportunity to develop practical solutions that they could take with them into national life'.[136] In his letter of application, Robert had given the Master of Balliol College as his referee. The latter remembered Oakeshott as 'an enthusiastic eager type of young man ... a young man of intelligence and personality'. He did not recall his being 'actively interested in social service', though he had 'a wide spread of interests in many directions'.[137] Robert's new-found interest in the unemployed, however, combined with his father's reputation, may

---

[133] *Sunderland Echo*, 7 March 1958, p 19.

[134] *Balliol Archives*, OakeshottRNW+4, RO to the Master, n.d. (c. early March 1958).

[135] (See Chapter 14).

[136] https://www.toynbeehall.org.uk/about-us/our-history/ [accessed 23 July 2021].

[137] *Balliol Archives*, Oakeshott RNW+8, Sir David Keir, Master of Balliol College, to AE Morgan, Warden of Toynbee Hall, 12 March 1958.

have influenced the Toynbee Board, who offered him accommodation on a temporary basis.

And temporary was all that Robert required, for he soon fixed himself up, sharing a flat with his Oxford friends Antony Martin, James Hughes and Charles Keen. They were all still in what Charles Keen referred to as their 'formative years' – mid-twenties – and sharing a flat with Robert could never be anything but great fun. Charles was later to recall a week's holiday in Dublin in 1959, staying with the Fitzherberts and the Martin family, where Robert displayed his unique gift of initiative in combination with his enormous sense of fun. It was a fine day in the summer that called for being both on the beach and drinking draught Guinness. Robert solved the conundrum by going to a hardware shop and buying a two-gallon galvanised bucket, then to a pub to have it filled with 16 pints of Guinness and finally to a stationer's for a packet of 100 drinking straws. And, as Charles recalled,

> ... off we went. There were more than two of us, but I must admit, less than 16, and a good many were female, with well-shaped, but not hollow, legs. It was a lovely afternoon.[138]

A year or two later, when Robert was one of the *FT*'s foreign correspondents, Charles lent him his dinner jacket to go to an important reception at the Foreign Office, despite the fact that Robert was the shorter by a good many inches:

> It must have been a very good diplomatic party, since he emerged next day from Bow Street police station, still in my dinner jacket, the trousers of which had worked their way down round the heels of his shoes and attached themselves to the soles.[139]

---

[138] Charles Keen, 'Robert Oakeshott, In Memoriam, a Sermon' (The Chapel, Balliol College, Oxford, 3 December 2011.)

[139] Keen, 'Robert Oakeshott, In Memoriam'.

CHAPTER 8

Financial Times
1958–1964

Robert began work at the *Financial Times* in April 1958. The editor, Gordon Newton, had no intention of wasting his newly-minted 'highflyers' in an apprenticeship of general journalism, and Robert's recent success at the *Sunderland Echo* earned him the role of 'Labour Correspondent'. This covered trade union matters and wage disputes, which were numerous, especially among dock workers and bus drivers. He also covered rising levels of unemployment, which the Transport and General Workers' Union (TGWU) laid at the door of deliberate Government policy.[140] He later co-authored a book with fellow journalist George Cyriax on modern trade unionism.[141] After serving as Labour Correspondent for a little over a year, Robert was shifted to Commonwealth and Foreign Affairs, where he thrived.

His new role involved a good deal of travel, by air, which Robert always enjoyed. Besides numerous trips to Africa, his assignments over the next few years took him to Jamaica, Japan and India, with en route visits to Hong Kong, Singapore, Tehran, Baghdad, Cairo, Beirut and Istanbul. Jamaica was a light assignment, involving a visit to a bauxite factory and an interview with Jamaica's first Prime Minister, Norman Manley QC. Robert found Manley charming, comparable in leonine features and long flowing locks to Russell Meiggs. The highlight of that trip was Robert staying for a few days in a luxury hillside villa as a guest of an aristocratic contact. There were other

---

[140] See, for instance, Robert's reports, *Financial Times*, 6 and 10 December 1958.

[141] George Cyriax & Robert Oakeshott, *The Bargainers. A Survey of Modern Trade Unionism* (Faber and Faber, 1960).

guests and numerous servants, and Robert particularly enjoyed swimming in the villa's glass-panelled pool – eight times in one day – 'a tally which I reckon I'm not likely ever to exceed'. Nearby was the holiday villa of Noel Coward. Robert and guests ventured over to visit the famous flamboyant actor, composer, director and wit, but he was not in residence.[142]

Armed with romanticised ideas of an exotic 'Far East', Robert was surprised to find Tokyo much like any Western industrial capital, although he was pleased to see a few Japanese women still wearing the kimono. On assignment to India in 1961, he first came across the implementation of a National Development Plan – something he had hitherto associated with communist rule, but which he soon realised was perhaps the only way to meet the high-development aspirations of newly-independent nations emerging from decades of colonial neglect.[143] He would not yet have imagined that in a few years' time he himself would be drawing up just such a development plan for an African country about to attain its independence.

In January 1963, Gordon Newton asked Robert to write an in-depth assessment of India's development plans – the country was on its third five-year plan by then, which in the critical opinion of some was bankrupting the state, to little positive effect. Robert felt the person best placed to write such a piece was his Uncle Pendy, who had not only served with distinction in the Indian Civil Service before independence, but had been called back by Prime Minister Nehru to help set up the Planning Commission that drew up India's First Five-Year Plan in 1950. On Robert's recommendation, the *FT* commissioned Sir Penderel Moon[144] to write 1,500 words on India's development planning. With its focus on education and agriculture, Moon judged Indian planning to have achieved 'succès d'estime', noting that by the early 1960s, '"planning" on the Indian model has become not merely respectable, but fashionable, and is being

---

[142] *Oakeshott Letters*, RO to his mother, 14 September 1960.

[143] *Financial Times*, 'Our Own Correspondent' reporting from Bombay, 26 September 1961, p 1.

[144] He was knighted in 1962, for services to Britain/India relations.

actively encouraged in "under-developed" countries by the IMF and the World Bank'.[145] He praised India's massive gains in agricultural production and irrigation, and believed these more than outweighed the rundown of foreign reserves and the high levels of unemployment, which he put down partly to rapid population growth. The *FT*, however, wanting to cut the piece by 100 words, excised whole paragraphs without consulting the author. This left Penderel Moon 'rather disgusted to find [when the article was published] that the *FT* had so emasculated [his carefully balanced] article' as to remove most of the positive aspects and make it read like a negative critique of the Indian model.[146]

Robert was highly embarrassed by the *FT*'s treatment of his much-admired and beloved Uncle Pendy and this may have sown the seed of a feeling that perhaps a long-term career in journalism was not for him. At this time, in the early 1960s, Robert's work for the *FT* was mainly concerned with issues around the decolonisation of Africa, which may thus be seen as an appropriate apprenticeship for his work to come.

* * *

In 1960, 17 African countries gained their independence, most of them former colonies of France, and the year was designated 'The Year of Africa' by the United Nations (UN). The *FT*'s resident correspondents in the Ghanaian capital Accra and in Kenya's Nairobi dealt with West and East African affairs respectively, while its Johannesburg correspondent had his hands full covering what was a seminal period in South Africa. This left room for Robert to become, in effect, the special roving correspondent for Central Africa, covering mainly the Belgian Congo and the British Central African Federation.

The Federation had been founded in 1953, largely in the interests of the white settler colony of Southern Rhodesia (present-day Zimbabwe). It combined that territory with the British Protectorates of Northern

---

[145] *Oakeshott Letters*, typescript of his *Financial Times* article, enclosed in Penderel Moon to his sister Noel, Bangkok, 23 February 1963.

[146] Penderel to Noel, 23 February 1963.

The British Central African Federation, 1960 (by the author).

Rhodesia (present-day Zambia) and Nyasaland (present-day Malawi). Control was exercised from Salisbury (present-day Harare), the capital of Southern Rhodesia, with the Northern Rhodesian 'Copperbelt' providing much of the Federation's export wealth and Nyasaland being treated largely as a labour reserve for white settler interests. One of the principal objects of the Federation was to shore up white settler rule in British Central Africa.

79

In January 1960, as the principal African nationalist leaders of the Belgian Congo were arriving in Brussels for a round-table conference on the course of the Congo towards political independence, Robert Oakeshott was flying in the opposite direction, aboard the inaugural flight by Boeing jet from Brussels to Leopoldville (present-day Kinshasa), the capital of the Belgian Congo. Of that experience, he wrote to his mother, 'I don't expect ever to travel so fast or so lavishly'. He spent half the flight 'lunching … drinking cocktails, eating about eight courses, and then drinking coffee & brandy'. He was particularly impressed that as they flew at 30,000 feet, and at three-quarters of the speed of sound, the fresh steaks were cooked inflight. Was it too good to be true? he wondered, as he sat back with his coffee and another brandy, '… suddenly I found myself thinking of the Titanic!'[147]

From Leopoldville Robert flew on to Elisabethville (present-day Lubumbashi), the capital of Katanga Province, the heart of the Congolese 'Copperbelt', where he spent a few days trying to assess the likely impact of the anticipated Congolese independence, which was then being discussed in Brussels. He was travelling with the *Manchester Guardian* correspondent and the two of them invited four young well-educated Congolese – of whom there were precious few in the country – to dinner at the upmarket Sabena Guest House. Conversation, however, was somewhat stilted, as the *lingua franca* of the Congo was French and neither Robert nor the *Guardian* man had sufficient French for the task. Robert joked that if he threw in 'se trouver' at regular intervals, it helped cover his lack of vocabulary – and this from a man who in a few years' time would be the *FT*'s chief correspondent in Paris.[148]

Next stop Ndola, the provincial capital of the Northern Rhodesian Copperbelt. Robert was immediately struck by the level of racist contempt shown by local white people towards Africans, regardless of their education or age. In his opinion it made the racism in the Congo seem relatively benign. To take an African to dinner in a hotel of any description in Ndola

---

[147] RO to his mother, 22 January 1960.

[148] RO to his mother, 22 January 1960.

would have been impossible: 'Right of Admission Reserved' posted over the door meant in local white parlance, 'Kaffirs Keep Out'. Robert was particularly disgusted by the contempt and bullying shown by many white people towards their black servants.

This African trip was linked to the timing of Prime Minister Harold Macmillan's six-week tour of 'British Africa', which was designed to show both Africans and white colonists that Britain was embarking on a course of decolonisation in Africa. Robert flew on to the Federal capital Salisbury in time for Macmillan's arrival in late January. His assignment was essentially to assess the chances for the survival of the Central African Federation. By the time he reached Salisbury, Robert realised that a clear majority of white people in the Federation regarded Africans as 'irredeemably inferior beings', and any political talk of racial 'partnership' was a complete sham. Which answered the principal question of his mission: '… the Federation is certainly doomed'.

Under the circumstances, Robert considered Macmillan handled the inevitable 'white' press conference adroitly, though showing off in a 'bouncing manner' – 'Dad would certainly have been bored by some of his jokes' – but he retained his good humour 'in the face of some decidedly acid questions'. Robert raised the question of the franchise in the three territories:

> … after looking surprised at the fact that the question came from the *F.T.*, he answered fairly civilly'.[149]

Macmillan's next stop was South Africa, where he delivered his famous 'wind of change' speech before the South African Parliament in Cape Town:

> The wind of change is blowing through this continent. Whether we like it or not, this growth of national consciousness is a political fact.

This did not go down well in white-ruled South Africa, already well-embarked on its apartheid policies, with no intention of allowing any movement towards African majority rule.

---

[149] RO to his mother, 29 January 1960.

Meanwhile, still in Salisbury, Robert had an interview with the Federal Prime Minister, Sir Roy Welensky – 'who has bushy eyebrows like Mr Meiggs & a very big bulk indeed'. In response to Robert's question as to why the Federation did not have the confidence of Africans, Welensky declared this to be nonsense and blustered about his efforts to get rid of the colour bar not being properly presented in the media. Robert's conclusion: 'humbug … all talk, no action'.[150]

On Saturday 30 January 1960 Robert flew to Lusaka, the Northern Rhodesian capital, a 'city' with one wide main street (Cairo Road), laid out north-south, with a couple of lesser streets to the west, comprising the '2nd class trading area', and to the east, the railway station. Clustered around the city, mainly to the south and west, were numerous 'African townships', official and unofficial, while beyond the station on a slight rise to the east were numerous new government buildings and the Ridgeway Hotel, five-star by any standards. It was a city with which Robert was to become familiar, but on this occasion it was a brief stop. As he wrote to his mother,

> I have two more days in which I hope to meet perhaps the most important of the African nationalist leaders – a man called Kaunda who has just come out of prison and apparently lives in the neighbourhood.[151]

He failed to meet him on this occasion, but his opportunity would come.

Robert undertook numerous other trips to Africa over the following three years, mostly concerned with the inevitable break-up of the Central African Federation. The main pressure for the latter came from the African nationalist leaders of Northern Rhodesia and Nyasaland. They believed the only route to majority rule and independence lay in their separation from the white settler dominance of Southern Rhodesia. Of the Southern Rhodesian white settlers, even the Chief Justice of the Supreme Court in Salisbury, Sir Robert Tredgold, recognised that the white 10 per cent of the population could not continue to rule the 90 per cent black population in the changed circumstances of the 1960s. As he told Robert prophetically:

---

[150] RO to his mother, 29 January 1960; see also *Financial Times*, 1 February 1960.

[151] *Oakeshott Letters*, RO to his mother, 29 January 1960.

... if they don't hand over power voluntarily it will ultimately be wrested from them by force. That must be the key fact in the situation, and not the low level of African education or their tendency to spit in public.[152]

On a more positive note, in December 1960 Robert spent a couple of nights in Dar-es-Salaam where he met, in the bar of his hotel,

... the delightful charming and moderate African leader in Tanganyika Mr Julius Nyerere. I was extremely impressed. He is certainly far the most likeable – and quite possibly the most able of the various African leaders I've met.[153]

Nyerere, at the time Chief Minister of Tanganyika (the mainland part of present-day Tanzania), was as strongly anti-racism as he was anti-colonialism, stressing that he was keen not to allow race prejudice against whites in Tanganyika. He was to become Prime Minister of Tanganyika the following year and lead his country to independence on 9 December 1961.

Robert was back in Lusaka in October 1962 for Northern Rhodesia's first General Election on a widened, though still restricted, franchise. The colonial authorities laid on lavish entertainment for the 'world's press' – drinks with the Governor and an 'El Alamein Ball', for which one official offered to lay on girls for anyone wishing to attend. 'I may say that I declined,' Robert assured his mother.[154] Robert realised the irrelevance of this surreal atmosphere. The real event was playing out on the streets, with Kenneth Kaunda, leader of the United National Independence Party (UNIP), at the fore.

Some of us [wrote Robert] attended a rally he held here on Sunday and he's clearly a person of the highest moral principles. His audience was 99% African. Yet he devoted over three quarters of his speech to arguing the case that Europeans would be really welcome to stay on in the country after a

---

[152] RO to his mother, 'en route to Nairobi', 5 December 1960.

[153] RO to his mother, 5 December 1960.

[154] RO to his mother, 30 October 1962.

Kenneth Kaunda leads the Northern Rhodesian delegation before the United Nations' Special Committee of Seventeen, appealing for independence from British colonialism, with (on Kaunda's left) Arthur Wina and (on his right) Sir Stuart Gore-Brown and Mr Desai, April 1962.
(From the Stuart Gore-Brown Archive, Shiwa Ngandu,
by kind permission of Charlie and Jo Harvey)

nationalist government had been returned to power. 'It's not that we want them to stay because of their capital or technical knowledge' he said, 'it is because they are our fellow human beings: children of the same father.' In its way it was one of the most moving things I have ever heard. And, quite evidently, he meant it.[155]

Clearly Robert was smitten by the Kaunda charisma.

His final visit to Africa as the *FT*'s correspondent was for the Victoria Falls Conference of June 1963, which led to the final winding up of the Federation at the end of that year. He stayed at the North Western Hotel in Livingstone, five miles upstream of the Falls on the Northern Rhodesian side of the Zambezi River. He hired a small Japanese car to drive himself to and from the conference at the Vic Falls Hotel on the Southern Rhodesian side. Remarking, 'I don't suppose I shall get another

---

[155] RO to his mother, 30 October 1962.

opportunity', he took time off at the weekend to drive 40 miles west to the ferry crossing at Kazungula where, at the confluence of the Chobe and Zambezi rivers, Northern and Southern Rhodesia met, in mid-river, with Bechuanaland (present-day Botswana) and the Caprivi Strip in South West Africa (present-day Namibia). Robert took the small car ferry across to Bechuanaland on the south bank of the Chobe and drove the few miles upstream to Chobe Safari Lodge, opened in 1960, where he had a very pleasant lunch followed by a trip aboard a paddle steamer to view the abundant hippos and elephants.[156] Three years later he did indeed get another opportunity to cross the Kazungula ferry to Bechuanaland – riding in the back of a Land Rover, heading south on a very different mission.

But for now, the Vic Falls Conference was his last journalistic assignment in Africa. A week later, on 8 July 1963, he took up the post of the *FT*'s chief correspondent in Paris.

* * *

On an earlier visit to Paris, in about 1960, Robert had met Catherine 'Kate' Shuckburgh, whose father, Sir Evelyn Shuckburgh, was a senior figure in NATO, based in Paris. Robert was later to recall a musical evening in Paris at that time, when Kate played the clarinet and Sir Evelyn the guitar.[157] It is not clear whether this was their first meeting, but it was clear to his close friends that Robert was smitten, and with a lot of interests in common, the attraction appeared to be mutual.

Robert was aware that several of his Oxford friends had been getting married in recent years and it seems to have occurred to him that this was his opportunity. He does not appear to have given much thought to what sort of commitment marriage would involve, beyond the idea that 'one got married', and it was highly romantic. He kept in touch with Kate from the London flat he shared with Antony Martin and Charles Keen, and sometime in early 1961 he proposed marriage to her. According to Charles Keen, Robert took a taxi from London to the Shuckburgh family home

---

[156] RO to his mother, 27 June 1963.
[157] RO to his mother, 23 August 1969.

near Watlington in Oxfordshire, where he spent the night in a telephone box, so that he could present his written proposal in an envelope to the butler in time for breakfast.[158]

He must have pictured her opening the envelope and her eyes lighting up with excitement, but he was too late: she was already engaged to John David Caute, a Fellow of All Souls College, Oxford. Although Kate indicated that under different circumstances she might have accepted, it was a commitment she could not break, and she turned Robert down.

* * *

There is no doubt that Robert's 1963 appointment to Paris was a promotion, but it lacked the thrill of international travel and was not that exciting from Robert's point of view. He found lodgings in Paris, but his 'office' was usually one of several favourite cafés where, like a regular Parisian, he could be found perusing the pages of *Le Monde* – which soon became the main source of his reports from Paris. Much of the British interest in French news at the time was related to President Charles de Gaulle's '*Non*' to British entry to the then European Economic Community (EEC), which consisted at the time of France, West Germany, Italy and the three Benelux countries. De Gaulle was at the height of his political career, intent on re-establishing France as a major power, especially within the EEC.

The height of Robert's social life in Paris was always visits from his friends, whom he enjoyed entertaining in the French capital. And on occasion he would take them riding in the nearby French countryside. His main complaint about his life in Paris, as he related to his Oxford friend John Jolliffe who was visiting for a few days, was the absence of public clocks in the streets of Paris, such as were to be found in most English cities; since he rarely if ever wore a watch, he never knew the time. Jolliffe reckoned Robert was out of his depth in Paris, mainly due to his lack of fluent conversational French; he apparently made no effort to improve this.[159]

---

[158] Charles Keen, interview, 29 September 2020.

[159] John Jolliffe, interview, 28 October 2020.

At the time he was still set on marriage, which he assumed was the natural course of a young man's life, and during one of his regular trips to London, in the early months of 1964, he met, fell in love with and quickly became engaged to Tessa Head. She was the daughter of Viscount Anthony Head, GCMG, British High Commissioner to Malaysia. Robert was 30; she was 25.

Robert loved the company of women. He had many great and lasting friendships with women, who were attracted by his charm, his humour, his respect for their intellect and perhaps, too, his great listening skills. But his attempts to establish a lasting romantic liaison seemed always doomed to failure. Not only was there his neglected clothing and personal hygiene, which Charles Keen warned him about, to which Robert responded, 'What on earth is wrong with the aroma of honest sweat?' But he knew next to nothing about sex, and it took Charles's sister Geraldine to educate him in this regard. She stayed with him in Paris; they went riding together; and they had deep conversations about relationships. Despite her efforts, however, Robert remained 'much too idealistic'.[160] He was instinctively shy with girls, until he had befriended them on a platonic level, and he did not know how to pursue a romantic relationship, as evinced by the manner of his proposal to Kate Shuckburgh. With Tessa, however, he believed he had made it. He had got to know her well enough for a direct, face-to-face proposal, and she had accepted. This was his great whirlwind romance. He threw a party to celebrate and, carried away by his good fortune, he got very drunk. It is thought this may have contributed to Tessa thinking better of her hasty acceptance; she called off the engagement.[161] As Robert later told Francis Nichols over a long lunch, 'I took her to dinner in the Place de la Victoire; it should have been the Rue de l'Humilité'.[162]

He was deeply distressed by the failure of his engagement and it ultimately led to his reassessment of his life's direction.[163] He decided

---

[160] Geraldine (Keen) Norman, interview, 9 December 2020.

[161] Geraldine Norman, interview, 9 December 2020.

[162] *Oakeshott Papers*, 'Robert', a typescript of memories by Francis Nichols, 2011.

[163] Charles Keen, interview, 29 September 2020.

he needed to do something completely different, more worthwhile than flitting between Paris and London and writing about de Gaulle's latest policy change, or the progress of the French economy.

Robert had turned 30 in 1963 and he wanted to leave his mark. In doing so he hoped to help make the world a better place. An element of Utopianism was creeping into his vision, and in this frame of mind he considered going into politics. His family, especially on his mother's side, had a long tradition of being on the Liberal side of British politics. Indeed, Noel's father had stood, though unsuccessfully, as Liberal candidate for Oxford in the 1929 general election. Robert's own instinct was to favour the Liberals, for he felt there must be a middle way between the bureaucratic, state-controlled socialism of Labour and the self-satisfied capitalism of the Conservatives. And there was a feeling in the air in 1963/64 that it was not only across Africa that the 'wind of change' was blowing.

Robert was a great admirer of Jo Grimond, leader of the Liberal Party since 1955. They had met through family and Balliol connections and they soon became firm friends.[164] Although holding only six seats at the 1955 and 1959 elections, the Liberal star was rising, and under Jo Grimond's leadership their share of the vote had doubled to 5.9 per cent. With a general election due to be called not later than October 1964, the Liberals were determined to up their game and contest at least half the seats in the country. Robert was an obvious potential candidate and might well have stood for the Liberals in the 1964 election, were it not for two events which occurred at about this time.

First, he received a substantial and unexpected financial legacy from the Belgian artist Georges van Houten. It had come about through his father's connection to the artist. In 1960, the septuagenarian van Houten wanted to find a permanent home for his 300 or so paintings, and his collection of Far Eastern antiques. Having been turned down by institutions in Belgium and France, he offered them, together with half his financial fortune, to the University of Oxford on the understanding that they be put on display. Walter Oakeshott was asked to review the artwork and he played a key role

---

[164] Trevor Smith, *Workhouse to Westminster* (Caper Press, London, 2018), p 258.

in the University Council's decision to accept the legacy. In gratitude, van Houten offered to bequeath Walter the other half of his personal fortune – something like £250,000, a very considerable sum in 1960. Walter's scruples would not allow him to accept, but he did, with considerable hesitation, accept van Houten's offer to divide the legacy equally between Walter's four children, on condition that it remain a secret until van Houten's death, which occurred in the early months of 1964.[165]

The bequest gave Robert considerable financial security. He was not a man to spend money on 'unnecessary' luxuries for himself – as evidenced by his attitude towards his clothing – but a legacy such as this gave him the financial freedom to leave the security of his well-paid job with the *Financial Times* and take up whatever attractive offer came his way; this happened in May 1964, when a fortuitous meeting offered his life an exciting and completely new direction.

---

[165] Dancy, *Walter Oakeshott*, pp 238–242.

CHAPTER 9

Zambia

1964

It was the first weekend in May 1964 and Robert was on one of his visits to London. Kenneth Kaunda, the African nationalist leader whom Robert had on two occasions tried to meet during fleeting visits to Lusaka, was also in London. Northern Rhodesia's first universal franchise general election in January 1964 had given Kaunda's United National Independence Party (UNIP) a decisive majority of seats in the National Assembly. Kaunda became Prime Minister and formed the country's first all-African cabinet. He was now in London to negotiate the final constitution under which Northern Rhodesia would gain its independence within the Commonwealth as the Republic of Zambia.

Anthony Grigg, younger brother of the politician and journalist John Grigg, had spent some time in Northern Rhodesia. Knowing of Robert's interest in Kaunda, he brought him round to the London flat that Robert shared with Charles Keen and Antony Martin. Charles noted that Kaunda gravitated towards Robert Oakeshott, and few others got a word in.[166]

The forty-year-old Kaunda, described in an obituary over half a century later as 'one of the most humane and idealistic African leaders in the post-independence age',[167] was in a difficult position. His country was in desperate need of development, but this had to be directed towards those who needed it most. Among the African population of 3½ million, the vast majority of whom scratched a subsistence living in the vast underdeveloped rural areas, there were high levels of illiteracy and a 40 per cent infant mortality.

---

[166] Charles Keen, interview, 29 September 2020.

[167] *The Guardian*, 6 July 2021.

Kenneth Kaunda in 1962.
(From the Stuart Gore-Brown Archive, Shiwa Ngandu,
by kind permission of Charlie and Jo Harvey)

Throughout the country there were fewer than 100 college graduates and barely 1,000 had graduated from secondary school. Kaunda's problem was compounded by the fact that the colonial civil service he inherited had colonial priorities. Their focus was on the maintenance of law and order and satisfying the needs of the copper mining corporations. These and other aspects of the 'modern sector', mostly a small amount of commercial farming along the line of rail, were dominated by the country's 70,000 Europeans. They had little understanding of the development needs that Kaunda envisaged for his people.

With independence scheduled for 24 October 1964, Kaunda was looking for special advisers who could be relied upon to override old colonial prejudices and prepare a Transitional Development Plan that would start to answer the needs of the African majority. What he saw in Robert was an intelligent, energetic, charismatic young man, with journalistic experience at the *Financial Times*, which had covered the fall of the Central African

Federation. It was also clear that Oakeshott appreciated human values and had the imagination to see beyond the hard numbers so beloved of professional economists – just the sort of man to join the team of radical young development officers Kaunda was collecting in Lusaka. By the end of the evening, he had offered Robert a job. It was all very personal and informal: Robert would be sent an airline ticket and contract details would be sorted out after his arrival in Lusaka.

Kaunda returned to his constitutional negotiations in Lancaster House, leaving Robert to contemplate, with some excitement, what had just occurred. But there was no hesitation: he would accept the job. All that remained was to serve a month's notice with the *Financial Times*, and to explain to Jo Grimond that he would not be able to stand for the Liberal Party in the forthcoming election, scheduled for October, the same month as Zambian Independence. He appears, however, to have assured Grimond that he would stand at the following election, and if he was abroad, he would come home for it.

* * *

Robert arrived in Lusaka on the last weekend of June 1964. Initially, he found accommodation with Theo Bull, 'one of the lesser heirs of Alfred Beit's [South African Gold Mining] fortune'. Bull had arrived in Southern Rhodesia from England in the late 1950s and in 1960 he had bought the *Central African Examiner*, a monthly magazine of comment and opinion. Under Theo's editorship, the *Examiner* slanted increasingly towards the African nationalist viewpoint.[168] Robert would almost certainly have met Theo during one of his journalistic visits to Rhodesia in 1960–63. Theo, seeing the writing on the wall in Southern Rhodesia, decamped to Northern Rhodesia in 1963. He was a few years younger than Robert, but like him, he was an eccentric Englishman with an enthusiasm and idealism

---

[168] Anthony King, '*The Central African Examiner, 1957-1965*', *Zambezia* (1996), XXIII (ii), p 138.

which would have appealed to Robert.[169] In Robert's terms, Theo was a good egg, and it is easy to see they would have got on well together.

It took more than a month for Robert's contract to be sorted and he spent much of that time reading, and exploring Lusaka on foot. What appealed to him about Lusaka was 'the delightful informality of the place', as he explained to his mother:

> Returning from a walk yesterday evening I was passing Dr Kaunda's house just as he drove up. He very decently called out asking how one was & we had an agreeable exchange of shouts – against a high wind – over his garden hedge.[170]

By August 1964, Robert was established as one of a small team of radical young expatriates in a sub-department answerable to the Minister of Finance, Arthur Wina. The nature of the work was not immediately clear, but Robert was excited by the prospect that, 'given one's inclusion in the team one should be as well placed as possible to learn about & perhaps, within limits, influence the business of development'.[171] Among his colleagues was the economist Mike Faber, who went on to play a major role in Zambia's early economic development. Robert soon became close friends with Mike and his wife Didon. The civil servants of the old Northern Rhodesian establishment considered Robert and Mike to be Marxist revolutionaries, intent on upsetting their comfortable colonial applecart.[172]

* * *

One of the more important tasks facing the government in the run-up to independence was how to recover the country's mineral rights from

---

[169] John Matchikiza, 'A fabulous original', *Mail & Guardian*, 24 February 2003: https://mg.co.za/article/2003-02-24-a-fabulous-original/ [accessed 8 September 2021]. With thanks to Hugh Macmillan for directing me to this site.

[170] *Oakeshott Letters*, RO to his father, Lusaka, 12 July [1964].

[171] RO to his father, Lusaka, 12 July [1964].

[172] T. Grundy, 'Kenneth Kaunda and the White Boys', 23 October 2014 (50th anniversary of Zambia's independence): www.politicsweb.co.za/about/kenneth-kaunda-and-the-white-boys – [accessed 23 June 2021].

the British South Africa Company (BSAC), also known as 'Chartered'. The Company, founded by Cecil Rhodes in 1889, had been granted a Royal Charter for the purpose of colonising 'the Rhodesias', which it did in the 1890s. Its claim to mineral royalties was based on an agreement signed in 1890 by the Lozi King Lewanika of 'Barotseland' in the west of the country – which did not cover the Copperbelt region – and on some dubious other 'concessions' signed by illiterate African chiefs. The British Colonial Government had recognised these claims in the 1920s, when industrial copper mining began on the Copperbelt. By 1963–64 £1 million a month, in the form of copper-mining royalties, was being drained from the country into the BSAC's private bank accounts in London.

Fearing an incoming Zambian Government might seize the country's mineral rights by compulsory acquisition, the BSAC offered to sell them for £50 million, spread over 20 years. Kaunda's UNIP Cabinet was, however, determined not to pay a penny. Suspecting the dubious conditions under which the royalties were acquired, they commissioned the London-based economic and banking consultancy Maxwell Smart Associates (MSA) to investigate the whole historical and legal background to the BSAC's claim. The MSA team of lawyers, historians and others with Rhodesian and South African expertise conducted a very thorough investigation and produced a report which revealed not only that the BSAC had no sound grounds on which to claim the royalty rights, but that the colonial government had known this all along. Finance Minister Arthur Wina placed the MSA evidence in the public domain by revealing its basic features in the Lusaka Parliament in August 1964.

Robert Oakeshott and Mike Faber were given the task of interpreting the MSA evidence, in the form of a political White Paper that would present the Kaunda Government's case to the British Government and the BSAC. Interviewed fifty years later, Faber forgot to mention the pivotal role played by MSA, with the clear implication that it was he and Robert who uncovered the evidence.[173] On one point, however, there is no doubt; it was Robert Oakeshott who took the lead and wrote most of the White

---

[173] Grundy, 'Kaunda and the White Boys'.

Paper, with Mike, the professional economist, handling the statistical material. Robert clearly relished the task and produced a 'forcefully argued' document. As locally-based journalist and friend Richard Hall, co-founder and editor of the *Central Africa Mail*, and later editor of the *Times of Zambia*, recalled of Robert's White Paper:

> Written in a style which contrived to be both elegant and fierce by a former *Financial Times* staff man who was part of the Wina entourage, the document indicted both Chartered and Britain through a close examination of events from 1890 onwards.[174]

The White Paper was published on 21 September 1964, just over four weeks before Zambian independence. By now the BSAC had dropped its selling price from £50 million to £18 million, but they had missed their chance. With the issue now in the public domain, and with MSA promoting their cause in England, things began to swing in the Zambians' favour. Robert used his contacts on the *Financial Times*, *The Guardian*, and *The Observer*, even writing some of their leaders for them, in what was a highly effective propaganda campaign.[175]

With the BSAC rapidly losing all credibility, Wina offered a gift of £2 million, purely as a gesture of goodwill: if the Company expected recompense, they must seek it from the British. At which point, the British general election of 15 October brought a change of government, with Harold Wilson's Labour winning a small majority. Wilson, aware of impending problems with Southern Rhodesia, was determined to start his administration with a smooth transition to Zambian independence, and he took a hard line with the BSAC. With the clock ticking on the eve of independence, the elderly president of the BSAC finally caved in and accepted Wilson's offer of £2 million, less than an hour before midnight.

Robert and Mike Faber had been hanging around at Government House on the periphery of these tense negotiations. Mike sped down to

---

[174] R. Hall, *The High Price of Principles. Kaunda and the White South* (Hodder and Stoughton, London, 1969), p 81.

[175] John Pell (a former employee of Maxwell Smart Associates), interview, 5 February 2021.

Independence Stadium, where he presented a huddle of international journalists with the details of the deal written on a piece of crumpled blue paper.[176] Minutes later, with the lowering and raising of flags, the Republic of Zambia was born in full legal possession of its own mineral rights. And Robert had the satisfaction of knowing he had played a not insignificant part in these crucial and dramatic events.

* * *

One of the closest friendships that Robert made in Lusaka was with Mick Pearce. Mick was a young architect in his mid-twenties who had been born in Southern Rhodesia in 1938. After earning a diploma with distinction from the Architectural Association in London in 1962, he found he could not stomach the political direction of his home country on the break-up of the Federation and, like Theo Bull, he decamped to Zambia. On first meeting Robert in Lusaka in 1964, Mick thought him 'the most pompous Brit ever'. But he gradually learned to look beyond Robert's upper-class manner of speech and 'see the soul underneath'. Robert's stay with Theo Bull was only ever intended to be on a temporary basis and by late 1964 or early 1965, Robert and Mick had decided to buy a house together, although ultimately, with Robert's administration of his finances always being somewhat chaotic, it was Mick who ended up paying for the house.[177]

The house they selected was a large colonial-style bungalow about five miles beyond the northern fringes of Lusaka. Named 'The Stoep' (Afrikaans for 'verandah'), it consisted of a large, central living room with a high ceiling, up to the roof, surrounded by a verandah which, at the rear and sides, was partly filled in to form several bedrooms. With an extension at the rear for a kitchen and bathroom, this left the front 'stoep' open for socialising and reclining of an evening with cheap South African wine, or several bottles of local beer. The house was situated in a large plot, with a lawn and trees at the front and sides, servant's quarters at the rear, and a paddock beyond. Robert saw it as a great place for having friends to stay

---

[176] Hall, *The High Price of Principles*, p 84.

[177] Mick Pearce, interview, 12 December 2020.

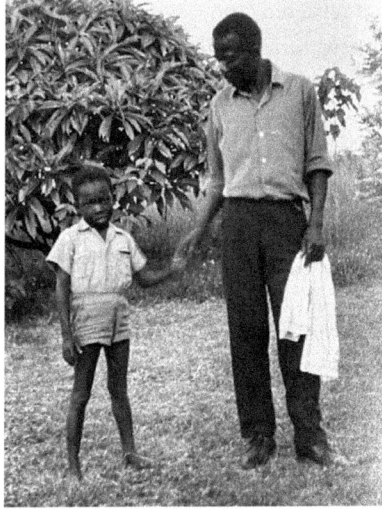

Time, the cook at the Stoep, whom Robert referred to as
'Father Time', with his son Meat.
(By kind permission of Johnny Grimond)

and for throwing parties, while the paddock put him in mind of getting a horse. Although reputed to be no great shakes as a horseman, Robert had always enjoyed a good hack, and there was plenty of open ground and dirt tracks for carefree riding.

As Mick has recalled, Robert was great fun and had the ability to bridge cultural problems with humour.[178] He had a talent for drawing people together. Robert and Mick and friends who congregated at the Stoep led 'a bohemian existence' and the house soon became 'famous [in Lusaka social circles] for its unique parties'.[179] These tended to start about noon on a Saturday or Sunday and last for much of the rest of the day, with Robert

---

[178] Mick Pearce, interview, 12 December 2020.

[179] Andrew Sardanis, *Africa. Another Side of the Coin. Northern Rhodesia's final years and Zambia's nationhood* (IB Taurus, 2003, this edition Bloomsbury Academic, London, 2019), pp 174–5.

organising what he considered appropriate games outside on the lawn. The parties usually consisted of a vibrant mix of the Lusaka liberal elite, Zambians and expatriates.

Zambians with whom he mixed loved Robert, drawn to him by his charm and generosity, his humour and freedom from racial prejudice – something that Zambians were only beginning to get used to in this age of independence. Robert counted the Wina brothers, Arthur and Sikota, both ministers, among his personal friends. He loved playing games with the politicians, partly perhaps because he could never imagine the same informal atmosphere occurring back home in England. On at least one occasion he invited the whole Cabinet to a Stoep party. (It would not have been seen as appropriate to have invited the teetotal President Kaunda.) After a meal and a fair bit of drink had been consumed, they played skittles along the front stoep with balls and empty bottles, and then Robert challenged the Cabinet to a tug-of-war, the Cabinet versus the rest. The result, if there was one, is not remembered.[180]

Any of Robert's friends who were visiting or passing through Zambia, and there were many, would always find a welcome at the Stoep. Antony Martin, who was working in Johannesburg for a South African financial magazine and the *Financial Times*, was a fairly regular visitor. Antony had been urged by Robert's friends to try to get him to cut down on the drink, a hopeless task, as in those days Antony was just as heavy a drinker, although in due course he was to recognise the problem and come off the drink for good – something that Robert never did.

An early additional resident at the Stoep was Peter Mackay, whom Robert referred to as 'Bwana Revolution'. An ex-Guards officer who had tried to make his home as a farmer in Southern Rhodesia in the early 1950s, Mackay soon became enmeshed in 'fighting for the African cause in one way or another', and following the break-up of the Federation, he was jailed for four months for refusing to register for duty with the Rhodesian territorial forces. On his release he was forced to leave the country and came to Zambia:

---

[180] Mick Pearce, interview, 12 December 2020.

Peter Mackay ('Bwana Revolution') at the Stoep, 1965.
(By kind permission of Johnny Grimond)

> Outside literature [wrote Robert], I have never met anyone who refuses so
> unequivocally to compromise with what he believes to be wrong; and yet
> he manages to do that with almost continuous good humour & with only
> the rarest trace of priggishness.[181]

It was through parties at the Stoep that Peter Mackay introduced Robert to
James Chikerema and George Nyandoro, exiled leaders of the Zimbabwe
African People's Union (ZAPU), and Herbert Chitepo the exiled leader
of its rival, the Zimbabwe African National Union (ZANU). Thus began
Robert's low-key and clandestine assistance from time to time in the
cause of the exiles and their struggle for freedom, although he was never
trusted with too much of their information, for it was feared that with his
gregarious nature he might not be able to keep it secret for long.

---

[181] RO to his mother, 3 February 1965.

CHAPTER 10

Development Planning
1964–1966

Following Zambian Independence, Robert's team became the Office of National Development Planning (ONDP) and was shifted from Arthur Wina's Finance Ministry to a department answerable to the office of Vice-President Reuben Kamanga. This brought it closer to the ear of President Kaunda, as an ideas team that was not too closely tied to the constraints of national budgets. The department was headed by Canadian economist Gordon Grounding, who appreciated Robert's imaginative free thinking, which more than made up for his not being a qualified economist. The ONDP was tasked with producing a Transitional Development Plan in a hurry.

Robert was to apply his fertile imagination to the business of development, soon proving himself 'one of the stars of the National Development Office ... standing out as very bright, very eccentric and very unconventional'.[182] As a convert to the concept of development planning on the Indian model, influenced no doubt by the views of his Uncle Pendy, Robert argued passionately for a government-led interventionist policy with a focus on education and agriculture. This, he saw, was the only way to counter the colonial policy of the Federation, which had deliberately held back African education in order to give preference to the white colonists, and had totally neglected African farming.

As with the mineral rights White Paper, Robert did most of the drafting, with Mike Faber providing much of the statistical material. It is said that Robert completed the drafting of the Transitional Plan in five

---

[182] Sardanis, *Another Side of the Coin*, p 174.

days, working day and night. That is characteristic of Robert's style and may well be true, but he did have the back-up of the whole team providing the statistical information on provisional costings, population levels and regional centres, with a particular focus on the rural areas beyond the line of rail, where most of the population still lived. Besides a wide spread of health clinics, Robert proposed the building of twenty new secondary schools, at least one in every regional centre and several more in the larger towns and cities.

Once the Plan was drawn up, it had to be fully costed before being presented to the Vice-President and then to the politicians and their departmental advisers. After some modifications, it was published in the first week of January 1965. Robert proudly posted a copy of the Plan to his mother, telling her, 'By and large, like the Mineral Royalties White Paper, it is a Faber/Oakeshott document.'[183]

Implementing a plan on this scale would involve a level of external investment that only the World Bank could provide. And as this would be outside the scope of Zambia's national budget, negotiations with the World Bank would need to be led from the ONDP. Gordon Grounding did not have the relevant experience, but it immediately became obvious to Robert: this was a job for his Uncle Pendy. Sir Penderel Moon – knighted in 1962 for services to Britain/India relations – had the relevant experience in India, and more recently in Thailand, and the Zambians were persuaded. Robert telegraphed his uncle, who expressed interest on a six-month basis. Once the World Bank had agreed, Sir Penderel Moon was contracted as a Deputy Director of the ONDP, alongside Gordon Grounding. Robert was hugely excited at the prospect of working with his Uncle Pendy, of whom he was always so proud.[184]

Robert did not think 'the ménage at the Stoep' would suit his uncle 'for residence purposes' and on Moon's arrival in mid-February, on Robert's recommendation, he was put up at the Ridgeway Hotel.[185] He thoroughly

---

[183] RO to his mother, 16 February 1965.

[184] RO to his mother, 22 January 1965.

[185] RO to his mother, 3 February 1965.

enjoyed dinners and parties at the Stoep but was thankful for the privacy and comfort of the Ridgeway.

The pressure was now on to implement the plan with immediate effect so that, for example, secondary schools, to which Robert had devoted particular attention, would be ready for their first year's intake the following January (1966). So keen were the rural districts to have a secondary school that a number of them started their school immediately, housing it in some temporary building. Moon quickly got things moving with the World Bank for funding the secondary school programme and road-building. He urged the team not to wait for World Bank approval, but to 'get the game started' with architects and surveyors.

Penderel Moon before departure from Amritsar, 1943.
(British Library India Office Library and Oriental Collections,
Newsletter, No. 39,1987)

Robert was to spend much of the first half of 1965 getting out into the countryside, visiting the provinces, the sites of his planned secondary schools, and helping to solve many of the initial logistical problems of this massive building project: sourcing cement, tarpaulins, lock-up storage and trucks. The first of Robert's 'provincial tours' was to Barotseland in January 1965, accompanied by Mike and Didon Faber. They flew to nine different places in three and a half days. Robert was disgusted to find that pompous colonial officialdom was still well-represented in Mongu, the Barotse capital. At a party laid on for the visitors from Lusaka, not one African had been invited. But this was made up for by their having an audience with the Litunga, King of the Lozi people. His stockaded palace, built on a mound in the Upper Zambezi floodplain, was accessible only by boat.

On the way back from that flight, Robert informed his mother:

> … the door of the aeroplane (next to which I happened to be sitting) flew open about 300 ft. above the Zambezi. Fortunately, I still had my seat belt fastened & there was no serious danger. However, it proved impossible to shut the door again up aloft, so we had to land and do it.[186]

This story got embellished in the retelling, in the way that Robert's stories often did. One version related that the exiled Zimbabwean novelist Doris Lessing, who had become a good friend to Robert, had been on the plane. According to this version Robert, somewhat the worse for drink, did not have his seatbelt fastened, the door flew open, he partially fell out and was only dragged back in by the efforts of Doris Lessing! This Robert story may have been mixed with a true one, in which Robert took Doris Lessing for a drive in Mick Pearce's VW to view some sights. The car struggled near the top of a hill, and everyone got out to push, leaving Doris to steer. But Doris got out to help push, the car slipped back, the door knocked her, and she fell and broke her pelvis. Mick recalls that as he nursed her on the sofa at the Stoep, Doris remarked, 'Robert seems to be in permanent conflict with the physical world'.[187] She had to use crutches for the rest of her trip.

---

[186] RO to his mother, 22 January 1965.

[187] Mick Pearce, interview, 12 December 2020.

Doris Lessing, on a visit to Zambia in 1964.
(By kind permission of her daughter Jean Cowen and
her granddaughter Susanna Cowen)

Robert was generally judged to be a hopeless driver. On another occasion when he borrowed Mick's VW, he arrived back at the Stoep with the whole side of the car severed by a truck. In August 1965, when his uncle completed his first stint at the ONDP, Robert inherited the rather grand Austin Metropolitan that Sir Penderel Moon had purchased from a departing British High Commissioner. Unused to handling such a powerful car, Robert misjudged the turning for the Stoep and the car ended upside down in the ditch. When Mick came out to find what the commotion was about, Robert, standing unharmed next to the wreck, exclaimed,

Oh my god, old fellow! I obviously turned too soon![188]

Among those who turned up at the Stoep for a few days in early 1965 was Jo Grimond's younger son, Johnny. He had just left school and had

---

[188] Mick Pearce, interview, 12 December 2020.

volunteered to teach in Zambia for five months before going up to Balliol. He was posted to a new secondary school in Lundazi in the far east of the country near the border with Malawi. Shortly after he had settled in, Robert, Mick Pearce and Mike Faber set off one weekend to drive the 500 miles to Lundazi to deliver a second-hand VW to Johnny. The school had started in January with 70 boys in two Form I classes temporarily housed in a Community Development Centre, previously used by the colonial education department to train girls to be domestic servants – instead of desks they had kitchen sinks and draining boards.

Robert was pleased to see that the ground had already been cleared for the new school buildings. He asked the students about their career hopes for the future and when he suggested farming, a student asked why the government was sending them to secondary school if it wanted them to be

Mick Pearce, Robert and Mike Faber outside Mulla Store, Lundazi.
(By kind permission of Johnny Grimond)

farmers.[189] They viewed education as a route to well-paid jobs in the formal sector, like the Europeans who had dominated Zambia for so long.

On returning to Lusaka, Robert began to draft a document outlining the range of career opportunities potentially available for secondary school leavers. Besides pushing careers in agriculture, he hoped to get Zambia moving towards self-sufficiency in electricians and mechanics. It was unbelievable, he wrote to his mother, that up to five years ago Africans were not permitted by law to be apprenticed to a trade. As a result, there were 150 apprentices in the country, but 5,000 to 10,000 clerks and typists.[190] He subsequently ran a 'fairly successful' propaganda campaign to promote alternative careers to the office jobs that most school leavers seemed to have in mind.

By June 1965 Robert had finally got round to purchasing a horse: a 'fine black stallion', a 'magnificent looker', all of sixteen to seventeen hands, named 'Secret Service'.[191] It had all the virtues of speed, power and a relatively tranquil temperament. Robert was excited at the thought that as it had been raced in South Africa and won three flat races, he could perhaps recoup the purchase price by winning some races in Lusaka, as well as use the horse for his personal hacking. Uncle Pendy, who had offered some advice on racehorse training, was keen to ride him in his first race that August. He was an accomplished rider who in his youth had won races on the Governor of Punjab's horses,[192] but neither he nor the horse was fit for racing. The horse had only four days pre-race training, and Uncle Pendy none. The latter, then in his early fifties, was dissuaded from riding in the race, his place being taken by a stable lass. The horse showed great promise with his long strides, but was not placed.[193]

At the end of August 1965, the ONDP lost the services of both Sir

---

[189] RO to his mother, 26 May 1965.

[190] RO to his mother, 26 May and 5 June 1965.

[191] RO to his mother, 5 June 1965; Sardanis, *Another Side of the Coin*, p 175.

[192] *Oakeshott Papers*, Philip Mason, 'Moon, Sir (Edward) Penderel', typescript dated 22 September 1992.

[193] RO to his mother, 8 and 29 August 1965.

Penderel Moon and Gordon Grounding. While Grounding went back to his university in Canada, Moon was to return to Zambia for a further six-month consultancy the following year. Grounding's replacement was a Mr Heseltine, an Irishman with experience in Madagascar, who arrived in mid-September. In the opinion of Robert, Heseltine was an autocrat, 'stuffy, pompous and inflexible', the opposite of Gordon Grounding.[194] In his first week in post, Heseltine 'had the cheek to suggest' that Robert should take his economics degree, 'as if I haven't fully thrashed out the various pros and cons of doing so'. It led Robert to reflect that if Heseltine was going to 'use one as little more than a glorified research assistant and collector of statistics then clearly it may be sensible to reconsider whether it is a good idea to stay on'.[195]

Fortunately, that weekend Robert was cheered by the prospect of attending Theo Bull's wedding to Lozi historian Mutumba Mainga in Mongu. It was a long trek by car, Robert and Mick travelling as part of a large party along 400 miles of poor dirt road. Having underestimated the time it would take, they finally arrived at 7.30pm, four hours late, 'but the wedding feast … still had a long way to go', and it was a most enjoyable break from frustrations at the office.[196]

* * *

It soon became apparent that the logistical problems in Zambia's huge range of construction projects were far more difficult than anticipated. The buildings were going up faster than expected and needed an extra 13,000 tons of cement a month. The railways from the south could not cope with the extra tonnage and Robert was obliged to make numerous trips to the Congo, Angola and even Malawi in search of alternative sources of cement and transport routes.

By October it was clear that the biggest potential logistical problem that could set back the whole of Zambia's carefully-laid development plans was

---

[194] RO to his mother, 10 October 1965.

[195] RO to his mother, 10 October 1965.

[196] RO to his mother, 20 September 1965.

the possibility that Ian Smith's Rhodesian Front Government in Salisbury might make an illegal Universal Declaration of Independence (UDI) as the only way to ensure continued white control over the African majority in Southern Rhodesia. If that happened, Britain and the UN would impose economic sanctions on Rhodesia. Zambia's whole import/export economy was geared towards the south, the source of almost all its industrial and consumer goods. Zambia would have great difficulty in imposing sanctions, to say nothing of finding alternative routes for its copper exports. There was also the very real possibility that the Rhodesians would hold Zambia to ransom by threatening to close the border between the two countries.

Robert did not believe that Smith would be so foolish as to cripple his own economy and he began taking bets of £5 against UDI being declared.[197] Cultural sentiment and years of racial prejudice overruled economic logic, however, and Robert lost his bets: UDI was declared on 11 November 1965. UN sanctions were imposed, the Smith regime did not collapse as foreseen, and Zambia received little of the promised aid from Britain.

At this crucial point Robert, brimming over with ideas, found himself continually blocked by Heseltine, who was trying to get him transferred to the Department of Information. When Robert refused to go, Heseltine demanded that he resign. But here Heseltine had overstepped his powers.[198] Besides, Robert had friends in high places, including Valentine Musakanya, the Head of the Civil Service. Musakanya recognised that Robert was too valuable an asset to lose at this critical time and he suggested to Andrew Sardanis that he take him on. Sardanis was Managing Director and Chairman of the board of the state-owned Industrial Development Corporation (Indeco), and had just been appointed Director of Imports and Controller of Supplies, responsible for dealing with the impact of UDI. Musakanya argued that Sardanis had 'so many pressing problems, between Indeco and the transport routes that [he] could do with an "ideas person"'.[199] Sardanis recognised the worth of a man with Robert's talents, and despite his having

---

[197] RO to his mother, 2 November 1965.

[198] RO to his mother, 16 November 1965.

[199] Sardanis, *Another Side of the Coin*, p 175.

broken 'umpteen regulations with his behaviour' while in government employ, he agreed to take him on; but with two conditions:

> ... that he promised to wear a belt – until then most of the time his trousers were held in place with an old tie. Also, that he would wear jacket and tie at the office.

Robert promised to comply, and kept his word, though Sardanis was to recall,

> ... I cannot even begin to describe his suits. They were cotton 'tropical suits', which were quite common in those days – but they must have had rough treatment. Sometimes they looked as if Robert had forgotten to take them off before he went to bed the night before.[200]

Sardanis never regretted his decision. Robert was 'a likeable person, with a great sense of humour', and was never short of ideas:

> Was I thinking of a new railway to Dar es Salaam? Within 24 hours [Robert] produced a detailed memorandum on the economics of a timber-fired railway to Dar. Timber plantations all the way, thousands of workers employed to cut trees and chop wood and load it onto the trains.[201]

When Sardanis introduced petrol rationing, Robert was 'exultant'. He felt that was how it should be: 'People in Lusaka did not need cars and they should not be using them, he said'. In Robert's view, 'Bicycles were the answer, but as far as he was concerned, he would be coming to the office on horseback'. And he did, 'even though it was the rainy season':

> Sometimes he walked into the office smiling as always and looking very pleased with himself, despite being dripping wet, as if he had just had a shower with his suit on.[202]

---

[200] Sardanis, *Another Side of the Coin*, p 175.

[201] Sardanis, *Another Side of the Coin*, p 175. The railway was eventually built by the Chinese in the 1970s, oil-fuelled, not wood-fired.

[202] Sardanis, *Another Side of the Coin*, p 175.

After barely a month of riding his horse to work, Robert started dreaming of riding in a small gig or cart. He had his eye on 'a sturdy little mare who [looked] as if she would do a tremendous job between the shafts'.[203] In due course he bought her and had a governess cart sent out from England. Neither pony nor would-be driver had any experience of pulling or driving a cart, and on first being fitted between the shafts the horse, without blinkers, panicked and bolted down the drive. Robert had no control and the cart failed to make it through the gateway.[204] Robert, standing beside the wrecked cart, probably remarked in customary fashion: 'No-one's fault, old boy! No-one's fault!'

The petrol rationing affected the ménage at the Stoep in other ways too, but never Robert's habitual good humour. They soon ran out of petrol for the water pump and diesel for the electricity generator. For the former, Mick installed a hand pump, and as the gardener was a bit too old and frail to manage the pump, it became an early-morning exercise for Robert and Mick on alternate days.[205] After nine months of this, Mick erected a 40-foot steel windmill to run the pump. Robert, no good with a spanner at 40 foot, spent a day pouring concrete for the base: a far more useful skill, in his opinion, than anything learned in the Cadet Corps at Tonbridge.[206]

One of Robert's more controversial tasks was drawing up lists of essential imports in the event of a complete border closure. Everybody had their own idea of what was essential. The Ministry of Commerce and Industry insisted on spaghetti and vermicelli, but Robert removed them from the list, along with manufactured breakfast cereals. There was some debate about cheese, which his mother argued in favour of as an essential source of protein; but Robert got it banned, on the grounds there was an almost unlimited supply of meat locally available. Besides, 'cheese can never be *preferable* to meat (except by vegetarians)'.[207]

---

[203] RO to his mother, 16 January 1966.

[204] Johnny Grimond, interview, 12 January 2021.

[205] RO to his mother, late January 1966.

[206] RO to his mother, 6 August 1966.

[207] RO to his mother, 16 January 1966 (his emphasis) and 19 February 1966.

By the beginning of 1966 Sardanis had a full complement of staff, some of them Indians from Tanzania:

> Intellectually, they may not have been as smart as Robert Oakeshott's group, but they certainly played better poker. Or maybe they drank less during the sessions and thus took a lot of money off Robert's friends.[208]

In the event, the Rhodesian border was never totally closed until 1973, when the war for Zimbabwean independence was gathering pace. In the meantime, people gradually got used to general shortages. And while an oil pipeline was being constructed along the thousand-mile route from Dar es Salaam to the Copperbelt, fuel was trucked in 44-gallon drums down the Great North Road, known as 'the Hell Run', due to the poor quality of the road and the number of accidents. Vehicles on the return journey northwards carried heavy bars of copper, often slung under the chassis so as not to unbalance the truck. The fuel supply remained precarious and petrol rationing was only gradually eased over the next couple of years.

---

[208] Sardanis, *Another Side of the Coin*, p 182.

CHAPTER 11

Politics and a New Beginning

1966

The focus of Robert's life shifted beyond problem-solving in Zambia when on 28 February 1966 British Labour Prime Minister Harold Wilson called a general election for 31 March. It was not unexpected. For sixteen months Wilson had been governing, competently, with a precarious parliamentary majority of only five. By going to the country now, he was confident of gaining a larger, more stable majority.

Robert was excited to hear the news and felt he must play his part, especially as he may have felt he had let Jo Grimond down by not staying in the United Kingdom to fight the 1964 election. On that occasion, the Liberal share of the vote had doubled to 11.2 per cent. Although they only had nine MPs, the party was optimistic and there was a feeling within Liberal circles that they were on the cusp of a breakthrough.

After a week of telegraphic communication with Jo Grimond and Liberal Party headquarters, Robert vowed to return to England and stand in whatever constituency the party chose. He reckoned he would need three weeks' leave for campaigning and at least a further week to visit family and friends. But how would he get approval for a month's official leave? The previous year it had not gone down well when, at only a week's notice, he had asked for a fortnight's leave to go home for social reasons and had been restricted to only one week. Now, although he had leave owing, he would once more be giving barely a week's notice. Robert prevaricated, which reduced the potential notice even further. In the end he decided, as he had with Balliol and the trip to Hungary in 1956, that he would simply *inform* his department when it was too late to stop him. He told only Mick and one or two of his closest friends and on Saturday 12 March, when nobody else was in the office, he left a note on his desk indicating that he was going to England to stand in the general election. On the Sunday evening he caught the direct flight to London. If he won the election, he would not be returning anyway; if he lost, he would face the consequences on his return.

* * *

Robert arrived in London to a cold Monday morning on 14 March 1966 and went straight to Liberal Party headquarters. Here he learned he was to stand in the North Eastern constituency of Darlington, in County Durham. He was handed a copy of the national party manifesto and was asked to draw up his own personal manifesto, to be printed as his campaign leaflet on arrival in Darlington.

The next day, having purchased a new suit, he took the train north to Darlington, where his agent had arranged for him to be photographed leaving the station. The photo selected to front his campaign leaflet shows him posing beneath the station sign for 'DARLINGTON', sporting a Liberal rosette on the lapel of his new light-grey suit and waving to the electorate. In his left hand he is holding a large tartan suitcase with the label 'LON' for London Airport still affixed to the handle, confirming his recent arrival from Africa, come specially to represent the people of Darlington. He was taken to the party office in the centre of town, where a group of enthusiastic Liberals had assembled to meet their candidate, and handed over his draft for the campaign leaflet for immediate printing.

The latter bears the personal imprint of Robert Oakeshott. He blames both Tory and Labour parties for the British economic malaise of the past fifteen years. Both were too wedded to their financiers: big business and the trade unions, respectively,

> ... I make my appeal therefore to all progressive and radical people regardless of their former party allegiance. I believe that by voting Liberal

you will be acting decisively to improve the quality of Government and of British life in all its aspects.[209]

The party was looking for 'an enlarged contingent of vigorous Liberals'. The three main points of his personal manifesto were to get into the Common Market;[210] to introduce strong and effective measures to end the rebellion in Southern Rhodesia; and to oppose Labour's plans to nationalise steel, on the grounds that it was irrelevant to the problems of the British economy.

He found accommodation at The Cross Keys, a 'delightful pub' in the village of Gainford, not far from Darlington. On Thursday 18 March Jo Grimond's daughter Grizelda arrived to witness Robert's formal adoption by the Liberal Party as their candidate for Darlington. Her presence 'boosted Liberal morale all round and completely charmed the people at headquarters'.[211] The next day, Friday, he was joined at The Cross Keys by his brother Evelyn, who observed that 'Rods is getting on tremendously well with everyone' and enjoying it. On the Saturday night all three candidates submitted to a Question-and-Answer session in a Quaker Hall, and in the partial opinion of his twin brother, 'Rods was very good indeed all through, and the assembly often applauded his answers which were clearly stated, obviously made good sense and on several occasions much better than the others'.[212]

Several of Robert's friends made an appearance on the campaign trail, including Tom Bingham, Christopher Files and Giles Fitzherbert. Each made open-air public speeches in Robert's support and although these were poorly attended, they were mentioned in the following day's paper. And Evelyn who, in Robert's words, 'worked like a Trojan' and 'converted' numerous people to Liberal, 'did a little bellowing through a loud-speaker mounted on a car'. All the while, Robert's agent was a 'continued source of

---

[209] Oakeshott's Darlington campaign leaflet, copy in *Oakeshott Letters*.

[210] The colloquial name for the EEC (European Economic Community), now the EU (European Union).

[211] *Northern Despatch*, 18 March 1966; and RO to his mother, 7 July 1966.

[212] *Oakeshott Letters*, Cargs to his mother, 20 March 1966.

Robert Oakeshott, Liberal Party candidate, 1966 General Election.
(By kind permission of the Oakeshott family)

inflated optimism'. In the event, although nationally the Liberals increased their number of MPs from nine to twelve, Robert failed to increase the Liberal vote in Darlington; but by attaining 8.2 per cent of votes cast, he managed to save his deposit.[213]

The sitting Labour candidate was returned with an increased majority, which was not surprising considering the strength of the Labour machine and the presence of a large, unionised factory workforce. Robert's post-election assessment recognised that an anti-Tory vote alone was not enough where Labour was entrenched. Robert's team had only managed to canvass ten per cent of households and might have done better given another week, but as people pointed out to canvassers, it was a big error not to have included a potted history of Robert in his campaign leaflet. On a lighter note,

> I am told, [he wrote to his mother] that the election photograph showed my trousers held up by a belt! One couldn't really have reckoned on that! (I did, incidentally, follow your advice and get an early haircut. ... So, I think we can rule that out as a vote loser).[214]

What his critics probably objected to was that Robert's belt was worn conspicuously over the outside of his trousers, which rather spoiled the effect of his new suit. These were still the days when the trousers of a man's suit did not have belt loops and were expected to be held up by a pair of buttoned-on braces, something Robert could never be bothered to affix. He probably considered that at least he wore a belt, and not his customary old tie or length of string.

On a more serious note, Robert believed the most important lesson he had learned from his Darlington campaign was that,

> ... neither the Tory nor Labour parties is ever going to have any attraction for me. ... I was continually struck (even on detailed things like rates & pensions) by the good sense of the Liberal Party policies.[215]

---

[213] Cargs to his mother, 4 April 1966; and RO to his mother, 2 April 1966.

[214] RO to his mother, 2 April 1966.

[215] RO to his mother, 2 April 1966.

Robert with Grizelda Grimond, Orkney, with Maeshowe,
a Neolithic burial chamber, in the background, April 1966.
(By kind permission of Johnny Grimond)

Robert extended his home leave by a further week. The Grimonds had invited him to spend a week at their family home in Orkney; there were people to see in London, a weekend to spend with his parents in Oxford, and a stop-off in Rome where Rose and her husband David Gaunt had lived and worked since 1964. Robert did not return to Zambia until Sunday 17 April.

* * *

Had he still been in direct government employ, Robert would probably have been dismissed for his unapproved 5-week absence; but Sardanis forgave him, as much for his humour and eccentricity as for his intelligence and imagination. It was clear, however, that Robert's usefulness to Zambia was drawing to a close. Times were changing and many younger expatriates were arriving from the British Overseas Development Institute (ODI) to take over from Robert and his friends. The difference, observed Sardanis,

> ... was that these kids were much younger, fresher in their outlook and ideas and ready to mix with the people as opposed to just congregating in the 'Stoep' like Robert and his friends, observing and pontificating. They frequented the fashionable bars in and around Lusaka like Tambalala,

Saika Daka etc., always in the company of young Zambian colleagues and got to know Zambia at grass roots.[216]

Robert began wondering what he would do when his two-year contract ended in August (1966). He fancied continuing to work somewhere in Africa.

On a short visit with Antony Martin to the mountain kingdom of Basutoland (present-day Lesotho), it had been suggested by a man there from the ODI that he should come and work with them; but that would require an economics qualification and Robert was not prepared to follow the example of his brother, who was about to undertake a year's post-graduate degree in Economics at the University of East Anglia in Norwich.[217]

Alternatively, there was the Liberal Party. Jo Grimond wanted him at Liberal headquarters as personal assistant to himself and the Liberal chief whip. Robert was flattered to be asked. He was certainly tempted but would prefer to leave it until halfway through the present parliament, at the beginning of the build-up to the next general election. That would leave him two years in which to find something a bit more exciting.

And then there was Patrick van Rensburg.

* * *

Robert had first heard of Patrick van Rensburg from Antony Martin, who had visited the exiled South African in Bechuanaland (present-day Botswana) in 1963. Antony had found van Rensburg and his work to be truly inspirational and he passed on his enthusiasm to Robert. Many years later, in presenting the valediction at Antony's funeral, Robert expressed the great debt he felt he owed to Antony,

> … for what has unquestionably turned out to be the most important introduction in my life: to Patrick and Liz van Rensburg and to the great works of education which they started in faraway Botswana in the 1960s.[218]

---

[216] Sardanis, *Another Side of the Coin*, p 240.

[217] RO to his mother, 14 August 1966.

[218] Robert Oakeshott, 'A Valediction Spoken at the Funeral', in *Antony* (privately published, 1997), p 178.

Patrick van Rensburg was a former member of South Africa's diplomatic service, who had resigned his position in 1957 on the grounds that he could no longer defend his government's apartheid policies. He had subsequently been exiled from South Africa in 1960 because of his leading role in the London boycott campaign that gave birth to the Anti-Apartheid Movement. Regarded as an Afrikaner traitor in the country of his birth, van Rensburg had settled in Serowe, in the neighbouring British protectorate of Bechuanaland, with his radical British-born partner, Liz Griffith, who was shortly to become his wife. Despite being the largest town in Bechuanaland at the time, with a population of 30,000, Serowe, the capital of the Bamangwato chieftaincy of the Batswana,[219] had no local secondary school until van Rensburg decided to correct that anomaly.

The school, Swaneng Hill, which he set up in 1963, initially with almost no money, challenged the educational establishment, which van Rensburg regarded as 'creating a ladder to privilege'. It was built partly by the students themselves, offering their labour voluntarily on Saturday mornings in term time and at work camps during the school vacations. Building Skills was among the innovative subjects on the school curriculum. The ethos of the school embraced the concepts of self-sufficiency and voluntarism in the broadest sense, with the students involved in some of the running of the school, including growing much of their own fruit and vegetables, doing their own cleaning and cooking their own meals. Van Rensburg's commitment to development encapsulated the whole of the local community and the consumer cooperative, founded at Swaneng Hill in late 1963, became the first registered cooperative in the country.[220]

Throughout 1965, Robert had been too involved in Zambia to visit Serowe and view 'the van Rensburg set-up', but he was prompted to action by the arrival in May 1966 of his great friend Lady Jane Willoughby. She was travelling under the auspices of Save the Children Fund, researching

---

[219] The Batswana are the Setswana-speaking people, who form the great majority of the population of Botswana.

[220] Kevin Shillington, *Patrick van Rensburg. Rebel, Visionary and Radical Educationist. A Biography* (Wits University Press, Johannesburg, 2020), pp 125–159.

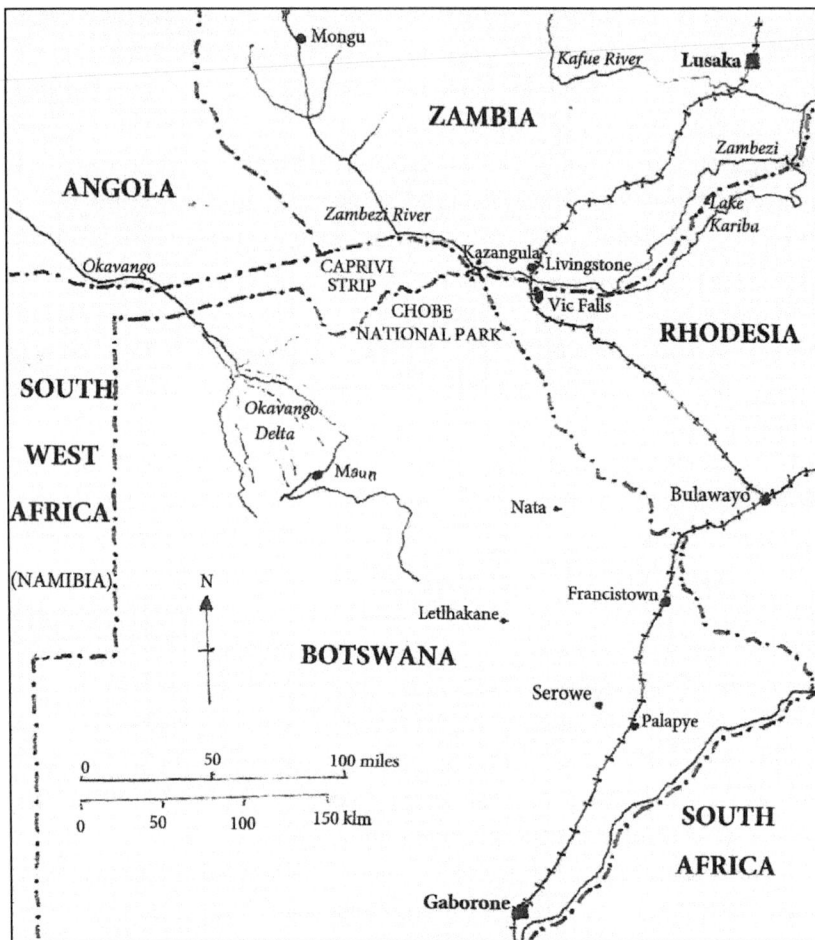

Zambia and Botswana in the 1960s (by the author).

possible water projects to irrigate vegetable gardens at rural primary
schools in Zambia and Bechuanaland.[221] Robert decided that Jane needed
an escort and the two of them got a lift in the back of Peter Mackay's Land

---

[221] Jane Willoughby, interview, 6 April 2021.

Jane Willoughby, Robert Oakeshott and refugee Atwell Bokwe take
a rest at Nata, on the 'freedom road', north-eastern Botswana.
(By kind permission of the Peter Mackay Archive, University of Stirling)

Rover. Mackay was on a mission to collect refugees from Francistown
in Bechuanaland. The journey south from the Kazungula ferry, recalled
Robert, 'was really memorable for its discomfort'. The 'freedom road', as it
was known to South African and Rhodesian refugees escaping to Zambia
and other points north, was little more than 'a donkey track', at times only
yards from the Rhodesian border. It took them thirteen hours of 'bucketing
up and down' to complete the 300 miles to Francistown. According to
Robert, Jane 'bravely took the line that the discomfort at any rate relieved
the tedium of the journey'. Robert, however, finding it impossible to read,
did not believe discomfort was capable of suppressing tedium.[222]

---

[222] RO to his mother, 25 May 1966.

Liz and Patrick van Rensburg, Serowe, Botswana.
(By kind permission of Benny Wielandt)

Travelling through the eastern third of Bechuanaland, where most of the country's half-million population lived, they were struck by the harsh severity of six years of drought. The evidence was everywhere: leafless trees, grassland turned to sand and the occasional skeletal cow or goat. The World Food Programme was supplying three-fifths of the population with drought relief rations.

They spent two nights in Serowe, about 130 miles south-west of Francistown, where Jane spoke with several primary school principals while Robert visited Swaneng Hill School, where he met Patrick and Liz van Rensburg and some of the staff. Most of the latter were from British, Danish and Dutch volunteer agencies, a few Peace Corps Volunteers from America and a few from South Africa, a couple of them refugees.

That evening Robert and Jane were dinner guests of Patrick and Liz in their recently-completed house overlooking the school. Over dinner and many drinks, Patrick expounded his vision, both for the future of the school and for its role in the development of the local community. It was clear that Patrick was brimming over with ideas for equitable rural development in poor countries such as Bechuanaland, based on low-technology, self-help, cooperative principles and voluntarism.

Robert was captivated by the van Rensburg charisma, charm and vision, and on his return to Lusaka he wrote a short article for *The Economist* in which he praised the school as an encouraging ray of hope in this poor, drought-stricken country on the eve of independence. Thinking of his own efforts in Zambia, Robert wrote,

> ... even secondary schools can – given the right quality of leadership – be built partly on a self-help basis. In this case a boarding school has been built for the astonishingly low figure of £200 a place; a major achievement when one considers that Zambia's new secondary schools are costing about £550 a place.[223]

He sent the £50 cheque he received for the article to Patrick for the school funds. Swaneng Hill at this stage received almost no funds from government and was entirely dependent on grants and charitable donations. Patrick wrote back urging Robert to come and join them at Serowe when he had completed his Zambian contract at the end of August. And by mid-August Robert had more or less decided he would do just that. As he explained to his mother,

> ... [Patrick's] experiment is one of the most exciting & encouraging things that are being tried anywhere in these parts. ... it's a secondary school intelligently adapted to Africa's requirements plus a vast amount of community development work undertaken from the school.[224]

Before flying home to England in September, Robert made a second trip to Serowe to find out just what his role would be:

> Van Rensburg has really proved himself as one of those rare people who can make a reality of something which starts simply as a gleam in his eye.[225]

---

[223] *The Economist*, 18 June 1966, p 1300.
[224] RO to his mother, 15 August 1966.
[225] RO to his mother, 6 September 1966.

This was something that some years later could equally be said of Robert Oakeshott.

Patrick had three main tasks in mind for Robert. The first would be to prepare a development plan for Serowe and the neighbourhood: what would be realistically and modestly possible, aside from encouraging better cattle husbandry. Second, in collaboration with British volunteer Donald Curtis, 'to evolve a syllabus for teaching the boys [and girls] to understand the development problems which their country faces and the sort of ways in which these problems might be overcome':

> That is very much up my street. It would be immense fun selecting material from the history of industrialisation & economic transformation in other countries. It could also, I think, be quite useful.[226]

And finally, to take charge of something called 'the builders' brigade' for primary school leavers not in secondary school. This had been started on an *ad hoc* basis the previous year, with 30 trainees. With instruction overseen by Patrick's foreman, Todd Kuhlman, they had built their own training centre in the town. It was run partly in conjunction with the local community through the Serowe Youth Development Association (Syda), chaired by the chief, *Kgosi* Leapeetswe, with Patrick as secretary. Patrick now wanted to offload this responsibility to Robert, whose main role would be to find building projects that would bring in money to finance the brigade, as well as devising a classroom syllabus that would provide some level of elementary education alongside the practical work. Robert saw the brigade as a sort of glorified, self-financing apprenticeship scheme, and it set his imagination running.

He found it all 'highly enthralling'. He hated Zambia's obsession with 'modernisation'[227] and was particularly excited that he would be living in a thatched rondavel, a circular, single-roomed, 200-square-foot building that had cost only £100 to build, in complete contrast to the expensive staff accommodation that the Zambian Government insisted on for their

---

[226] RO to his mother, 6 September 1966.

[227] Caroline Cox-Johnson, interview, 6 November 2020.

Zambian staff. 'One realises,' Robert quipped 'what almost amounts to the *advantages* of being a poor country'.[228]

Robert awarded himself two months' home leave, during which he was able to visit all or most of his huge circle of friends, besides his brother Evelyn, his sister Helena and family in the Isles of Scilly, Rose and family in Rome, and his parents in Oxford.

---

[228] RO to his mother, 6 September 1966.

CHAPTER 12

Botswana, Education and Diamonds

On 30 September 1966 Bechuanaland gained its independence from Britain as the Republic of Botswana with Sir Seretse Khama, the uncrowned king of Serowe's Bamangwato, as President.

Six weeks later, feeling thoroughly refreshed from two months' leave, Robert arrived at Serowe airstrip.[229] Patrick van Rensburg was away for the day and Robert was probably met by Sheila Bagnall in the school truck. Sheila, Swaneng Hill School's new Vice-Principal, was a professional teacher with wide experience, unlike most of the expatriate volunteer staff. She had been sent by the charity Oxfam to help raise the academic standards of the school, something that at times under van Rensburg's leadership, tended to lose out to voluntarism and the greater concept of a broad and egalitarian education. She achieved her aim by maintaining an efficient day-to-day administration of the academic side of the school, and by mentoring the young and inexperienced, though enthusiastic and hard-working, volunteer staff.

Robert had paid for his own flight out, while the school provided him with accommodation and meals in the staff canteen and a small monthly stipend, the same as the other volunteer staff. Robert was just as unconcerned about his surroundings or possessions as he was about his clothes, and he was very happy to be accommodated, like other single volunteer staff, in an African style thatched rondavel with the bare minimum of furnishings – a

---

[229] Sandy Grant (ed.) *Sheila Bagnall's Letters from Botswana, 1966–1974* (Leitlho Publications, Odi, Botswana, 2001), 12 November and 17 November 1966, pp 32–33, hereafter cited as Bagnall, *Letters*.

126

bed and a chair, with a cardboard box acting as a table. The only possessions to which he did pay attention and which he would have considered essential, were a modest library of books, often sent out by his mother, and a record player, together with a small but 'fine collection' of classical records.

The impact of Robert Oakeshott's 'mighty personality'[230] was 'immediate and substantial'. In the words of Patrick van Rensburg,

> Robert's loud upper-class voice, and his invariably earnest conversation, scholarly style and intellectual speech, both amazed and amused what he doubtless regarded as the lesser mortals of the common room. In contrast with his high-minded, upper-class seriousness, his usually shabby dress and unkempt appearance created an image of absent-minded eccentricity, more especially as he seemed unaware and unconcerned about any incongruity.[231]

Robert found in Patrick a hard-working, hard-playing fellow spirit who loved a party, although Patrick was not quite the regular heavy drinker that Robert was.

American volunteer Mike Tiller, who lived in the adjacent rondavel and quickly became a firm friend, recalls an incident that impressed upon him something of the character of his new neighbour. Robert had arrived at a time when colonial era civil servants were making way for a new generation of Batswana. Robert by this time was totally opposed to the whole concept of colonial rule, but when he heard that District Commissioner Eustace Clark was retiring to South Africa, he laid on a farewell dinner for him and his wife, in recognition of Clark's 45 years of colonial service. Mike Tiller recalled this as a very decent gesture and typical of Robert's character. According to van Rensburg, the party ended late at night at his house, and as Mrs Clark grew nostalgic about 'the old days', 'Robert rose to respond with a loud raspberry, heralded by "My dear old Mrs Clark …". As he did so, the rope about his trousers loosened and they fell to his ankles. … It

---

[230] Tom Holzinger, interview, 19 March 2018.

[231] Patrick van Rensburg, *Memoir* (being an unpublished autobiographical typescript, with light editing by Liz van Rensburg), p 306.

was a happy, if raucous, note for the Clarks to leave on'.[232]

Petrol rationing in Zambia had impressed upon Robert the benefits of traditional forms of transport, which he felt were more suitable for the slow pace of life in Africa. The interconnecting sandy tracks of the spread-out town of Serowe made cycling very difficult, and within days of his arrival Robert bought a local horse called 'Joke'. It was stolen within 24 hours, but he seems to have got it back, although by then he had arranged to have his Lusaka horse, 'Secret Service', transported to Botswana by rail. The horse was put in a goods truck, clearly not properly secured, and suffered severe grazing to its flanks. It was also riddled with ticks. In the end 'Senior Service' seems not to have survived long and 'Joke' became Robert's main form of transport. He derived great enjoyment from him, always willing to gallop into town – about two miles – to go to the bank or on some other errand,[233] or enjoying a hack with his cousin John Moor, the resident doctor in Serowe.

* * *

Within two weeks of his arrival, and with the aid of the fourth form, Robert had conducted a preliminary survey of the human and physical resources of Serowe and surrounding villages, and presented his conclusions to Patrick as his proposal for a Serowe Development Plan. Following the model of the builders' brigade, with its focus on primary school leavers, he proposed an enlarged and diversified brigade project, starting with a farmers' brigade. This would teach modern farming techniques so that the trainees would learn how to make a decent living from the land. To help bring constructive development to the whole of Serowe, Robert proposed an expansion of brigades to cover a wide range of skills, from spinning, weaving and dressmaking to mechanics, carpentry, metalwork and engineering. While Patrick departed on a fund-raising trip to Europe in December, Robert completed full costings for the plan, which he forwarded to Patrick with the words, 'If you can get some backing for it, then the whole labour will

[232] Van Rensburg, *Memoir*, p 328; and Mike Tiller, interview, 12 November 2020.
[233] Bagnall, *Letters*, 27 October 1967, p 114.

have been immensely worthwhile'.[234] Charities and aid agencies were duly impressed. Oxfam became a capital funder for the project, as did the Danish agency Danida, which promised to send an agronomist and a stock specialist for the farmer's brigade, together with some capital funding.

Similarly, it did not take Robert long to come up with a clear proposal for the development studies curriculum, which, according to Patrick, had hitherto been taught by himself, Donald Curtis, and others in a rather makeshift fashion without a properly elaborated syllabus. Within a day or so of Robert having a look at it, he came up with a detailed outline of a course he proposed be adopted. Patrick immediately saw it as 'a great improvement on anything we had done before'.[235] Robert recognised that 'all societies continually evolve' and he proposed that the course study the transformation process from pre-industrial rural to urbanised industrial society, including technical advances, but also linking it to a country's pre-colonial and colonial histories. Alison Kirton, who went on to teach the new revised course, described it as 'an excellent synthesis of economics and history'.[236]

Robert was very much in tune with Patrick's ideas. They trusted each other implicitly, and Patrick was happy to delegate the expansion of the brigade programme to Robert, who spent much of the first term of 1967 getting his brigade plans up and running. Some of the finance came from his own resources. His Japan Airlines shares had done well and he sold some to pay for three looms for the weaving brigade, at £35 apiece. His father sent 'a dollop of £175' for the anticipated carpenters' brigade and helped search for other sources of finance for technical equipment that would be needed in the engineering workshop.[237]

By June 1967 they were ready to start setting up the brigades. The 'tribal

---

[234] Van Rensburg, *Memoir*, p 317.

[235] Van Rensburg, *Memoir*, p 305.

[236] Alison Kirton, 'Teaching Development Studies at Swaneng Hill School', in https://theswanengstory.files.wordpress.com/2015/09/development-studies-2.pdf [accessed 31 August 2021].

[237] *Oakeshott Letters*, RO to his father, 10 March [1967].

authority' allocated seventeen acres on the same site as the builders' brigade near the centre of Serowe for the textile workshop, and the mechanical and carpenters' brigades. The farmers' brigade was the largest undertaking, consisting of a dairy farm of 500 acres near Swaneng Hill School, and 6,000 acres further out in the country for a ranch. Robert was constantly working at getting the various projects moving, ahead of the receipt of funds, just as his Uncle Pendy had urged them to do in Lusaka. One Saturday morning, for instance, he drove to Palapye, the nearest railway station, to collect 25 pounds of unwashed mohair for carpets, before there was even a textile workshop to store it in. The mohair had come at Robert's own expense from South Africa and that afternoon, over lunch in the mess, 'Robert was doing abstruse sums which told him that with 500 goats [they] could produce X carpets and make a profit of Y Rand[238] and employ Z girls per year'.[239] Caroline Cox-Johnson, a volunteer teacher, recalls that a couple of years later, when the textile workshop was up and running, Robert acted as auctioneer at a public sale of their rugs and other produce. With much wit and humour, he managed to sell a lot, mostly to the volunteer teachers and visitors at the Serowe Hotel.[240] The farmers' brigade became Robert's particular responsibility. Much of the initial work involved de-stumping, clearing the ground and fencing the land. It was 'back-breaking' work and some of the farming trainees must have wondered what they were letting themselves in for. Robert thrived on the physical work, regarding it as important to set an example. As American volunteer Tom Holzinger, who became a good friend of Robert's, recalled,

> As we dug tree stumps and prepared land for ploughing, Robert loved to muse aloud on 'The Good', and what a good society would be.
>
> Conversation about prices he despised; gossip about people he mistrusted; debate over policy and philosophy galvanised him.[241]

---

[238] Rand = the South African currency which Botswana was still using at this stage, then at the rate of 2 Rand to £1.

[239] Bagnall, *Letters*, 4 June 1967, p 85.

[240] Caroline Cox-Johnson, interview, 6 November 2020.

[241] Tom Holzinger, from a posting at Robert's memorial service in 2011.

He would spend three hours in the morning on physical work and the rest of the day on administration, writing papers and planning. And occasionally he would enjoy an exhausting 'day in the saddle', riding out to check on the progress of fencing the ranch.

Robert's evenings were devoted to socialising, which to his mind meant talking and drinking. Sleep, he claimed, interfered with good conversation and all-night sessions, aided by alcohol and coffee, were not unusual. Sheila Bagnall found him 'terribly intelligent' and a little over-bearing,[242] but she was drawn to his company, as were others such as Tom Holzinger, and they both found conversing with Robert very stimulating. He would philosophise about the quest for a better world and throw out challenging questions on unexpected topics, often with a note of humour if he felt the dynamism was flagging. As Caroline Cox-Johnson recalls, 'he would swoop from highly intellectual talk to comic enactments of his life in the army, and tragi-comedies of his life in Rome and Paris'[243]. At times, his drinking sessions got the better of him. On occasion he became so drunk that he could not find his way to his own rondavel and would crash out on someone else's unoccupied bed, or the floor. But he was always up at first light, ready to throw himself into whatever task was at hand.

Later, when Robert was the founding principal of Swaneng's sister school, Shashe River, volunteer teacher Angela Mackay, who shared a neighbouring rondavel, was to recall with great humour how Robert's early morning movements began their days:

> First, the soft scrape of his rondavel door opening, the cough and occasional splutter, a groan or two – and then we tracked his shuffle to the ablution block. …
>
> The scrape of another door, then the sound of water running in the shower, and a moment of silence. By this time Georgie and I were already giggling under the covers. Then it came, in great gasps:
>
> "Ohhhhhh, ahhh, ahhh, Oh my god, shit!"
>
> The water was turned off. Robert was finished, after mere seconds

---

[242] Bagnall, *Letters*, 'Staff List, June 1967', p 87.

[243] Caroline Cox-Johnson, interview, 6 November 2020.

under the water. Minutes later he would emerge, damp haired and semi-dressed, trotting back to the rondavel for a sweater …

The sounds of an Oakeshott shower have clung to me for the rest of my life, like an aural miasma from a magic time.[244]

* * *

In mid-July 1967 Robert received a letter from his brother Evelyn with the 'magnificent news' that he and their father Walter were 'planning to converge on Botswana in the first few days of August'.[245] Evelyn would fly via Nairobi and Lusaka, where he would meet up with Antony Martin and other friends, while Walter would fly to Johannesburg. Robert was extremely excited and wrote off a string of letters to both father and brother with travel and clothing advice, warning that August in Botswana could be pretty cold.

By this time Robert had been barred from entering South Africa, as were many who worked with that 'arch traitor' Patrick van Rensburg, so he was unable to meet his father in Johannesburg; but he arranged for him to stay the night there with Scottish novelist, poet and social activist Naomi Mitchison and her husband while he waited for a flight to Botswana. On 3 August, the day Walter Oakeshott, the prestigious former Vice-Chancellor of Oxford (1962–1963), flew into Serowe, Sheila – who had already remarked that Robert '… has difficulty with his waistline, from which belts fall, shirts flap, underpants peep'[246] – suggested he smarten up a little before his father's arrival. No problem, Robert replied, he would turn his dirty woollen jumper inside out and drive out to the airstrip to meet him. Meanwhile, Evelyn was on his way by car from Lusaka, where he had met Sekgoma Khama, a cousin of President Sir Seretse Khama. Sekgoma knew Robert well and had offered to give his twin brother a lift for the 800-mile journey to Serowe. In Rhodesia they were regarded with suspicion, as the white man was observed to be sitting in the front next to the black driver;

[244] *Oakeshott Papers*, Angela Mackay, Ottawa, Canada, memories of Robert, November 2011.
[245] *Oakeshott Letters*, RO to his father, 12 and 17 July 1967.
[246] Bagnall, *Letters*, 'Staff List, June 1967', p 87.

they had difficulty finding places where black and white could eat together and they were relieved to reach Botswana. It was approaching midnight by the time they drove into Serowe. Evelyn stayed with Robert in his Swaneng rondavel, while Walter stayed at the Serowe Hotel.

Within a few days Walter came down with shingles, a painful and debilitating disease. The Serowe doctor, John Moore, who happened to be a cousin on the Moon side of the family, advised him to rest for the next week or two. Walter, however, was determined that 'the boys should not miss their hols together', so while he stayed in Serowe, well-tended by John Moore and the van Rensburgs, Robert and Evelyn took the train to the beautiful eastern highlands of Rhodesia, where they stayed with Pat Pearce, Mick's mother, with whom Robert had by now developed a close friendship. As Walter remarked in a letter to Noel, 'it will be a good thing for R. to get away; ... as usual, he's been working like a maniac on all the new farm development'.[247]

It is clear from Walter's letters to Noel that the work Robert was doing had made a deep impression upon him. Despite his son's numerous and forgivable foibles, the work he was doing now was so immensely worthwhile. Indeed, the most lasting emotion that Walter Oakeshott took away from Botswana was 'pride in Robert's work – just the kind of venture' that would have attracted him in his idealistic youth.[248] From this time, if not before, a much more relaxed and mutually appreciative relationship evolved between father and son.

After a fortnight's rest Walter was feeling well enough to fly to Livingstone, where he met up with Evelyn, who had come up from Rhodesia by train, while Robert had had to return to Serowe, as it was still term time. Walter and Evelyn spent a week in Zambia, viewing the Victoria Falls and visiting Lusaka, where they met many of Robert's friends and had a 'quiet dinner' at the Stoep.

Meanwhile, back in Serowe, Robert's journalistic antennae picked up rumours of a major diamond discovery somewhere to the north-west of Serowe. Anticipating a scoop, he hired a five-ton lorry to drive himself and

---

[247] *Oakeshott Letters*, Walter to Noel, 7 and 9 August 1967.

[248] Dancy, *Walter Oakeshott*, p 265.

a few friends along 135 miles of sandy tracks to the village of Letlhakane.[249] A prospecting party from the South African diamond conglomerate De Beers was operating at the nearby site of Orapa. On arrival at the site, Robert was undeterred by a sign telling them to keep out. They pitched their tent and lit a fire within sight of the geologists' camp; after supper Robert walked across and invited them to come over to his camp as he had some good whisky. They accepted the invitation and after a couple of hours of well-oiled talk, Robert had his story.[250]

The geologists had uncovered a 'kimberlite pipe' – the subterranean volcanic source of diamonds. They had not yet drilled to any depth, but on digging around near the surface they had collected several parcels of valuable-looking gemstones which they sent off to South Africa for evaluation. It could not yet be confirmed that they had discovered a major source of gemstones, but the excitement of the geologists was palpable.

Robert returned to Serowe, wrote a well-considered article on the find and sent it off to the *Financial Times* for publication. He highlighted some of the potential problems of large-scale mining on the northern edge of the Kalahari, such as the shortage of water, and the find's potential significance for the future of Botswana.[251] That weekend, Walter Oakeshott, back at the Serowe Hotel for a few more days before returning home, met up with a couple of the geologists who had come into Serowe for the weekend. He was so impressed by what he heard from them that he wired his bank to sell some stock and buy De Beers' shares.[252] A financially shrewd decision, for the Orapa find proved to be the single most valuable source of gem diamonds in the whole of the De Beers ambit, and a game-changer for Botswana's development trajectory. And Walter's son, Robert Oakeshott, had been the first to spring the news upon the world.

---

[249] Tom Holzinger, interview, 19 March 2018. Tom was one of the friends who accompanied Robert on the trip.

[250] 'The Letlhakane diamonds', by a Special Correspondent, *Financial Times*, 7 September 1967; and Tom Holzinger and Anstice Oakeshott, 'A brief account of Robert Oakeshott', (unpublished typescript, 24 June 2011).

[251] 'The Letlhakane diamonds', *Financial Times*, 7 September 1967.

[252] *Oakeshott Letters*, Walter Oakeshott to Noel, 3 September 1967.

CHAPTER 13

Shashe River School

1968–1971

Robert spent Christmas 1967 with the Pearce family in Nyanga, in the eastern highlands of Rhodesia, and on returning to Serowe he moved to a new rondavel on the site of the farmers' brigade, where he had easy access to an almost unlimited supply of poultry and dairy products. Farmers' brigade trainees drove a horse and cart around Serowe making daily deliveries of milk, yoghurt and other products from the farm. Robert had been looking forward to spending less time on the administration of the other brigades and more time on writing, but in January 1968 the government sprung upon them its approval for what Robert referred to as 'a second edition' of Swaneng.

Since before Robert's arrival, van Rensburg had been thinking beyond Swaneng Hill School and Robert's proposal to expand the brigade structure convinced the two of them that this sort of proactive, locally-based, rural development could, and should, be replicated widely across the country. They drew up detailed plans for just such a school in Maun, the largest town in the remote north-west of the country, where there was no secondary school.

Robert was carried away by a romantic vision of transporting cement by ox-wagon by the little-used direct route from Serowe to Maun, across 300 miles of the northern Kalahari. Serowe had many unused ox-wagons and to Robert it seemed logical to use 'traditional' technology wherever possible. The previous year he had bought a horse and cart in Johannesburg, and he and Mike Tiller had driven it all the way from Johannesburg, on the grounds that it was far more cost-effective for delivering the milk round

135

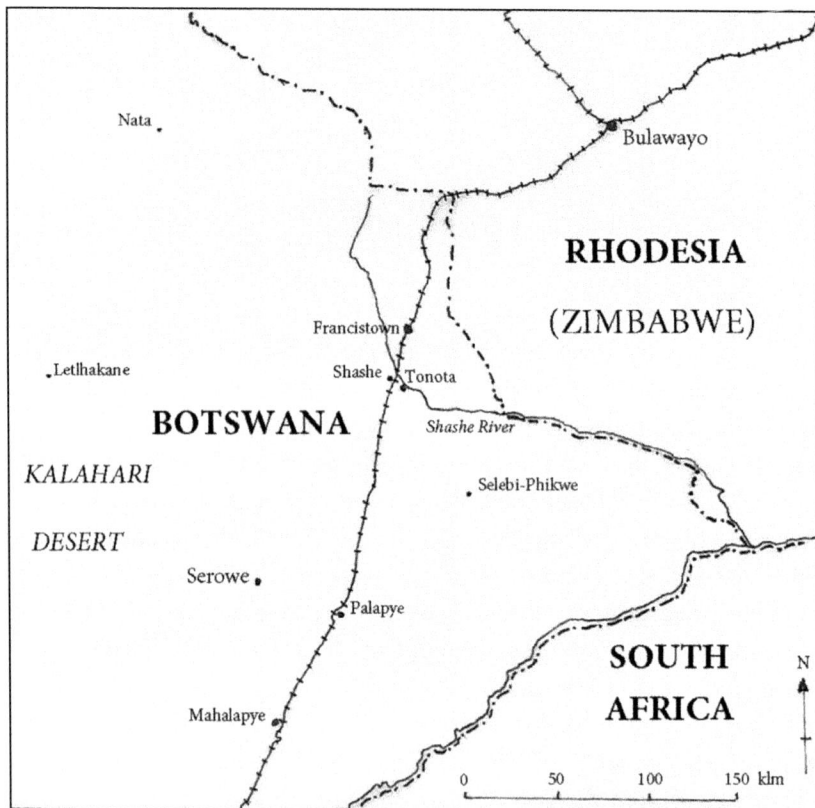

Northeastern Botswana c.1970 (by the author).

Serowe than using the Swaneng truck.[253] But Patrick knew something of the dangers of cross-desert travel and dismissed the ox-wagon idea as 'crazy', though 'typical of Robert'.[254]

When the government finally gave its approval for a Swaneng sister

---

[253] Mike Tiller and Gerry Pozzani, 'Fetching Mace, the carthorse that regularly went from SHS to Serowe' in www.theswanengstory.wordpress.com/change-log/ [accessed 24 November 2021].

[254] Shillington, *Van Rensburg*, p 182.

Early construction work at Shashe River School.
(By kind permission of Johnny Grimond)

school, in January 1968, it was for a school at Tonota, a small town on the line of rail, about 75 miles north of Palapye and 20 miles south of Francistown, and the Maun plans were simply shifted to Tonota. Robert, Patrick, Sheila and others went up to Tonota and found an ideal site overlooking the Shashe River, as a result of which they named the new school 'Shashe River School'.

A site manager and local labour were hired to start clearing the land and they were joined during the April school break by a work camp of students and staff from Serowe. Robert, the obvious person to head the new school, persuaded Mick Pearce and Erhard Lorenz, his architect friends in Lusaka, to act as 'consulting architects'.[255] Patrick's vision for the new school was not as radical in terms of cost-cutting as Robert would have preferred, however, and Robert soon realised that their ideas in general were, in his words, 'tending rather to diverge'. By March Patrick had made it clear that he was not going to offer Robert the job of principal at Shashe River. He would prefer to find a suitable African to take on the task. The whole turn

---

[255] RO to his mother, 6 and 25 January 1968.

of events was, in classic Robert understatement, 'a little disappointing', and he began planning to depart from Botswana at the end of 1968.[256]

In the meantime, he focused his efforts on drafting his development studies text. He had already made a start by getting his mother to send him two huge volumes on 'The History of Technology', which had many wonderful examples for teachers to use as case histories. And after in-depth research, he wrote up a chapter for submission to one of many weekend workshops with Patrick and Swaneng staff, including Alison Kirton, who were teaching the course in line with Robert's three-year junior secondary syllabus.

The research was an education in itself for Robert, who thoroughly enjoyed the task, particularly when his mother sent him, at his request for a 35th birthday present, Christopher Hill's radical new book, *From Reformation to Industrial Revolution*.[257] Hill, Master of Balliol College since 1965, was a leading left-wing historian of the post-war era and his interpretation of Britain's early modern history was a revelation to Robert. He knew of the horrors of child labour in early industrial Britain, but Hill's work introduced him, apparently for the first time, to the realities of the transatlantic slave trade, and he learned of the role of the 'triangular' trade in building the financial foundations of Britain's Industrial Revolution.[258] On his own account, Robert worked out that some of his Moon forebears, who owned ships in the eighteenth century, may have profited from that notorious trade. And in Hill's coverage of the seventeenth and eighteenth centuries, Robert found relevance to economic and social change in 1960s Africa.

From Christopher Hill, Robert turned to EP Thompson's *The Making of the English Working Class*,[259] another major work of social, economic

---

[256] RO to his mother, 17 March 1968.

[257] First published in 1967, and never out of print since.

[258] 'Triangular Trade': British manufactured products were shipped to West Africa, offloaded and exchanged for African captives, who were transported across the Atlantic to be sold into slavery in the Caribbean and North America. The third leg of the journey carried the products of slave labour (sugar, tobacco, cotton) back to British ports, mainly Bristol, Liverpool and Glasgow.

[259] First published by Victor Gollancz, London, 1963. Robert's mother probably sent him the new revised edition published in 1968.

Robert's preferred form of school transport.
(By kind permission of Johnny Grimond)

and cultural history. This was 'history from below', far from the kind of English History Robert had been taught at Tonbridge, where Wat Tyler and the Peasant's Revolt were dismissed by Mr Somerwell as 'a time when the Great Unwashed made one of their rare appearances on the stage'.[260]

Robert's enjoyable historical musings were rudely interrupted on 21 August 1968. Early that morning he heard on the radio that Soviet troops had invaded Czechoslovakia to crush the 'Prague Spring'. This movement for greater freedom within the communist system had been initiated earlier in the year by reforming First Secretary of the Czech Communist Party Alexander Dubček. For Robert, it was a repeat of Budapest 1956, with the so-called 'nuclear deterrence' rendering the Western powers impotent in the face of Soviet aggression. 'It seems a terrible thing', he wrote to his mother, 'that the Western Democracies can once again do nothing but stand idly by.' He recalled the Prague student conference of August 1956, when he and Jane Willoughby had had supper with an elderly Czech

---

[260] RO to his mother, 5 November 1968, 23 August and 1 November 1969.

139

translator and his wife, and how the old man's eyes had filled with tears as Dvořák's New World Symphony played on the gramophone.[261]

This melancholy mood was diverted some weeks later when Robert got hold of a copy of Julius Nyerere's booklet, *Education for Self-Reliance*.[262] Nyerere, President of Tanzania, was widely regarded as the guru of African socialist, self-reliant development, and from this booklet Robert realised they were already practising in Serowe just the sort of self-reliant education of which Nyerere wrote. He rushed round to the van Rensburgs with a bottle of whisky and he and Patrick excitedly discussed the subject well into the small hours. The experience seems to have restored the trust between them and it was not long before Patrick, who had had no luck in the search for a suitable African to take charge of Shashe River School, reversed his previous decision and offered the job to Robert. He even agreed to allow Robert to operate largely independently from Patrick's direct control.[263]

Robert could not resist accepting full charge of this exciting new project, and he, Patrick and Sheila travelled down to the Education Department in Gaborone to obtain formal approval for Robert's appointment. Robert had been persuaded to buy a new suit 'off the peg' for the occasion for, as he acknowledged,

> [The Education Department] are a highly cautious and conservative bunch. ... They were fairly friendly, but obviously guarded. They had in mind (& would have much preferred) a fellow with much more orthodox a background.[264]

Nevertheless, with Patrick's strong support, the Department agreed to the appointment, on a two-year contract, with a possible extension for a third year. It meant a shortened home leave for Robert, who was back in Botswana on 5 January.

* * *

---

[261] RO to his mother, 8 and 21 August 1968.

[262] Julius K. Nyerere, *Education for Self-Reliance* (Government Printer, Dar es Salaam, 1967).

[263] RO to his mother, 5 November 1968.

[264] RO to his mother, 23 November 1968.

Shashe River School opened in the last week of January 1969, with 100 students for Form One, a further 80 transferred from Swaneng for Form Two, and 80 trainees for the builders' and farmers' brigades. Other brigades would follow during the course of the year. The quality of expatriate volunteer staff was 'a bit of a lucky dip'; but Robert had the support of Sheila Bagnall, who would come over from Swaneng on occasional weekends to mentor the inexperienced volunteers and indulge herself with a night's liquid conversation with Robert.

In due course, Robert was delighted to welcome Mike Tiller who, having gone back to America to complete his degree, returned to Botswana to join the staff at Shashe. There was in addition one local Motswana teacher, Gets Moroeng, who was appointed Vice-Principal, with a view

Shashe River School, c.1970.
(By kind permission of the late Sandy Grant)

*Robert with his cousin Charles Gott who joined him at Shashe River
School and took over the running of the farmer's brigade, 1969.
(By kind permission of the late Sandy Grant)*

to succeeding Robert in due course.[265] The Swedish aid agency Sida had
agreed to underwrite the school, which meant that Robert got a salary
– enough for local living expenses and one trip to Europe a year. It also
allowed him to hire help with the accounts, to enable him to do other
things 'without getting totally exhausted'.[266]

Despite his rather chaotic administration, there were no major disasters
in Robert's first term at Shashe. His rondavel was packed full of textbooks,
sheets, blankets and a duplicating machine, leaving barely room for a bed;
but he was buoyed by the enthusiasm of the staff and their willingness,
together with the students, to work voluntarily on Saturday mornings,
laying the foundations for a textile workshop. Robert, as ever, led by
example, cheerfully wielding a pick and shovel.[267]

Robert's cousin Charles Gott, who had sold up his farm in South Africa
and joined the farmers' brigade at Swaneng, now moved to Shashe River
to manage the farm training there. According to Charles's elder brother
Richard, who was working in Tanzania at the time, Charles was fairly

---

[265] RO to his mother, 16 January 1969.

[266] RO to his mother, 5 November 1968.

[267] RO to his mother, 1 and 23 February 1969.

Robert at the official opening of Shashe River School, 1969.
(By kind permission of Anstice Oakeshott)

cynical about certain aspects of Shashe River School, believing that Robert was getting carried away with his socialistic idealism.[268]

In July 1969 President Sir Seretse and Lady Khama paid an official visit to the new school, and Robert borrowed a suit from Charles Gott for the occasion. Khama was an old Balliol man and had in fact just been offered an honorary fellowship at the College. Thus, much to Robert's relief, the small talk revolved around reminisces of Balliol characters, such as Russell Meiggs, and the day passed off well.[269]

After a successful first year at Shashe, and with the school expected to expand year on year, the new student intake for 1970 would take the total number up to 350 and there was much preparation to be done before the start of term. The South African Voluntary Service had sent a team of university students for a work camp to help with the building work at the school and Robert worked alongside them for a week, doing a full day's physical labour and eating only local food. This was a new experience for him, especially in the oppressive heat of a rainless January. Hitherto, he had enjoyed hard physical work as a form of relaxation for two or three

---

[268] Richard Gott, interview, 3 March 2021.
[269] RO to his mother, 29 July 1969.

hours of a morning or afternoon of his choosing. This experience taught him that working the full stretch between breakfast and lunch without a tea break was 'unendurable'.[270]

It also strengthened his empathy for those Botswana citizens for whom life was a daily struggle. The more he read about the sharp divisions of wealth and poverty in early industrial Britain, the more he feared for the future of developing countries like Botswana. He feared the country's new-found diamond wealth would drive up inequality in Botswana society, observing that 'living and working in a place like this is bound to push a person of any sensitivity to the left':

> For my part I am more and more convinced that Castro [of Cuba] has put his finger on the real key to economic development policy, namely income distribution.[271]

But he also had empathy for those Botswana citizens, like his deputy Gets Moroeng, who expected their well-educated children to have a far higher standard of living than the less-educated majority on the minimum wage.

* * *

Meanwhile, in the United Kingdom Prime Minister Harold Wilson called a general election for 18 June 1970. Jo Grimond had retired from leadership of the Liberal Party in January 1967, and Robert believed his successor, Jeremy Thorpe, whom he had met briefly in Lusaka, would bring ruination to the party. Unable to bring himself to stand for Mr Thorpe's Liberal Party, Robert decided on this occasion to stay put, to comment from afar. He had no great faith in Harold Wilson either, regarding him as a dissembler, although he much preferred him to Edward Heath and his Conservatives, who scraped through to a narrow victory. The Tories under Heath, Robert opined, would be 'unquestionably worse for this part of the world – and for race relations etc. in Britain'. He regarded their intent to resume arms sales to South Africa to be 'utterly perverse', as was their

---

[270] RO to his mother, 23 January 1970.
[271] RO to his mother, 14 March and 29 May 1970.

Robert in his office, Shashe River School.
(By kind permission of Johnny Grimond)

desire to come to terms with Ian Smith's Rhodesia.[272]

While worrying about the state of politics in Britain, and its implications for Southern Africa, Robert was faced with a more immediate crisis. In July 1970 the Shashe River students came out on strike, refusing to enter their classrooms as they marched around the campus voicing their complaints. The spark that set it off was the 'voluntary' duty of baking bread, which the students undertook on a rota basis. Robert was taken aback. He was aware that conditions at the bakery were poor, but had been reassured by the lack of vocal protest when he had not addressed the issue. He thought the *idea* of a strike might have come from Swaneng Hill, where six weeks previously the final-year students, the fifth formers, had gone on strike against doing voluntary work when their priority was studying for their end of school exams in November.[273] But he was unnerved by the thought that the real cause of the strike might have gone far deeper. He feared that

---

[272] RO to his mother, 29 May, 20 June and 23 July 1970.

[273] Shillington, *van Rensburg*, pp 212–217.

perhaps there were unresolvable cultural differences with a 90 per cent white staff making decisions for a 100 per cent black student body.

The experience strengthened his opinion that the role of principal should be localised. He reasoned that neither he nor the staff were authoritarian and they encouraged the students to think for themselves. But perhaps that was the point. In self-critical mode, he wondered whether he spent too much time trying to set an example, rather than *explaining* the school's philosophy.[274] Fortunately, the strike was short-lived, although he does not record how it was settled. On making enquiries he learned that school strikes were not that rare, and it made no difference whether the principal was black or white. Indeed, a couple of years previously a black school principal had had his car burned during a strike. 'Luckily,' quipped Robert, 'I haven't got a car'.[275]

Despite the strike, Robert lost none of his enthusiasm for the school and what he was trying to achieve. He stuck to his attempts to break down the students' prejudice against manual labour and made a point, as principal of the school, of being seen to be identified with hard physical work, which he always undertook alongside the students on Saturday mornings. He was also set on minimising the privileges normally 'enjoyed by the lucky minorities [who went to secondary school] in these countries'. Otherwise, he wrote to his mother, they will find themselves as a small minority running an economic system that is 'not doing anything about mass poverty'.[276]

A few months after the strike, Robert was pleased to report that Shashe's policies seemed to be taking root, as exemplified during a visit from Gaborone Secondary School's football team. After a night in Shashe student accommodation, the Gaborone students complained about having no milk in their porridge, to which the Shashe students responded, 'How many of you have fresh milk at home?' And to the Gaborone complaint about the thinness of their mattresses, the Shashe students asked, 'How many of you have mattresses at all at home?' Robert was thrilled with these 'splendidly

---

[274] RO to his mother, 23 July 1970.
[275] RO to his mother, 8 August 1970.
[276] RO to his mother, 23 August 1970.

sophisticated' responses. And to this was added the Shashe third formers' very critical reaction to the 50 per cent pay rise given to Botswana's MPs.[277]

In early 1971 a further Swaneng sister school, known as Madiba, was founded at Mahalapye with Mike Hawkes, a long-time Swaneng Hill volunteer, as principal. By this time Sheila Bagnall had become principal of Swaneng Hill, Patrick having moved on to focus on brigades and other cooperative organisations. Robert, Mike and Sheila were summoned to Gaborone for a Principals' Conference. In the dining car of the mail train south, Robert's loud and 'very English' voice attracted the attention of an elderly Rhodesian couple who, when they learned the three were teachers, launched into a racist harangue along the lines that African brain structure was different from that of white people and 'their learning capacity was limited to that of a white child of seven'. Robert was hypersensitive about racism and would not let that pass. And as Sheila in due course retired to bed, Robert and Mike continued their alcohol-fuelled, anti-racist 'discussion' with the couple until, around midnight, the dining car was decoupled at Artesia, about 50 miles north of Gaborone. Robert 'who had

---

[277] RO to his mother, 24 October 1970.

Shashe railway siding, c.1970.
(By kind permission of Johnny Grimond)

147

drunk copiously', had to be pushed out of the dining car where he fell 'flat on his face on the stones between the tracks and was covered in blood'. Undeterred, he climbed back onto the departing train and on arrival at Gaborone, the three intrepid travellers made their way by a shortcut through the bush in the dark to the house of a friend. Robert, wrapped in a sleeping bag 'kept tripping over the end of it and falling into thorn bushes'. Each time, his apologies for his 'imitation of a rhinoceros' sent Mike off into 'a bad attack of the giggles', and Sheila had her work cut out keeping the party together. To their delighted surprise, the conference turned out to be 'really rather good'.[278]

By this time, Robert had completed two and a half years as principal of Shashe River School and was eager to move on. He had planned to leave in April 1971, assuming he would hand over to his vice-principal, Gets Moroeng. Robert, however, had paid scant attention to the sensitivities of the school board, which consisted of the Director of Education and various appointed officials. According to Sheila Bagnall, Robert would turn up late for board meetings in a generally shambolic state, with 'a sort of grey knitted vest, riddled with holes, [and] dirty trousers with large hole in knee', while the board were all in smart suits with ties. They viewed Robert's behaviour on such occasions as unprofessional and they seemed reluctant to accept his recommendation of successor. Moreover, Robert had failed to prepare Gets for the role. Gets had 'never taken a staff meeting, looked at the accounts, recruited staff or written a school letter'.[279]

Gets recognised his own shortcomings and in January 1971, he had asked Robert to stay on until the end of the year. Robert agreed, and to give Gets more confidence, Mike Tiller agreed to provide support by taking over as vice-principal during Gets' first year as principal. The board seemed to accept the arrangement, until it was vetoed by the Minister of Education. Gets later revealed to Mike Tiller that he had expelled a student some years before, and that student happened to be the son of the man who was now Minister of Education! This impasse was only resolved when

---

[278] Bagnall, *Letters*, 13 June 1971, p 303.

[279] Bagnall, *Letters*, 12 November 1970, p 289.

Mike Tiller agreed to become principal for a year while Gets remained vice-principal.[280] This enabled Robert to leave at the end of 1971 confident that, for at least one year, the school to which he had given so much was in safe hands.

* * *

Robert had made a huge contribution to Patrick van Rensburg's alternative education project and had thoroughly enjoyed his time in Botswana. Although his administration of Shashe River School still left a lot to be desired, students and staff were inspired by his hands-on leadership. He enjoyed the teaching and was valued by some students for his 'discussions',

---

[280] Mike Tiller, interview, 12 November 2020.

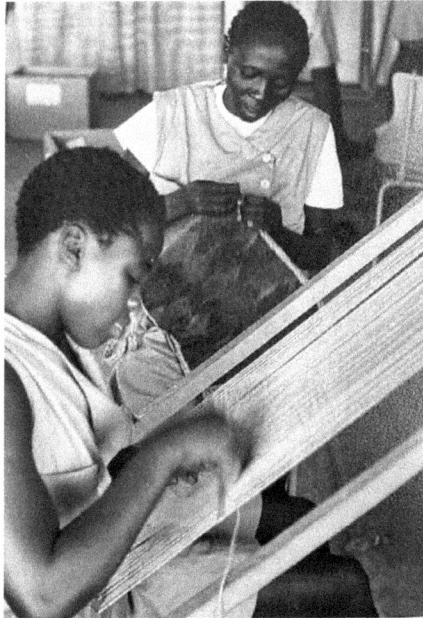

Trainees working in the Shashe River textile brigade.
(By kind permission of Johnny Grimond)

which was his way of introducing them to the concept of debating. He found the 'opening' of young minds enormously satisfying. And besides 'working like a maniac' on the brigade programme, the development studies curriculum and textbook, and the founding of Shashe River School, he always made time for a great social life and developed many new, lasting friendships. He had also given a lot of thought to the direction of his life after Botswana.

On his first arrival in the country, the thing that had inspired him most was the Serowe builders' brigade. Here was a highly flexible institution that was providing skills training for local youths who had little formal education: in effect, an apprenticeship scheme that was engaged in paying, productive work. Combined with a philosophy of voluntarism and cooperatives it was, at least potentially, a self-financing route out of local unemployment. And the success of his brigade diversification, especially at Shashe River, inspired his imagination – if Botswana, why not England?

CHAPTER 14

Planning a Builders' Cooperative

1972–1973

Since his time in Lusaka Robert had kept in close touch with Mick Pearce, often spending the Christmas holidays with the family at Nyanga or Lusaka. As ever, with Robert, these were occasions for philosophising through long conversations, and increasingly they concerned his plans for life post-Botswana. They were both inspired by Nyerere's promotion of self-sufficient, self-reliant communities and in Mick Pearce, Robert had found a potential partner in his enterprise.

He proposed the formation of a builders' cooperative somewhere in the de-industrialising North of England, where there were high levels of unemployment. And to raise the potential earning power of as many

Mick Pearce and Robert on holiday near Nyanga.
(By kind permission of Johnny Grimond)

young unskilled unemployed as possible, the project would have a heavy commitment to skills training. It would, in effect, be a British version of a builders' brigade. And in reaction to the 1960s tendency to demolish sub-standard housing and replace with soulless tower blocks, they decided to focus initially on upgrading Victorian era, working-class housing stock. This would also suit the sort of small- to medium-sized business they had in mind. As ever, with Robert the visionary, he had no doubt it would succeed and this would promote a new era of industrial democracy based on fairness and justice.

He arrived back in England in January 1972. After a month's holiday visiting friends and family, he found himself digs in Camberwell, south-east London and began researching businesses organised on a common ownership basis. Aside from the large and well-established John Lewis Partnership of department stores and the Scott Bader Commonwealth chemical company, he did not find many worker-owned enterprises in England, although the two he visited seemed to be doing well, with profits comparable to standard firms of a similar size. He contacted various cooperative organisations on the Continent – Norway, France, Italy and Spain – and resolved to visit many of them in due course.

While he waited for Mick to arrive on a recce, Robert took a job as a builder's labourer with a small firm in Peckham, a couple of miles to the east of Camberwell. His parents, while supportive of his ideals, thought this was going too far and his father suggested he would be better off writing articles for the *Financial Times*. But Robert was adamant: the hands-on experience would be invaluable. And while he found the long hours of physical work tiring, it was the monotony that struck him most:

> Working on a building site [he wrote to his mother] is not like knitting. You can't read at the same time. And you can't all that meaningfully *think* at the same time.
>
> … Of course, it's one thing to know this intellectually, it's something much more to experience it yourself.[281]

---

[281] RO to his mother, 1 May 1972.

He soon concluded that the general philosophy of the working labourer was to get maximum cash for the minimum of work, but he recognised that under the current system of complete divide between business ownership and hired labour, it was 'illusory to expect otherwise'.[282] After being with the firm for just a month, he was laid off without notice. He knew in principle about the precarious life of a casual labourer, 'as it is at present organised', but he consoled himself that it was 'no bad thing to have experienced it in practice'.[283] He had not, of course, suffered the real consequences of being fired and thrown back on the dole at a time of rising unemployment.

Apart from being able to fall back on his personal finances, Robert could always accept the hospitality of his well-off friends at weekends. And for all his talk of more equitable income distribution, 'it was impossible <u>NOT</u> to enjoy the comfort and easy good living' of Lawford Hall, the Grade I listed Essex home of Francis and Maureen Nichols, where over a weekend of good food and wine he was able to indulge in the irony of 'living in luxury while espousing the causes of reform'.[284] Similarly, over a weekend with Charles Keen and his family, Robert was delighted to find that despite his eight years absence in Africa, the old camaraderie had lost none of its lustre as they gathered round Charles at the piano and gave voice to the tunes of the Oxford Song Book.[285]

* * *

Mick Pearce arrived in May on a month's initial recce with his wife and two small children. The immediate aim was to identify a suitable site for the enterprise, their requirement being a town or small city in England with a population of at least 50,000 that was classified by the government as a 'special development area', for which government grants were available. Robert was also looking for somewhere with a 'supply of stimulating

---

[282] RO to his mother, 23 March 1972.

[283] RO to his mother, 1 May 1972.

[284] RO to his mother, 12 March 1972.

[285] RO to his mother, 23 March 1972.

people', a university or polytechnic, and a few professional people.[286] This was not just to make his life more congenial; if he was to fulfil his dream of feeding into and stimulating a cooperative culture and making it work, he needed much more than just an unemployed workforce.

It did not take them long to settle on Robert's old stamping ground, Sunderland on the North East coast. Apart from Robert's contacts and knowledge of the town, Sunderland satisfied their criteria in terms of size of population, with the highest youth unemployment anywhere in the UK. It had a good mixed social composition and a 'seemingly excellent Polytechnic', Wearside College, for the classroom side of the training. Sunderland had a large stock of sub-standard housing in need of upgrading and in the residential area of Millfield, just west of the city centre, they found a like-minded soul in Graham Dennis, a sociology lecturer at Newcastle University and town councillor for Millfield Ward. Dennis had recently published a book criticising the council's slum clearance policy,[287] and he welcomed their aim of involving and training local unemployed young people in the upgrading of what were known as the 'Sunderland (or Fisherman's) cottages'. Dennis was to become a supportive and invaluable contact.

Mick returned to Zambia with his family in June, due to return later for 'a much more detailed and intensive look' at Sunderland and the whole scheme, while Robert approached the Joseph Rowntree Charitable Trust for a grant of £500 towards a detailed reconnaissance survey for their enterprise.

The Rowntrees, a Quaker family, famous for their chocolate manufacturing in York, had a long tradition of concern for employee welfare and were supportive of cooperative principles in business. In 1905 the head of the family, Joseph Rowntree, formed three trusts, two charitable and the third, the Joseph Rowntree Social Service Trust (JRSST), was non-charitable and thus able to support causes engaged in political or

---

[286] RO to his mother, 5 June 1972.

[287] Graham Dennis, *People and Planning: The Sociology of Housing in Sunderland* (London, Faber, 1970).

economic reform. The JRSST, henceforth in this book referred to simply as the Rowntree Trust, provided financial support to the Liberal Party, especially under the leadership of Robert's friend and fellow co-op devotee, 'ex-leader' Jo Grimond, who in the 1970s and 1980s happened to be on the Rowntree Trust's board of directors, and it was to this trust that Robert applied for support. The Rowntree trustees already knew of Robert from his Botswana work, as they had been supporters of Patrick van Rensburg's projects since the early 1960s. Robert got his grant and in due course, once the Sunderland business got going, the Rowntree Trust was to become one of the principal financial underwriters for Robert's projects through the 1970s and 1980s.

With financial support from his old friend from Zambia days, Richard Hall at *The Observer*, for whom he promised to write articles on common ownership and industrial cooperatives, Robert visited France, Italy and Spain. France had a long history of cooperatives, some dating back to the nineteenth century, although they formed only a tiny proportion of French businesses. Antoine Antoni, secretary-general of the 'Société Coopérative des Ouvrière de Production' (SCOP), emphasised the importance of working with trade unions. He warned that the failure rate of new cooperatives was high, although if they survived the first six years they tended to prosper, with rates of production significantly higher than the national index.[288]

Towards the end of 1972 Robert visited the Mondragón cooperatives, 'that astonishing setup in the Basque country of Northern Spain'. Mondragón was a small town in the mountains south of Bilbao. In 1942 the local priest Fr José Maria Arizmendi had founded a small technical school to try to bring life to the town and stem the flow of young men and women to the larger towns and cities. In 1956, with Fr Arizmendi's leadership and encouragement, five of his original trainees who had gone on to higher technical education in Zaragoza returned to Mondragón, and founded the town's first industrial cooperative, manufacturing iron stoves and cooking equipment. It was named ULGOR after the initials of the founding five.

---

[288] Robert Oakeshott, 'The French Cooperatives', *New Society*, 1 March 1973.

It became the nucleus for the growth of the cooperative movement in Mondragón, a central ingredient of which was the cooperative savings and investment bank, the *Caja Laboral Popular*, founded by Fr Arizmendi in 1959. Its original capital was built from the small-scale personal savings of the local population, mostly the peasantry and working class. As such it provided a uniquely unifying factor in consolidating the Mondragón cooperatives into a single industrial culture.

At the time of Robert's visit in 1972, the original technical school had been upgraded to a Technical Institute and the number of cooperatives had risen to 55, with 90 per cent of them in manufacturing and construction. The largest was the original ULGOR group, now involved in the manufacture of refrigerators, with a workforce of 2,500 and an annual sales growth rate of 30 per cent since 1966.

Robert spoke with Fr Arizmendi, and a number of workers in several of the cooperatives, including the *Caja Laboral* and the Technical Institute. He judged the Mondragón cooperatives to have achieved a successful reconciliation of modern industry with social justice and democracy. As one of the foremen explained to Robert, 'You can't walk around as if you own the place'. The highest-paid, be they bank manager or professor at the Institute, earned no more than three times that of the lowest-paid worker. Capital was rewarded at a fixed rate of interest, 6 per cent in 1972, which left a high rate of profit for reinvestment and led to a high rate of growth that could not be creamed off in executive bonuses or payments to outside shareholders. Most of the small number of older inhabitants of Mondragón, including Fr Arizmendi, had been on the republican side during the Spanish civil war of the 1930s, and they were proud of their town as an 'oasis of democracy' in Franco's Spain.

Robert was hugely impressed by his Mondragón experience. Indeed, it was to become the inspiration for much of his future work in the field of employee ownership. To his mind, Mondragón proved that with the right leadership and favourable circumstances, employee ownership really could be the way to spread fairness and justice through industrial democracy in the workplace. He was to visit Mondragón again on numerous occasions, with friends, colleagues, bankers and businessmen, as he spread the word of Mondragón's success and the possibilities and benefits of employee ownership in the UK and elsewhere. Indeed, through his article on Mondragón in *The Observer* colour supplement in January 1973, and other writings through the decade, Robert effectively introduced Mondragón to the English-speaking world, and later to an international audience across Europe and beyond.[289]

In his search for a successful English cooperative enterprise on which he might model the Sunderland enterprise, Robert visited the Scott Bader Commonwealth. Scott Bader had been founded in 1921 as a family-owned, conventionally managed chemical company. Following the horrors of the Second World War, the company's Quaker founder Ernest Bader came to believe that every company should be owned by those who worked in it, and that 'labour should employ capital, not the other way round'. To achieve this, in 1951 Ernest and his family transferred 90 per cent of the company's total share value to the employees, and thus was formed the Scott Bader Commonwealth.[290] At the time, the company's lawyer, Hubert Munros QC, remarked, 'Gentlemen, I must remind you that the invitation cards to the funeral of capitalism have not yet been issued'.[291] Robert saw Scott Bader as an encouraging example to emulate. In 1958 Ernest Bader founded a membership organisation for like-minded businesses, which became the Industrial Common Ownership Movement (ICOM) in 1971.

It was through ICOM that Robert met Pete Smith, a trade union convenor, plant operator and technician at Shell Chemicals. As a member of the Institute for Workers' Control, as well as ICOM, Pete Smith was already firmly committed to industrial democracy in the workplace, and he agreed to join Robert and Mick in becoming a founder member of 'Sunderlandia Limited'. Mick Pearce was scheduled to wind up his

---

[289] R. Oakeshott, 'Spain's oasis of democracy', *The Observer* colour supplement, 21 January 1973.

[290] www.scottbader.com/corporate/history/ [accessed 17 October 2021].

[291] I am grateful to Andrew Gunn for this quotation from his typescript Obituary of Godric Bader who died 7 July 2022 aged 98.

architect's partnership in Zambia and arrive in England with his family in March 1973, while Pete Smith indicated that he would resign from Shell Chemicals, effective end of April. They set 1 May 1973 as a provisional starting date for Sunderlandia.

*   *   *

In January 1973 Robert bought one of the Sunderland working men's cottages for himself, 139 Rutland Street, in the inner-city Millfield district just to the west of the city centre. It had a front parlour and back room, with a kitchen galley leading to a back door and small yard that contained an outside privy. Stairs led up from the back room to an attic bedroom, small bathroom and a sort of anteroom that served as a spare bedroom. This was to become his home for the next four years, and although he loved to indulge in the fine living of his wealthy friends, personal comfort and tidiness were never high on his list of priorities, as was clear to the many friends who visited him in Rutland Street.

Anthony Gater, who stayed for several days, described Robert's home as 'a total shambles, which was normal for Robert'.[292] Johnny Grimond concurred, finding Robert 'living in squalor, but quite happy with it, guests tending to scrub up'.[293] Among Robert's many friends who visited him in Sunderland was Charles and Maurice Keen's sister Geraldine. She and her husband Frank Norman had spent part of their honeymoon in Botswana, where Robert had put them up in one of the Shashe River rondavels, and on their visit to Sunderland he vacated his bed for them. As Geraldine recalls, she had never seen such dirty sheets.[294] But that was Robert – a warm, welcoming and generous host in every other way. He loved entertaining and thrived on good company, no matter how disorganised he might be, and his friends always came back for more.

Jo Grimond described Robert's Sunderland home as 'very African', by which he meant sparsely furnished, but he thoroughly enjoyed Robert's

---

[292] Anthony Gater, interview, 14 October 2020.

[293] Johnny Grimond, interview, 12 January 2021.

[294] Geraldine Norman, interview, 9 December 2020.

'shake-down' of fish pie served on a tablecloth of pages from the *Financial Times*.[295] Caroline Cox-Johnson, who had worked with Robert in Botswana and visited him once or twice in Sunderland, recalls that his parents came up to have a look and Robert hired a car to drive them around:

> He crashed it and smashed the boot. His experience with cars was a chapter of accidents.[296]

His parents supported Robert's project and invested in Sunderlandia, but his mother never understood why he chose to live in such a small, rundown working-class home.

Other family who visited included Evelyn and his new wife Charlotte. They had married in May 1973 in Stonesfield Parish Church, near Woodstock, north-west of Oxford. The reception had been held in Stonesfield Manor, Charlotte's family home, and Robert was best man. He had been to enough weddings to know the drill, but as Charlotte recalls,

> … when the Major Domo said, 'Silence for the Best Man', Robert piped up 'Oh no, no, no!' There was no understudy, so Evelyn missed out [on the traditional best man's speech], which he was probably glad about, but the gorgeous little bridesmaids got no toast. I had my own 'best man', a friend from my publishing work, who stepped in at that point and gave me a toast, and Robert's lack of forethought or care was never mentioned again.[297]

After that inauspicious start, Robert did not feel 'completely at ease' with Charlotte when she and Evelyn visited Sunderland that October; but Charlotte did her best to smooth things over:

> … she was extremely helpful with the cooking and claimed (? diplomatically) that she found Rutland St. much less small, and less of a general shambles than she had expected from [his mother's] description.[298]

---

[295] RO to his mother, 26 September 1973.

[296] Caroline Cox-Johnson, interview, 6 November 2020.

[297] Charlotte Oakeshott, private communication, January 2022.

[298] RO to his mother, 31 October 1973.

Marie Little, singing for Robert and his guests.
(From Robert Oakeshott's collection, by kind permission of the Oakeshott family)

Marie Little, Pete Smith's wife, was a well-known local folksinger, and she and Robert became lifelong friends. Robert loved her songs for their combination of humour, pathos and social protest. He loved Marie's outspoken, no-nonsense attitude; she took people as she found them and did not bat an eyelid at Robert's eccentricities. Indeed, she was very fond of him and could see he was totally undomesticated so far as housework was concerned. One day, she and a friend put on rubber gloves and cleaned Robert's house while he was out. A couple of weeks later Marie found a copy of *Private Eye* pushed through her door. On the front was a picture of a naked streaker running across a football pitch, with the speech bubble, 'I want your advice on contraception'. Marie was pregnant at the time and presumed someone thought she should take the hint. She mentioned it to Robert, who said, 'Oh, I'm sorry – that was me. I thought a little thank you, for cleaning my house'.[299]

* * *

---

[299] Marie Little, interview, 11 January 2021.

Robert approached solicitor Bob Ayling for *pro bono* legal work to draw up Sunderlandia's 'Articles of Association'. At the time, Ayling, a future CEO of British Airways, was a junior partner in the solicitor's firm in London that had done the conveyancing on Robert's and Mick's properties in Sunderland. David Erdal relates Bob Ayling's story:

> When Robert came into the legal practice dressed in his usual shambolic manner, the very snooty senior partner asked, with contempt dripping from his aristocratic nose, who on earth this unprepossessing figure was. Bob told him it was the son of the Rector of Lincoln College, which changed the senior partner's tune.

When Bob explained to Robert that a company needs a Memo setting out the purpose and Articles setting out the rules, Robert came back the next day having written what Bob described as 'The Communist Manifesto'.[300] The Preamble to the Memorandum was Robert at his most left wing, still strongly radicalised by his African experience. As he saw it, he was simply reiterating the principles he had learned from Mondragón and Scott Bader, namely, that workers should be the owners of the enterprise, that they should hire capital at a fixed rate of interest and control the business 'in a true industrial democracy', one member one vote, with wage differentials 'much narrower than is now normal'. He could not resist adding that in his opinion the wages of most managers and professionals were far too high and should come down. The highest wage in Sunderlandia would be set at no more than twice that of the lowest-paid employee.[301]

---

[300] David Erdal, 'Robert Oakeshott: renewing the memory', 4 April 2019, typescript in *Oakeshott Papers*; and David Erdal, interview, 2 December 2020.

[301] A copy of the 'Memorandum and Articles of Association of Sunderlandia Limited' is to be found in both the *Oakeshott Papers* and the *Joseph Rowntree Charitable Trust Archives*, (Borthwick Institute for Archives, University of York), *JRRT*, Box 104.

CHAPTER 15

Sunderlandia

1973–1978

Robert estimated Sunderlandia would need £75,000 in starting capital. Part of this was to come in the form of loan stock from each of the three founders: Robert, Mick Pearce and Pete Smith. Pete brought in money from Shell Petro-Chemicals, while a considerable amount was raised from up to twenty of Robert and Mick's family and friends, including Robert's parents.[302] Investors would be paid no more than a fixed rate of interest, set in line with that of the Bank of England. Among the loan stockholders were Lady Jane Willoughby, a loyal supporter of Robert's schemes, and Baron Éric de Rothschild. Lady Jane had introduced the banker and owner of Château Lafite Rothschild to Robert at some time in the mid-1960s, and the two men formed a firm friendship. Éric followed Robert's work closely and willingly became a loan stock investor in Sunderlandia, regularly flying over from France to attend AGMs and some of the general meetings of the cooperative.[303] A further £5,000 investment came from the Scott Bader Development Fund, which brought the starting capital fund up to £50,000 by early March 1973.[304]

Robert applied to the Joseph Rowntree Social Service Trust for a further £20,000 and a three-man delegation of trustees visited Sunderland to assess the feasibility of the project. They reported back to the directors of the trust:

> Robert Oakeshott could best be described as a somewhat eccentric secular missionary – maybe even a secular saint.

---

[302] Mick Pearce, interview, 12 December 2020.

[303] Éric de Rothschild, interview, 18 January 2021.

[304] The figures appear on a handwritten note in Robert's handwriting in *JRRT*, Box 104.

They confirmed everything about Robert's estimate in terms of housing need, size of project and availability of unemployed young labour. But despite the commendable enthusiasm of those they met, the trustees concluded,

> … the project was totally devoid of any form of orderly management whatever.

Sunderlandia lacked a proper business manager to 'organise the enthusiasts', investigate government loans, keep financial control and 'generally provide a sense of order'.[305] The directors ruled that the trust could not support Robert's application, at least not until Sunderlandia had corrected these deficiencies. The unspoken problem was that financial management was in the hands of the innately disorganised Robert Oakeshott, the greatest 'enthusiast' of them all.

Nevertheless, enthusiasm prevailed and Sunderlandia went ahead, hoping to attract Rowntree support at a later date. While Mick Pearce, as works manager, prepared a portfolio of a number of different designs for upgrading cottages, mostly entailing a back extension for an inside bathroom, Pete Smith identified nine skilled tradesmen – bricklayers, carpenter/joiner, plumber, electrician, plasterer, and painter/decorator – who would undertake the basic work alongside training and supervising the work of the apprentices. This left Robert to go to the Labour Exchange and ask those at the back of the unemployment queue who would be interested in an apprenticeship in a cooperative building firm.[306] It did not take him long to recruit 31 recent school-leavers, at least two of whom were sixteen-year-old girls. Pete Smith, at Robert's urging, had managed to get trade union agreement for the girls to sign on as apprentice bricklayers, among the first females in the country to do so; and in May the 31 were sent on an eight-week, pre-work course at Wearside College. The actual building work did not finally get under way until mid-July 1973.

* * *

---

[305] *JRRT*, Box 104, 'JRSST, Memorandum to the directors of the Trust', unsigned, 25 April 1973.

[306] Mick Pearce, interview, 12 December 2020.

It was a fairly haphazard start, with Robert's idealism often clashing with practicality. As Mick Pearce has recalled,

> It was a great idea, getting 30 or 40 North Easterners to agree at a general meeting with one vote each, but actually, *managing people* wasn't Robert's thing. I used to argue quite a lot with him.[307]

From the beginning there was a conflict between profitability and Robert's insistence on maximising skills training. They started with nine tradesmen to 31 apprentices, a ratio of three or four to one. The tradesmen's time was to comprise one-third working on the project, one-third training and one-third supervising the work of the apprentices. With this regime, productivity inevitably suffered and there was no sign of ever making a profit. Even so, Robert was loathe to compromise on his commitment to maximising skills training, and six weeks into the work, he admitted in a letter to Johnny Grimond,

> It's not exactly 'easy riding'; at the moment it's more like pedalling uphill against a stiffish wind. Still, and with occasional reinforcement from Newcastle Brown Ale, morale remains high.
> … there is great charm and good humour among the lads and the two bricklaying lasses. In fact, I've already twice had that very good feeling which you get when working with people who don't have to be pushed to work at all.[308]

Robert was most at ease when he donned his old blue overalls and an ARP warden's helmet and joined the workforce, which he did once a week. Ian Smith, who had known Robert in Botswana and was a supporter and contributor to Sunderlandia, met Robert one day walking home from work, covered in soot from head to foot. 'I feel cleansed!' Robert declared.[309] Nor did he shirk from digging trenches in the pouring rain, although his favourite work was demolition. It could be hazardous when

---

[307] Mick Pearce, interview, 12 December 2020.
[308] *JJ Grimond papers*, RO to Johnny Grimond (JJG), 24 August 1973 and 3 January 1974.
[309] Ian Smith, interview, 17 December 2020.

Robert was around, swinging a hammer at a wall with no conception of the danger involved.[310] For Robert, this was leadership by example.

It was clear, however, that the tradesmen were 'carrying the business', and Robert was forced to face reality. The number of tradesmen was boosted to fifteen, and in December nine of the apprentices were laid off. This brought the ratio down to a much more manageable one or two per tradesman, and productivity increased dramatically.

Initially, membership of Sunderlandia consisted of the tradesmen, the three founders and a handful of other employees. Members were required to invest £50 in the business, payable over the first year. All decisions were made at regular general meetings where every member had a voice and a vote, and in September it was agreed to admit the apprentices to full voting membership. The result of their admission was remarkable. A month later a third of them decided, on their own initiative, to come in unpaid on Saturday mornings, taking it in turns on a three-week rota. Robert was ecstatic, for it 'brought back memories of voluntary work at Shashe', and he reported to his mother,

> A strong minority of the apprentices are, I think, developing very positive, responsible, and even warm feelings about SUNDERLANDIA. Of course, that's not a substitute for efficiency, skill, industrial discipline and the rest, [but it was clearly] a source of strength.[311]

In October 1973, three months into the work, Robert, as company secretary, called Sunderlandia's first Annual General Meeting, to be held at the Sunderland Catholic Club.[312] Robert's AGMs were very informal and there was always a party afterwards. The main business of the first meeting was the election of a board of directors. Hitherto the board had consisted of the three founders, Mick, Pete, and Robert. They remained ex-officio members, but three new directors were elected at the meeting: two tradesmen and one apprentice. Each year thereafter one of the founder directors would be replaced by an elected one so that in three years' time,

---

[310] Marie Little, interview, 11 January 2021.

[311] RO to his mother, 15 October 1973.

[312] *JJ Grimond papers*, RO to JJG, 29 September 1973.

the board would be an entirely elected body. In addition, two non-voting, part-time directors were co-opted onto the board: Bob Ayling and Éric de Rothschild.[313] The post-AGM party was judged a great success, with music and song provided by Marie Little.

Robert, as sociable as ever, would regularly host dinners at his Rutland Street cottage for visiting friends, as well as for some of the Sunderlandia workforce. He saw the inclusion of the latter as a way of building solidarity among the workers and the management. At the first AGM in 1973 he hosted twelve for supper, mostly for the investors who had come from out of town. He served what by then had become one of his stock dishes, 'FISH PIE!', with the pastry held up in the middle by one or two empty marmite pots, labels still attached. He was to become famous for his fish pies, and his tablecloths of pages from the *Financial Times*.

> On a related topic, [Robert wrote to his mother] how do you prevent Macaroni sticking to the bottom of the saucepan when you heat it up for MAC CHEESE? A second kitchen question: can you think of any objection to 'TOAD in the Mac Cheese': I tried it the other day when I had some sausages left over. It seemed not too bad to me. But there may be some reason for not offering it to guests.[314]

In complete contrast the following weekend, Robert, the Pearce family, Pete Smith and Marie were guests at Jane Willoughby's Scottish home. Robert had been there once before, and particularly enjoyed the 'wonderful local food like venison and salmon'.[315]

Marie Little recalls that Robert's parents came to the following year's AGM, and once more about a dozen dinner guests, 'some of them very posh', squeezed around the *Financial Times*-covered dinner table, on which Lady Jane had put out cards for the seating arrangement in the manner of a formal dinner. This time Robert excelled himself and served roast silverside of beef with barley. He cooked the barley separately and doled it

---

[313] Éric de Rothschild, interview, 18 January 2021.

[314] RO to his mother, 15 October 1973.

[315] RO to his mother, 31 October 1973.

out in great dollops, like porridge (or maize meal, African style). The drink flowed and his mother, ever loyal, said, 'Oh Robert, darling, this barley is absolutely delicious.'[316]

* * *

By Christmas 1973 Sunderlandia had completed twenty back conversions for a series of owner occupiers, with a dozen more in the pipeline. In the new year of 1974, they began a large contract for Durham County Council, worth £80,000, for twenty modernisations in a single block in a small mining village outside Sunderland. Despite the extra transport costs, work on a single site was much more manageable and cost effective. With two more such projects through 1974 and 1975, and the Rowntree Trust prepared to underwrite one of them, Sunderlandia edged towards breaking even.[317] To all outward appearances things seemed to be progressing well, the quality of work was improving and by 1975 the cooperative was attracting media attention.

Sunderlandia captured the Zeitgeist of the early to mid-1970s: the women's movement, squatters' movement, Friends of the Earth and Campaign for Real Ale. It was a time of self-help in this era of industrial conflict, inflation and rising unemployment, and there was a yearning for greater social justice in the workplace. Backpackers and others came to Robert's door seeking inspiration and a vision of a better world. Among them was Mary Clemmy, a former literary agent for socially progressive books in America and strong in the women's movement in London. She wanted to enter the building trade, which she saw as a bastion of male power. Sunderlandia's works committee agreed that in return for one week's unpaid work in the wages office, she could try her hand at various building skills for a week, to help her decide for which one she would undertake a professional apprenticeship.

Robert, whom Mary had previously met socially, offered free accommodation for the two weeks, and in the evenings she observed the arrival of young backpackers, who would simply turn up unannounced.

---

[316] Marie Little, interview, 11 January 2021.

[317] *JRRT*, Box 104, various correspondence.

There would be an enormous lamb stew on the hob and they would stay for supper and beyond. The drink flowed and Robert, in his questioning, Socratic style, would direct the conversation from an old armchair. As the evening progressed, and more and more alcohol was consumed, Robert would slip further down the chair until he was virtually prostrate on the floor, too drunk to get himself to bed. And as two young men carried the prostrate Robert up the stairs, he did not for a moment break the flow of his talk to the group below, '… and another thing you might consider, …'.[318]

* * *

At the 1974 AGM it was Robert's turn to step aside as ex-officio member of the board. He was eligible for election, but it was a salutary lesson for him when he was not even nominated for election to the board, which was now under majority worker control. The issue of class still mattered and no matter how hard he tried, Robert had never been one of the workers. He was dispirited to find that most had no interest in discussing management issues at the end of a long day's work on site. That was the management's job. Basically, 'We'll do our job, you do yours – and get us the work'.[319] As Mick Pearce has acknowledged, 'We came into their culture without understanding it'.[320]

But it was not all cultural misunderstanding. It was an unfortunate time to be entering the building trade, which suffered particularly from the downturn that followed the oil crisis of 1973/74. Despite Sunderlandia's early promise and Robert's inherent optimism, they struggled to achieve the profitability upon which the whole project hung. By 1975, some of the best craftsmen were beginning to look elsewhere. Sunderlandia had to rely more and more on the less efficient workers, a point that Robert, with his idealistic focus on maximising skills training and democratic control, was reluctant to acknowledge, no doubt partly because the less efficient workers tended to be more sympathetic to the cooperative concept.[321]

---

[318] Mary Clemmy, interview, 26 February 2021.

[319] Ian Smith, interview, 17 December 2020.

[320] Mick Pearce, interview, 12 December 2020.

[321] Mick Pearce, interview, 12 December 2020.

£7,000 for college training was a heavy burden to sustain, and with inflation soaring in the mid-1970s, it became increasingly difficult to make ends meet. Competition for contracts increased and Sunderlandia faced open hostility from standard building companies, who regarded Sunderlandia as interlopers, a bunch of amateurs poaching their trade, while the local Labour Party looked down on them with baffled condescension. Robert knew he had not got it exactly right, but the vision was still very much alive, and in response to the Labour Party's condescension he told journalist Robert Taylor that over the next decade the critique of capitalism must turn away from nationalisation and into 'industrial self-governing enterprises like [Sunderlandia]'.[322]

Pete Smith left Sunderlandia in early 1976, the first of the founders to do so. As a trade union man, he was more used to fighting for working men against the management establishment, and he never felt that comfortable in the role of company management. He had long been interested in the Chinese model of socialism and Mick Pearce's mother helped to arrange for him to visit China. On his return, Pete regarded Robert and Mick as 'enemies of the people'.[323] With their focus on profitability and worker dividends, they were trying to turn working people into petty capitalists. For Pete, cooperatives were primarily for 'the mutual benefit of participating members', and in this he had more in common with ICOM, a membership organisation formed to help and co-ordinate industrial cooperatives of the communal type.[324] Pete became Chairman of ICOM in 1977, and Robert helped him get a grant from the Rowntree Trust. This enabled Pete to set up ICOM's headquarters in a rent-free office in Woolwich, South East London.[325]

Robert had never intended to stay long term with Sunderlandia. As

---

[322] *JRRT*, Box 104, photocopy of published article, 'Be your Own Builder' by Robert Taylor, c. 1975, source unidentified.

[323] Mick Pearce, interview, 12 December 2020.

[324] *JRRT*, Box 111, Pamphlet, 'Industrial Cooperatives. A Guide to the ICOM Model Rules' (Registrar of Friendly Societies, 1977), p 23.

[325] *JRRT*, Box 111, correspondence between PW Smith and Pratap Chitnis of the JRSST.

with Shashe River School, he would stay long enough to see it set up with some level of stability and then move on. And it was in search of greater stability in 1976 that it was decided to reduce Sunderlandia to a smaller, more compact organisation of about twenty members. Although this left Robert feeling free to move on, the reality was that after a promising first three years, Sunderlandia was struggling to survive by 1976.

The lesson for Robert was that Sunderlandia was too much driven by its original promoters, himself and Mick, and that 'no new cooperative undertaking should normally be set up unless the prospective workforce takes a major role in the promotion exercise and makes a meaningful contribution'.[326] The proof of this was to be found in 'Little Women', a collective grocery store with infant-care facilities.

* * *

Little Women was the brainchild of Margaret Elliott, wife of Sunderlandia's leading bricklayer/trainer, Peter Elliott. She had met Robert at one of his dinners in 1974 and had been inspired by the principles expressed in his Memorandum, the so-called 'Communist Manifesto'. She saw that a small-scale cooperative store would be an 'opportunity for part-time work – and concurrent child minding – for young mothers', most of whom were wives of members of Sunderlandia.[327] As Marie Little, one of the Little Women, recalls,

> We got a shop on Hilton Road. It had a bench to sit on and chat. We bought and sold things for people who were very poor, who only had pennies to spend on essentials like food. They couldn't afford a half pound of butter? – we would cut it in half and sell them a quarter.
>
> There were eight of us altogether. There would be three women at any one time, two in the shop and one minding the small children in the flat upstairs.[328]

Little Women was formally structured on the Sunderlandia model, with Robert

---

[326] R. Oakeshott, *The Case for Workers' Co-ops* (Routledge & Kegan Paul, London, 1978), p 93.

[327] Oakeshott, *Case for Workers' Co-ops*, p 92.

[328] Marie Little, interview, 11 January 2021.

acting as mentor. All ideas that Margaret had, she would bounce off him.[329] As Robert admitted, the principle of the co-op may have come from middle-class outsiders like himself but, unlike Sunderlandia, the thrust to establish it came from the women themselves. They were totally committed; it was they who pushed it along. And one of the keys to its success was that each of the women had a 'significant capital stake' through the overdraft guarantee their husbands had offered the bank. Furthermore, the women agreed to be paid just 25p an hour, well below the market or trade union approved rate, 'until their enterprise was strong enough to afford an increase'.[330]

The enterprise lasted for four years and then only closed because the children were old enough to go to school. The shop was sold, all debts were paid, and the women took up other employment. Margaret, who remained in close contact with Robert, went for an education degree at a London polytechnic before starting another small cooperative – Little Women Household Services – which grew into Sunderland Home Care, now providing elderly homecare throughout Tyneside and the North East, with a cooperative workforce of 400 women.[331]

As Margaret Elliott explained in interview for this book, cooperative work changes lives for the better. The users benefit from a better quality of service, and the workers benefit from running their own company. They have more control over their lives:

> … there's no 'them and us'; there's 'us and us'. It's a great way of working.[332]

* * *

Robert left the full-time management of Sunderlandia in October 1976, after that year's AGM. He still visited Sunderland, spending a few days at a time, as and when required to give assistance. Mick got a local man to help with the management, and in 1979 he asked a large general meeting

---

[329] Margaret Elliott, interview, 19 December 2020.

[330] Oakeshott, *Case for Workers' Co-ops*, p 93.

[331] Margaret Elliott, interview, 19 December 2020.

[332] Margaret Elliott, interview, 19 December 2020.

of the Sunderlandia workforce whether they wanted to go back to a more conventional structure. The overwhelming vote was 'Yes'.

Mick mortgaged his house to keep the cooperative going long enough to pay off all Sunderlandia's debts. It was wound down through 1979 and closed with all debts paid.[333]

* * *

On the face of it, Sunderlandia may have appeared to have been a failure, because it struggled to make a profit and it closed after six years. But the majority of conventional new businesses failed to last that long; and in terms of what it achieved against adverse conditions, and its legacy, it was far from a failure. Sunderlandia's cooperative of skilled workers and their apprentices completed scores of high-quality housing conversions, and in doing so turned unemployed youths into skilled craftsmen, with an additional understanding of some of the workings and responsibilities of management. Self-esteem was boosted and all of them moved into good jobs after Sunderlandia or set up as self-employed, several as small-scale cooperatives. As one of the apprentices, Bill Brown, was to recall many years later,

> For the last 24 years I have worked in the field of Construction Training since the days when I worked in Sunderland. I often find some of the things done at Sunderlandia which were controversial at the time are now a part of so many peoples' everyday lives.[334]

As for the founder members, as Mick recalls, 'We had a marvellous time and did amazing things for about four years'. He returned to newly-independent Zimbabwe in 1980 and continued with pioneering architectural work. Pete had the chairmanship of ICOM. As for Robert, besides the practical and direct experience of running a worker-owned business, Sunderlandia had provided the foundation, and 'Little Women' the proof of success, from which he was able to go on to become an internationally-recognised expert in the promotion of worker-owned productive enterprises.

---

[333] Mick Pearce, interview 12 December 2020.

[334] *Oakeshott Letters*, Bill Brown to RO, January 2011.

CHAPTER 16

The Founding of Job Ownership Limited

Job Ownership Limited (JOL), Robert Oakeshott's flagship consultancy for spreading the economic alternative of worker ownership, was a logical progression of his professional life from Botswana in the 1960s and through Sunderlandia in the 1970s.

Robert had indicated to the Rowntree Trust that when he left Sunderlandia in October 1976, he intended to work 'in the field of industrial democracy … acting as a kind of freelance promoter of the common ownership idea through writing, speaking and developing new projects'.[335] The Rowntree trustees had always had a high regard for Robert, as Rowntree's Pratap Chitnis indicated,

> … my Trustees have for some years been very impressed by the selfless work which you have put into the projects with which you have been involved in the school in Botswana, Sunderlandia Limited, and work you have done in the field of common ownership.[336]

The trustees regarded Robert as someone who was 'particularly good at getting value for [their] money' and they agreed to grant him an unconditional personal award of £3,000 for a year: 'as a token of their appreciation for all that you have done'. It was to be paid quarterly from mid-November 1976, with a further £2,000 for expenses, to cover anything involved with his work.[337] This gave Robert the freedom he wanted,

---

[335] *JRRT*, Box 125, JRSST Memorandum, Chitnis to all trustees, 2 July 1976.

[336] *JRRT*, Box 125, Chitnis to RO 9 August 1976.

[337] *JRRT*, Box 125, Chitnis to RO, 9 August 1976.

especially to travel, as he sharpened his ideas through visiting successful, and some not so successful, examples of worker-owned businesses in England, Ireland, France and Spain.

* * *

Although Robert did not immediately sell his house in Sunderland, from mid-November 1976 his father's home at 'The Old Schoolhouse' in Eynsham near Oxford became his main address. Walter Oakeshott had bought the former primary school in 1969 and converted it in time for his and Noel's retirement from Lincoln College in 1972. The building was large enough to contain a separate unit for Walter's widowed sister Maggie Denham who moved there to live alongside them, supported by a monthly stipend from Walter.

Noel had suffered from poor health for much of her adult life; but she was considered fit enough to go into hospital in May 1976 for what should have been a routine operation to relieve the internal pain she had been suffering for some time. But something went wrong; she contracted peritonitis and had to have a second operation, from which she never fully recovered. She died in hospital on 19 June 1976.[338]

The family were devastated. Walter confided to a friend the following year, 'I'm ageing rapidly'.[339] Evelyn was so unsettled by his mother's death that he left his civil service job in London and moved to Scotland where he became fisheries economist in the Department of Agriculture and Fisheries in Edinburgh.[340]

It was a heavy blow for Robert, too. In his mother's death he had lost the parent with whom he had felt most at ease. With a little editing of his news at times, he had always been able to share with her his experiences and dreams, knowing he had her full support. She had taken a direct interest in all he did, offering suggestions and gentle advice.

Now, as executor of her Will, combined with his having left Sunderlandia

---

[338] Dancy, *Walter Oakeshott*, p 296.

[339] Dancy, *Walter Oakeshott*, p 319.

[340] Charlotte Oakeshott, personal correspondence, 22 January 2022.

within months of his mother's death, Robert was able to spend time in his father's company in Eynsham, which would have been a great comfort to them both. His relationship with his father had become much closer, since at least his time in Zambia and Botswana, and they found they had much in common, besides a love of Mozart and Handel. They shared a concern for social justice for working men, and they loved the company of family and friends over dinner. Robert moved to London in 1977, where he stayed for a few years in a basement flat in Lloyd Baker Street that belonged to Willie and Anne Charlton, before moving to Finsbury Park in North London. Over the following decade Robert often visited Eynsham for the weekend, or invited his father to join him and a few select friends for dinner at his London flat.[341]

* * *

Robert made full use of his expenses allowance from the Rowntree Trust. Besides a tour of cooperatives in France and Spain, which included another visit to Mondragón, he visited two of the 'Tony Benn cooperatives', Rowen-Onllwyn, a street furniture factory in South Wales for ex-miners laid off through injury, and Kirkby Manufacturing and Engineering near Liverpool, a cooperative attempt to save an ailing factory. These had both been formed at Benn's initiative when he was Secretary of State for Industry in 1975. Although it was not clear in 1976 that both would ultimately fail, Robert was to conclude that successful worker-ownership must be based on profitable or potentially profitable industry. And in December 1976 he found just such a model in Bewley's Café in Dublin.

Publication of his *Financial Times* article on Bewley's was timed to coincide in January 1977 with the publication of the Labour Government's Bullock Report on industrial democracy.[342] Bullock recommended worker

---

[341] Dancy, *Walter Oakeshott*, p 314, quoting a letter by Walter to his elder daughter Helena.

[342] Robert Oakeshott, 'A cooperative café', *Financial Times*, 26 January 1977; and 'Bullock Report': *Report of the committee of inquiry on industrial democracy* (HMSO 1977, Cmnd 6706). Sir Alan Bullock, prominent British historian, best known for his biography *Hitler: A Study in Tyranny* (1952), was founding master of St Catherine's College Oxford (1962–1981), Vice-Chancellor of Oxford University (1969–1973), and was created a life peer in 1976.

representation at company board level, whereas Robert, in citing Bewley's Café, described an alternative approach in which 'ownership is changed rather than the management'. Bewley's was a case of benevolent conversion whereby the Quaker ownership of this profitable old family business, founded in 1840, had been handed over to the workers in 1972, though with the old management remaining in day-to-day charge, at least for the time being. It was a successful business model, and although profits were as yet modest, worker satisfaction was high.

While Bewley's made good press for countering the theme of the Bullock report, Robert was searching for something that was not primarily dependent upon the benevolence of family owners, and he was more than ever convinced that Mondragón was the model to follow. He was aware that conventional wisdom in Britain, based on the socialist writings of Sidney and Beatrice Webb, was that democratically-controlled enterprises either failed commercially or failed to remain democratic. Robert believed the contrary was true: if correctly structured, democratically controlled enterprises could be 'outstandingly successful', as in the Basque country.[343] To counter the negativity, he needed a two-pronged strategy. He would start with a pamphlet to promote the Mondragón economic model and follow it up with a book on the practical experience of industrial democracy in Britain and on the Continent.

Robert persuaded his friends Charles Keen, banker, and Geraldine Norman, journalist at *The Times*, to accompany him on a research trip to Mondragón in early 1977, funded by a grant from the Anglo-German Foundation for the Study of Industrial Society. They were joined by Alastair Campbell, who had former experience of Mondragón. Although it was agreed they would be co-authors of the resultant pamphlet, it was ultimately written by Geraldine, the journalist, with banking advice from her brother Charles. The manuscript was 'corrected' by Robert, who liked to have the last word in matters of language and style.

The aim of the Mondragón pamphlet, due out in October 1977, was to provide the basis for a high-minded debate; to generate pre-publication

---

[343] *JRRT*, Box 125, Oakeshott Report to Trustees, 12 July 1977.

publicity, Robert took a high-profile delegation to Mondragón in late September. This was headed by Jo Grimond, 'ex-leader' as Robert liked to refer to him, who was by then in the House of Lords. The rest of the delegation was made up of Martin Smith, banker with the First National City Bank, and two prominent businessmen, David Guinness of GEC and Ian Backhouse of Shell. Robert had no illusions that GEC or Shell might convert to worker ownership, but he hoped that exposure to the Mondragón experience on the part of representatives from two of the country's largest industrial conglomerates might help to soften hostility from the mainstream capitalist world. And in David Guinness he gained a personal convert. Finally, there was Robert's cousin Richard Gott, journalist at *The Guardian*, who travelled as Jo Grimond's interpreter – he had spent some time in Latin America and was familiar with Mondragón. Richard had been close to Robert when he was running Sunderlandia and he recalls the Mondragón visit as 'very enjoyable', as one would expect of a trip organised by Robert Oakeshott.

The Mondragón pamphlet – *Worker Owners. The Mondragón Experience* – was duly published the following month.[344] It was widely circulated and followed up by two full-page articles from Geraldine Norman in *The Times* on successive days in late December, cleverly timed to fall within that week between Christmas and New Year when people are generally not too busy to think. Her first article was about 'The machines and inventions that have made slaves of us all', with a focus on the intolerable working conditions set in train by the Industrial Revolution. And despite the raft of new technology, capitalist industry had not improved its attitude towards its workers:

> … we have as yet hardly paused to consider the spiritual degradation of living with these technologies.

She argued that the modern worker's inability to control his environment resulted in frustration, nervous pressure and insecurity,[345] a point borne out

---

[344] Alastair Campbell, Charles Keen, Geraldine Norman and Robert Oakeshott, *Worker Owners. The Mondragon Experience* (The Anglo-German Foundation, 1977).

[345] *The Times*, 28 December 1977.

a year later by the 'Winter of Discontent' of 1978/79. The following day, in an article entitled 'How ownership involves the community in the work that keeps it alive', Norman presented the alternative, as argued through the pages of *The Mondragón Experience* pamphlet, of which she herself had been the principal author.[346] Robert's book, *The Case for Workers' Co-ops*, was finally published in the autumn of 1978.[347]

In the meantime, on 11 December 1977, Robert had called a meeting at his South Islington basement flat in Lloyd Baker Street to discuss the 'Next Steps'.[348] Robert's vision was to set up a small, high-powered group consisting of a lawyer, accountant, banker, engineer, and someone experienced in industrial management. The group's aim would be to midwife, guide and protect small- and medium-scale worker-owned enterprises, whether initiated from the bottom up or converted from conventional business.[349] Present at the meeting, besides Robert, were Bob Ayling, Alastair Campbell, Richard Gott, Jo Grimond, David Guinness, Martin Jay, Charles Keen, Geraldine Norman and Martin Smith. They called themselves the Mondragón Job Ownership Group.[350]

Robert recognised there were other players in the field, such as ICOM and the Co-op Union and Bank, and that the Labour Government was pushing ahead with its own Cooperative Development Agency (CDA); ICOM was, however, lukewarm towards individual job ownership by workers which was at the heart of the Mondragón model. And as Robert pointed out to Rowntree's Pratap Chitnis, his 'midwifery' group for worker owners was offering something that was 'small, new, and potentially quick acting', as opposed to something large and bureaucratic like the Co-op Union and Co-op Bank, or the government's proposed CDA.

The group began regular monthly meetings from January 1978, held informally in Robert's basement flat, which was also his office for the time

---

[346] *The Times*, 29 December 1977.

[347] Oakeshott, *The Case for Workers' Co-ops* (Routledge & Kegan Paul, 1978).

[348] The flat belonged to his great friends Willie and Anne Charlton.

[349] *JRRT*, Box 125, RO to Chitnis, 7 October 1977.

[350] RO to Chitnis, 13 December 1977.

being. Their main work in the early months of 1978 was to devise a list of principles and best practice for the successful establishment of a worker-owned enterprise. The name Mondragón was soon dropped from the group's title to indicate that there was no direct connection between the proposed British model and the Basque original. It was agreed that once they had secured funding, they would structure themselves as a limited company, Job Ownership Limited (JOL), with the existing members forming a company board. JOL was deliberately not set up as a charitable organisation, which might have affected its freedom of action, although it did later set up a research branch – Partnership Research Limited – as a charity.

Robert approached the Rowntree Trust to fund two full-time paid executive staff (one of whom would be himself) and a secretary, and their office, travel and other expenses, for a trial period of two years. He hoped by the end of that period they would be at least partially self-funding through feasibility studies and selling packages of integrated legal, accountancy and planning advice.

It was a sign of the depth of Rowntree's trust in Robert that in June 1978 they agreed to a grant of £45,000 spread over two years, paid quarterly from that September.[351] Three new members joined the group to represent the Rowntree trustees: James Cornford, David Shutt and Trevor Smith, the latter two being prominent Liberal Party politicians, and Jo Grimond was elected chairman.

The tasks ahead were threefold: promotion of the Mondragón-type model, combined with public and professional education through media exposure, articles and conferences; provision of feasibility studies and integrated packages of professional advice and back-up services to interested enterprises; and political lobbying for changes in legal and tax arrangements which would benefit this particular type of cooperative enterprise. As part of his effort to fulfil the first of these, public education, Robert wrote in the *Co-operative News*,

> The world of work is of much greater importance in today's Britain
> than the world of shopping, and thus cooperative production, if it can

---

[351] *JRRT*, Box 199, Chitnis to RO, 9 June 1978.

be successfully organised, is of far greater consequence than cooperating among consumers.[352]

During the six-month hiatus between Rowntree's confirmation of their grant and the registration and launch of Job Ownership Limited (JOL) that November, besides proof-reading the manuscript of his book, *The Case for Workers' Co-ops*, and preparing for its launch that autumn, Robert got married.

* * *

The pain of the failure of Robert's engagement to Tessa Head in 1964 had stayed with him throughout his time in Africa, during which he does not appear to have attempted any other romantic liaison, despite the wishes of Caroline Cox-Johnson in that regard.[353] Indeed, when in 1968 his mother sent him news of Maurice Keen's engagement, together with the suggestion that he himself might consider 'settling down', Robert replied that besides the 'after effects of what happened four years ago', he considered he was possibly 'temperamentally unsuited to the kind of "settling down" programme' his mother had in mind.[354]

On his return to England in 1972 he had met with Tessa Head for the first time in eight years, whether by chance or design is not clear; but when she revealed that the announcement of her engagement to a master at Eton was about to be published in *The Times*, Robert wrote to his mother,

> … though the news is painful I am pretty sure that he will be able to give her more nearly the sort of life which would suit her best than I could'.[355]

By the age of 45, Robert was widely perceived to be a confirmed bachelor with a strong social conscience and a romantic heart, who loved to spring surprises on family and friends. And the biggest surprise of all came on

---

[352] *Co-operative News*, 7 June 1978; copy in *Oakeshott Papers*.

[353] Caroline Cox-Johnson, personal communication, 1 October 2022.

[354] *Oakeshott Letters*, RO to his mother, 12 April 1968.

[355] RO to his mother, 1 May 1972.

Robert and Kate's wedding, outside the registry office, 30 June 1978.
(By kind permission of the Oakeshott family)

30 June 1978 when he married Kate Shuckburgh, seventeen years after she had first turned him down. She had two teenage sons from her marriage to John Caute, which had ended in divorce in 1970, and it seemed the boys had a good relationship with Robert.

The marriage was a small registry office affair, with family and friends invited to a reception hosted in Chiswick by Gemma Nesbit, a friend to both Kate and Robert, the latter from his Oxford days. The invitation to the reception was the first that most of the guests had heard about the marriage. As Charlotte Oakeshott recalls, there must have been about fifty people present, mostly friends,

> … I don't recall his father being there; Helena certainly wasn't; the Gaunts were there, and Evelyn and I. Kate wore a simple flowery summer dress. Robert looked tidy![356]

---

[356] Charlotte Oakeshott, in consultation with Rose Gaunt, private communication, 22 January 2022.

Robert was clearly making an effort. They went to Paris for their honeymoon, staying in Éric de Rothschild's flat. Rothschild was in residence and vacated his bedroom for them while he slept on the sofa.[357]

The marriage was, however, destined to last only a few months.[358] The nearest we have to Robert's thoughts on it at the time is in a report to the Rowntree Trust, written two weeks after the wedding:

> On 30 June I married Catherine Caute (born Catherine Shuckburgh). In the very short term, the change in my position could only reduce the time and energy I was able to devote to work. In the longer term I am hopeful that it will have beneficial effects all round.[359]

He appears to have anticipated 'in the longer term' being able to develop a balance between his normal life's pattern of 'working like a maniac' and socialising around alcohol-fuelled lunches and dinners with friends and colleagues, and the responsibilities of marriage, with the added advantage now of sharing his work, dreams and social life with his life's partner, with whom he felt he had so much in common. But it did not work out like that. When the late Charles Keen phoned Kate Shuckburgh on my behalf, she declined to be interviewed for this book, but recalled that Jo Grimond had said to her at the time, 'You know, you are marrying a saint'. Perhaps that was part of the problem.[360] Mary Clemmy recalls visiting them for supper one evening that summer and being 'staggered' to find Robert in an apron and behaving in a 'domesticated' way such as she had never seen before. She felt Robert was 'being groomed by Kate to be someone he wasn't'.[361]

Two months later, Robert revealed in a letter to Pratap Chitnis's secretary that his wife Catherine had applied to Ealing Borough Council for a bursary

---

[357] Éric de Rothschild, interview, 18 January 2021.

[358] An approach was made to Kate Shuckburgh through a third party, but she declined to be interviewed for this book.

[359] *JRRT*, Box 125, Report to Rowntree Trust, 15 July 1978.

[360] Charles Keen, private communication, 21 February 2021.

[361] Mary Clemmy, interview, 26 February 2021.

'in connection with a degree course at the London Poly'.[362] This is the last mention of his wife in any of Robert's surviving correspondence, personal or official, although her name does appear – 'and for Kate' – on the dedication page of his *The Case for Workers' Co-ops*, published that autumn, alongside that of his father and his late mother. Her attendance at the London Polytechnic that autumn was probably the time that, in John Jolliffe's words, she 'walked out on him … It was a frightful blow to him when she left – pushed off, abandoned him'.[363] Robert's niece Helena Gaunt recalls him turning up at their house in Harrow that evening, desperately upset.[364] He had always assumed that one day he would marry, and he was devastated when it failed. He hoped for a long time that their issues could be resolved; but eventually, he had to chalk it up as another painful episode in his life. It was something that he very rarely talked about, consoling himself in later years that his lifestyle did not suit marriage; it was not, for him, a reality.[365]

He did not, however, allow this major disappointment to interfere with the job at hand. He was still dedicated to making the world a better and a happier place; his humour and his *joie de vivre* were soon restored, and he quickly re-established the old familiar pattern of hard work and his customary social life. Nor did it put him off the concept of marriage for other people. He was always extremely compassionate and supportive of his friends in this respect, especially when a relationship was failing or one was in mourning. Geraldine Norman, for instance, recalls that when her husband Frank died just before Christmas in 1980, Robert took her on a two-to-three-week holiday on the Continent the following spring, 'to cheer her up'. It was a generous gesture that Geraldine felt was 'so typical of Robert'.[366]

Accompanied by the former Labour politician Michael Lord, they

---

[362] *JRRT*, Box 125, RO to Lois Jefferson, 25 September 1978.

[363] John Jolliffe, interview, 14 May 2021.

[364] Helena Gaunt, interview, 4 January 2021.

[365] Robert's thoughts revealed in conversation with David Wheatcroft in the early 1990s: David Wheatcroft, interview, 24 November 2022.

[366] Geraldine Norman, interview, 9 December 2020.

travelled by train through France, Italy and Spain, inevitably calling in at cooperatives along the way. They visited Éric de Rothschild at Château Lafite in Bordeaux. And at dinner that evening, one of Éric's guests was the world-famous film star Greta Garbo, renowned for having once said, 'I want to be alone'. Robert, famous for his conversational skills, was placed next to her and Éric recalls there was no lack of conversation; they appeared to get on very well.[367] When asked on return to England what it was like meeting Greta Garbo, Robert replied, 'Not a patch on Aunt Emilie', a reference to his much loved, down-to-earth, diminutive and strong-minded maternal aunt who ran a farm.

---

[367] Éric de Rothschild, interview, 18 January 2021.

CHAPTER 17

The Growth of Employee Ownership

Job Ownership Limited (JOL) was registered and formally launched in mid-November 1978, with Jo Grimond as Chairman and Robert as Company Secretary. They got good publicity from *The Sunday Times*,[368] and Robert's book, *The Case for Workers' Co-ops*, was published the following week.[369] This was followed in early 1979 with a Job Ownership pamphlet, *Owning Your Own Job*, a guide to setting up and operating a business owned by its workers. *The Sunday Times* described JOL as espousing 'socialism without the State', whereby profits are shared between labour and capital, in contrast to conventional capitalism where labour and capital are fundamentally divided, with all the advantages accruing to capital and top management. Robert was quoted as saying,

> It is surely impossible to believe that rational and intelligent people, starting from scratch, would choose such a structure [as conventional capitalism] when organising activities which depend on teamwork for their success.[370]

From Mondragón he had learned three crucial conditions for success: first, the main thrust to get an enterprise going must come from the potential workforce, unlike Sunderlandia, which was founded through 'high-minded paternalism'; second, the workforce commitment must be secured through 'a meaningful capital stake', such as the equivalent

---

[368] Graham Searjeant, 'What is a worker's co-operative?', *Sunday Times*, 19 November 1978.

[369] Published by Routledge & Kegan Paul, London, 1978.

[370] *The Sunday Times*, 19 November 1978.

of several months' wages, paid over a reasonable period; and third, the manager or management team must be at least as good if not better than that of a conventional enterprise.[371] As Robert pointed out, with the full commitment of the workers and management in such enterprises, from shop floor to head office, productivity invariably increased; he offered it as a solution to the so-called 'British disease' of low productivity.

* * *

The 'Winter of Discontent' of 1978/79 set many minds searching for economic alternatives and combined with publicity for JOL and Mondragón, this set Robert's 'doorbell … jingling'. The quality woodworking firm WH Ryder of Reading, a banking client of Charles Keen's, sought assistance on conversion to worker ownership. *The Times* Chapel of the National Union of Journalists requested a feasibility study to look into the possibility of converting Times Newspapers Limited into one or more workers' cooperatives. Other interested parties included a group of helicopter pilots who specialised in flying businessmen to the Continent, a group of tanker drivers from the Shell depot in Hamble, and the Gay Hussar restaurant in Soho.[372]

In the early winter months of 1981 Robert gave up the basement flat in Lloyd Baker Street and bought a lease on a top-floor flat in Queen's Drive near Finsbury Park in North London. And in order to retain office space in Central London, JOL took a lease on a third-floor office in Hanway Street, just north of the eastern end of Oxford Street and a short walk from the Gay Hussar in Soho, which soon became Robert's favourite haunt for elongated business lunches and dinners. Robert's main work at the time was publicity and searching out new projects. Charles Uridge was employed as JOL's General Manager, while Gemma Best was an invaluable full-time Secretary who took on much more than general secretarial work

---

[371] *Case for Workers' Co-ops*, p 243; and *JRRT*, Box 199, Minutes of JOL meeting, 18 December 1978.

[372] *JRRT*, Box 199, Minutes of JOL meetings, 18 December 1978, 29 March and 26 April 1979.

and was in practice Robert's Personal Assistant.

By this time the BBC had taken an interest. With Robert's help their *Horizon* team visited Mondragón, from which they produced a documentary in which Robert featured quite prominently and included reference to his work in Botswana. The BBC aired the documentary twice in the autumn of 1980 and that really set Job Ownership's bells ringing. JOL was requested to organise several trips to Mondragón during 1981, and *The Guardian* reported that Britons interested in co-ops were 'flooding to Spain' to learn from the Basque experience.[373] Indeed, a Basque politician confessed that he had known nothing of the reputation and fame of the Mondragón cooperatives 'until he heard about them from England'.[374]

* * *

Robert spent much of his time during the first five years of Job Ownership Limited publicising the concept of employee ownership through a series of speaking engagements at universities, polytechnics and business schools across the country and this, combined with other publicity, elicited 500 enquiries, although only a minority resulted in a completed employee-owned enterprise. The process of converting a company to employee ownership often took at least two years, with a role for JOL throughout the process. Among those that fell by the wayside were the Shell tanker drivers, who faced trade union opposition, the helicopter pilots, who had to postpone because of the economic downturn, and *The Times* journalists, whose promising efforts were swept away by Rupert Murdoch's takeover in 1981. Indeed, in December 1981 a Rowntree Trust minute noted that while Robert Oakeshott was 'particularly good' as a propagandist, JOL had not yet set up a single cooperative.[375] Nevertheless, they agreed to support him for another three years, saving themselves some expense by offering JOL the free use of their grace and favour offices at 9 Poland Street in Soho for up to ten years.

---

[373] *The Guardian*, 9 January 1981.

[374] *The Guardian*, 1 December 1981.

[375] *JRRT*, Box 199, JRSST Minute, 11 December 1981.

A serious problem for some promising employee ownership projects was trade union opposition. Robert saw the Thatcher Government's drive for privatisation as an excellent opportunity for genuine worker control, something that was missing from the bureaucracy of the nationalised industries. But any form of privatisation was anathema to both the trade unions and the Labour Party at that time, who viewed Robert's form of worker ownership as a weakening of worker solidarity in the face of the capitalist assault on workers' rights that characterised the Thatcher years. The effect of this conflict is illustrated in the case of the Liverpool refuse workers.

When Liverpool City Council decided in 1982 to outsource its refuse collection services the workers, facing redundancy, decided to form a cooperative and tender for the contract. This was just the sort of enterprise that Robert had in mind and JOL conducted a feasibility study for them. It looked a promising enterprise: the initiative had come from the workers, who had each pledged £500 from their anticipated redundancy payments, and the work was guaranteed. The 36 Liberal councillors voted in their favour, but the 42 Labour councillors voted against them, arguing that going down this road would weaken trade unionism. Council officials ruled against them, on the ground that they had used a residential council house address for their 'business' application. And the 21 Conservative councillors cast doubt on the validity of the tender because the paperwork – produced with the aid of JOL – was far too professional to have been written by the workers themselves.[376] With this level of prejudice against them, the Liverpool refuse workers were not even allowed to submit their tender.

Overall, however, from 1982 onwards, the number of JOL clients who successfully completed conversion began to rise. After a shaky start the Gay Hussar restaurant finally completed, as did Manchester Cold Rollers (a small manufacturer of cold rolled steel), but both of these had very small workforces. More significantly, Richard Baxendale & Sons, manufacturer of

---

[376] Polly Toynbee, 'How democracy is trying to put the lid on the dustmen cleaning up the contract', *The Guardian*, 7 March 1983.

domestic heating appliances with 800 employees near Preston, and Cleggs Limited, an industrial laundry service on Merseyside with 80 employees, both successfully completed conversion to employee ownership in this period. Both were secure, profitable companies who were converting from positions of strength,[377] and both were to become important financial and professional supporters of JOL. Indeed, on completion of his firm's conversion to employee ownership the following year, Philip Baxendale, of what was now the Baxi Partnership, was invited onto the board of JOL, and in due course he succeeded Jo Grimond as Chairman.

Another important name in employee ownership at this time was Tullis Russell, manufacturers of high-performance industrial coatings and specialist papers, then based in Scotland. David Erdal had taken over control of the family firm from his uncle and was prompted to consider employee ownership from the example of the John Lewis Partnership. He met Philip Baxendale who introduced him to Robert, whom he found to be 'a highly unusual individual'.[378] David was impressed by Robert's depth of knowledge and understanding of employee ownership, and he commissioned him to come to Glenrothes to address the Tullis Russell board. As David was later to recall,

> ... Naively, I thought that Robert would dress formally to meet a group of directors of a moderately sizeable company. However, Robert arrived in Scotland wearing an old jacket, which he took off for the meeting, and a pink pullover which he had reversed, exposing the holes in the elbows, now at the front. And the zip closing his flies was open: it had broken that morning, he explained. In those days of nappies made from terry toweling you could buy very large safety pins, with heads that slid back and forth to fix them closed. Robert had bought one of these to close his zip, but it was far too big. Moreover, it was a pin designed for a girl baby, and the sliding head was bright pink. The main effect was to draw attention to the still open flies. You can imagine the impression made on the directors by Robert's appearance. It was worse when he started speaking, since his voice

---

[377] *Financial Times*, 31 March 1983.
[378] David Erdal, interview, 2 December 2020.

retained what seemed to these Scotsmen, several of whom had worked their way up from the shop floor, to be pure affectation. But by the end of the allotted hour Robert had their respectful attention, and the meeting proved an important step on the way to employee ownership for Tullis Russell.[379]

With Robert acting as David Erdal's mentor, the firm was able to distribute some shares free to all employees in 1985. The sceptical board had to be convinced that it would work, however, and the move to 100 per cent employee ownership was not completed until 1994. David Erdal joined the board of JOL and became an important promoter of employee ownership.

Numerous other smaller companies followed the trend through the 1980s, most with some form of input from JOL. An interesting case, and one in which Robert played a key role, was that of the Provincial Bus Company of Fareham and Gosport, a subsidiary of the state-owned National Bus Company (NBC). What is remarkable about this conversion is that, under pressure from a rival bid, it took just three months from conception to delivery.

When James Freeman, the young managing director of Provincial, heard in February 1987 that Harry Blundred of the predatory bus company Devon Central had put in a bid for Provincial, and that his bid was expected to be accepted within the next ten days, he contacted Robert Oakeshott. He had heard 'this very extraordinary chap' speak to a meeting of senior managers of NBC the previous year and had warmed to both the man and his message.

Although when he had joined Provincial in November 1986, Freeman had found the workforce unionised, militant and threatening strike action; by working on the ground alongside the men through some severe winter weather he had built up a good working relationship with union convenors John Speed and John Early by February 1987. They were happy to hear there might be a way to upstage Blundred's hostile bid, and that there was

---

[379] *Oakeshott Papers*, David Erdal, 'Robert Oakeshott: Renewing the Memory, hero and friend' (unpublished typescript for a lecture, 2019).

this chap in London who would be willing to help them. And sure enough, when Robert heard from Freeman about Blundred's bid, he dropped everything and invited him and his trade union convenors up to London to meet specialist lawyers at the New Bridge Consultants of Clifford Barnes. There, besides Robert, they met lawyer Laurie Brennan, and Ann Tyler who was to guide them through the process of securing the bid.

The next evening Robert came down to Gosport to help convince the workforce. It is a credit to the level of trust which Freeman had built up within the company that almost the entire workforce of 212 turned up on that freezing February night, after the last bus was in, to hear what this man from London had to say.

In what Robert was later to describe as 'well after his normal bedtime', he stood on the back of a pick-up truck in a bitterly cold bus depot that had seen better days and spoke in his usual cut-glass accent, which may have been somewhat tempered in the eyes of the men by his dishevelled appearance. He explained in very plain terms what the project would involve and explained the benefits of owning one's own job. They could see he was not metaphorically talking down to them, and his heartfelt passion both inspired and reassured his sceptical working-class audience. By the end of the evening, he had the support of at least 80 per cent, and by a show of hands, an overwhelming majority of those present accepted 'that it would be reasonable for everyone who took part to subscribe a sum of £750',[380] a little over a month's wages. This brought in £150,000 towards the Government's valuation of £750,000. The rest would have to come from loans.

The Unity Trust offered to lend them £40,000, but by the final day, Friday of the following week, they were still short by nearly £600,000. The primary aim at this stage was to halt the acceptance of Blundred's bid, and they arrived at NBC's headquarters in London that Friday afternoon, shortly before the Department of Transport officials packed up for the weekend. Ann Tyler put an envelope on the table and announced they had

---

[380] Robert Oakeshott, *Jobs and Fairness. The logic and experience of employee ownership* (Michael Russell, Norwich, 2000), pp 275–276.

come to buy the Provincial Bus Company. In fact, the envelope contained nothing more than a blank sheet of paper.[381] The officials, caught unawares, said they would have to discuss it with the other bidder and asked them to return a week later. Before leaving, Ann retrieved the envelope. They had a week's breathing space, but even then, the money was not raised, and Robert said, 'We've got a firm proposal – simply structure a letter as though we've got the money'. This time the officials did open the envelope, but they did not fully understand the letter and asked them to come back the following week.

That left a weekend of incredible string-pulling with a range of influential colleagues. Somebody, possibly Robert, leaked the story to BBC News who did a vox pop around Gosport and Fareham and found a very favourable response to the idea of the drivers owning their own bus company. It was broadcast on 'South Today' that Monday night; the next day, Freeman got a telex and promises of funding began to come through. By the end of the week Blundred had withdrawn from the competition, and the Department of Transport accepted Provincial's bid.

A long weekend with Robert, Ann Tyler, Laurie Brennan, Freeman, Speed, Early and a few others sorted out the structure of the enterprise, with an ESOP trust[382] holding the majority of shares on behalf of the employee owners. A key feature of the structure, for which Robert pushed hard, was that ownership of shares must be egalitarian, unlike many of the NBC's buyouts, which were management-led and from which management benefited disproportionately.

On 8 May 1987 the new owners of the renamed People's Provincial Bus Company drove up to London in one of their buses to the Department of Transport, handed over their cheque and formally took control of the company. Then, with Robert and Ann Tyler on board, they drove around London drinking champagne to celebrate.

---

[381] Ann Tyler, interview, 2 December 2020; James Freeman, interview, 11 December 2020.

[382] Employee Stock Ownership Plan: the ESOP concept was invented by US economist and banker Louis Kelso in the 1950s to enable the employees of a newspaper chain to buy the company from its retiring owners.

The new ownership proved very successful, popular among both drivers and customers. From being a company in which James Freeman had found the workforce to be militant and uncooperative, they became a team of people who could look management in the eyes and smile, and they never had another strike in the time of employee ownership.[383]

Freeman considers that Robert Oakeshott was 'absolutely instrumental' in bringing about this transformation, which began with the mass meeting that cold February night at the bus depot. Relating the story in his book *Jobs and Fairness*, Robert is typically modest about his own role, but he does acknowledge being immensely proud to have been 'present at the creation' of this most promising of enterprises.[384]

Similarly, in the case of the local authority-owned buses of Chesterfield in Derbyshire, although the original initiative for an employee buyout was management-led, it did not become management-dominated; indeed, quite the opposite. In 1986, as part of the restructuring that followed the legal requirement that bus companies held by local authorities become 100 per cent share ownership, William Coupar and James Miller were appointed managing director and finance director of Chesterfield Buses respectively. In 1988 they formed a joint working party consisting of two from management (Coupar and Miller) and four representing the three trade unions involved. They became known as 'the buyout team', and in 1989 they formed a new company, Chesterfield Transport. It was this company that made the offer to the local authorities to buy Chesterfield Buses, and because of their strong trade union representation, Labour-controlled Chesterfield Borough Council and Derbyshire County Council viewed their bid favourably. The company was valued at £300,000, the bulk of which was raised by contributions from the 350 employees, the balance coming from an Employee Benefit Trust.

What particularly impressed Robert about this management/trade union-led buyout was their decision to hold 51 per cent of the equity in an ESOP Trust on behalf of the community of workers. As elsewhere, this

---

[383] James Freeman, interview, 11 December 2020.

[384] Oakeshott, *Jobs and Fairness*, p 276.

added long-term stability to the company and enabled it, to some extent, to weather the storm of the economic decline that accompanied the pit closures in the Derbyshire coalfields.[385]

Although Robert had no direct role in Chesterfield's conversion to employee ownership, it is worth mentioning here because when it came to the rush for privatisation that accompanied the fall of communism in Central and Eastern Europe, Robert came to believe they could not do better than to follow the model of Chesterfield Transport, which became employee-owned in the spring of 1990. And it was through the Chesterfield case that Robert found a valuable friend and colleague in the trade unionist bus driver David Wheatcroft, who joined the board of JOL and assisted him when it came to promoting employee ownership in Eastern Europe, as well as in America.[386]

---

[385] Oakeshott, *Jobs and Fairness*, pp 287–293.

[386] David Wheatcroft, interview, 24 November 2020.

CHAPTER 18

Spreading the Word

Robert was a brilliant networker, and he applied this assiduously to his political lobbying. He had an advantage through the contacts and influence of Jo Grimond, initially in the House of Commons and then in the House of Lords. Robert's political aim was twofold. First, he needed recognition in legislation of employee-ownership as a distinct class of business, separate from the normal class of cooperative that did not allow individual share purchase or ownership; and second, he sought business and individual tax relief for employee owners and their businesses. He believed that money spent on owning one's own job should be just as eligible for tax relief as home ownership, which earned mortgage tax relief in those years.

By the early 1980s Robert was moving with ease among cross-party backbenchers and junior ministers. In 1982 he introduced Philip Baxendale to Nicholas Ridley, then Financial Secretary at the Treasury, and the latter was able to point to a loophole in tax law that eased Baxi's transition to Partnership status the following year. On occasion he invited junior ministers to lunch at the Gay Hussar, among them future Chancellor of the Exchequer Norman Lamont. Indeed, on several occasions Robert's name was mentioned in debates in both Houses of Parliament.

The focus of the Thatcher Government, especially after the 1983 landslide, however, was fighting the trade unions and mass privatisation. Nuances concerning the exact shape of privatisation were not something that most Conservatives considered worthy of attention. Indeed, *The Daily Telegraph*, with reference to the employee-owned Manchester Cold Rollers, commented:

Mrs Thatcher, if she went there, would be almost bound to detect a genuine flowering of her much-loved Victorian self-help values. ... What she seems so far to have largely missed is that those values make real economic sense when workers become worker-owners.[387]

Thus, despite his efforts and the support of sympathetic Conservative backbenchers such as Nigel Forman MP and Ian Taylor MP, the most Robert got at this stage was a promise each year that JOL's proposals would be considered in the following year's Budget.[388]

Robert was not one to give up, however, and thanks to his persistent lobbying, employee share ownership trusts (ESOTs) were finally granted statutory recognition in the Finance Act of 1989 as a new type of corporate entity. Companies were slow to respond to the new opportunities, however, and Robert, in conjunction with Ian Taylor MP and Graeme Nuttall, a partner in the specialist law firm Fieldfisher, pushed for further changes that would provide equal representation by employees and management on boards of trustees. Robert called it 'paritarian composition of trustees'. Thus, 'paritarian', a word Robert had invented to suit his case, made its way into primary legislation and into specialist articles and textbooks.[389] It became a recognised word, despite its absence from any dictionary, although Wikipedia offers a definition of 'paritarian institution', giving its etymology as from the French '*paritaire*', to be managed on an equal (parity) basis, but with no mention of the man who invented the word.[390]

Furthermore, correspondence between Robert and Tessa Keswick, Political Adviser to Chancellor of the Exchequer Kenneth Clarke, helped lead to a relaxation of the rules in the Finance Act of 1994, which for the

---

[387] *The Daily Telegraph*, 14 May 1984.

[388] *JRRT*, Box 199, RO Annual Reports to JRSST trustees for the years 1980–1989.

[389] Graeme Nuttall, 'How Robert Oakeshott made paritarian governance good practice for employee ownership trusts', *Ownership of Work*, June 2021, pp 1–3 [https://www.lawgazette.co.uk/news/fair-shares-the-measures-taken-in-1994-to-make-employee-share-schemes-more-attractive-to-companies-/19885.article] – accessed 10 February 2022, with thanks to Graeme Nuttall for this reference.

[390] https://en.wikipedia.org/wiki/Paritarian_institution [accessed 2 March 2022].

first time made the distribution of shares through employee trusts tax-deductible.[391]

* * *

Robert thrived on holding and attending conferences and seminars. He believed these, combined with visits to successful employee-owned businesses, were the best way to spread the word about the benefits of employee ownership and how to achieve it.

In 1982 Job Ownership Limited was invited by Plater College, a Catholic adult education establishment in Oxford, to co-host a seminar to discuss the history and level of Christian involvement in cooperatives as a way of solving the social and economic problems of industrial society. Robert saw this as a great opportunity to get his message of job ownership to a wider audience and he willingly became involved. The seminar was held at Plater College that July and JOL was represented by Robert, Geraldine Norman, Jo Grimond and Gemma Best. Philip Baxendale attended, as did Margaret Elliott of Little Women Home Care.[392] While Robert headlined the proposals and invitations, and his name drew many people in, he was a great delegator and it was Gemma who worked with the college on most of the practical organisation.

Robert was very aware of the prejudices and scepticism attached to the cooperative concept and thus the importance of being able to headline examples of success. And to be sure of future successes, he always stressed the potential pitfalls in the way of setting up an employee enterprise. His paper for the Plater College seminar, for instance, was entitled 'Obstacles and overcoming them'.[393] The seminar opened new avenues in the field of job ownership and Robert decided that 'the Christian response to industrial capitalism' was a subject worthy of a book. His Roman Catholic

---

[391] Anonymous, 'Fair shares – the measures taken in 1994 to make employee share schemes more attractive to companies', *The Law Society Gazette*, 8 March 1995 [https://www.lawgazette.co.uk/news/fair-shares-the-measures-taken-in-1994-to-make-employee-share-schemes-more-attractive-to-companies-/19885.article] – accessed 10 February 2022.

[392] *JRRT*, Box 199, July 1982, papers concerning the Plater College seminar.

[393] *JRRT*, Box 199, RO to JRSST, 15 July 1982.

friend Willie Charlton, who had a particular interest in theological history, agreed with him and they approached Tatiana Mallinson to see if she would take it on.

As Tatiana has recalled, Robert and Willie came to see her and suggested the need for a book on Christianity and industrial capitalism. Robert said to her: 'You're not doing anything – why don't you do it? It would be a good thing to occupy your time.'

Her husband said, 'She's got a job already.' And Tatiana said, 'I haven't time. I've too much to do. Why don't you do it?'

Robert gave his characteristic cackle with head thrown back. He then turned to Willie and said, 'Why don't you do it?' So, it was decided, they would all three do it, and in the manner of joint authorships, especially with Robert, a stickler for detail, it became a three-year project.[394]

In January 1986 Robert, through JOL, began what was to become a series of international conferences at Oxford, with financial support from the John Lewis Partnership, the National Freight Consortium (employee-owned since 1972), the Baxi Partnership and the Industrial Participation Association (IPA). The first conference was held at Balliol College, where accommodation was available during the winter vacation. Robert's contacts were such that delegates came from America, as well as the Continent, and a wide range of interested parties in the United Kingdom, including senior politicians from each of the three main parties, who voiced their active support.[395] The conference was judged a great success and was repeated at Balliol in January 1988. Again it was attended by representatives from a wide range of high-quality enterprises, that year including the Weirton Steel Corporation, Avis and White Pine Copper Mine from the United States, John Lewis Partnership, National Freight Consortium, Baxi, Tullis Russell and People's Provincial Buses from the United Kingdom, Mondragón from Spain and Zeiss from West Germany. Sandy Anson,

---

[394] William Charlton, Tatiana Mallinson and Robert Oakeshott, *The Christian Response to Industrial Capitalism* (Sheed & Ward, London, 1986); with thanks to Tatiana Mallinson (interview, 2 October 2020) for her recollections and a copy of the book.

[395] *JRRT*, Box 199, RO to JRSST, July 1986.

senior staffer of the Institute of Directors reported that the 1988 Balliol conference was decisive in securing his support for the concept and he subsequently wrote a paper arguing for the removal of legal obstacles to the spread of employee ownership.

In January 1989 the conference shifted to Merton College and thereafter Robert's JOL Merton College conferences, held at first every two or three years, and later annually, became a notable feature of international employee-ownership calendars, gaining favourable write-ups in the *Financial Times*, *The Economist*, *The Guardian* and *The Observer*. The conferences would run from Friday to Sunday lunchtime. David Erdal, a regular attendee, recalls they were free, with college accommodation cheap, though very cold. But Robert was a terrible organiser and it was all a bit chaotic. He would invite huge numbers, eighty or more, some of them very distinguished, including a couple of Nobel laureates, and very often there were so many speakers scheduled during the day that there was little time for discussion. It was only with the ruthless chairmanship of James Cornford, whom Robert knew from his directorship of the Rowntree Trust's Outer Circle policy unit, that they managed to get through the daily schedule. But this was more than made up for by the socialising and discussions over alcohol-fuelled lunches and dinners.

On one occasion, recalls David Erdal, a ditch for pipework had been dug across the Merton College courtyard and as Robert returned from late night drinking with participants, he fell into the ditch and spectacularly bruised his face. But he did not let that hold him up for a moment. Next morning, with not a care for himself or his bruised appearance, and with a safety pin holding his glasses together, he got on with the work of the conference.[396]

* * *

By the time of the January 1989 Merton conference, there were clear signs of imminent major changes on the Continent. And while none foresaw at that stage that the Soviet Union was less than three years off total collapse,

---

[396] David Erdal, interview, 2 December 2020.

it was clear that the Gorbachev reforms opened opportunities for an end to centralised control in the Soviet satellites of Eastern Europe. The doors of privatisation were about to be opened and Robert saw this as virgin territory for employee ownership.

Among those at that year's Merton conference was David Ellerman, American economist and philosopher, who presented a paper on the legal and other preconditions for the successful development of an employee-owned sector. Over the previous twenty years Ellerman had, in Robert's words, emerged as 'the most forthright and unequivocal advocate of a labour theory of property'. Ellerman argued that people had 'an inalienable right to enjoy the fruits of their labour' and that right could only be satisfied if labour (management and non-management) were the legal owners of businesses, the governance of which must be democratic.[397] Ellerman's 'elegant and convincing analysis' was published the following year as *The Democratic Worker-Owned Firm. A New Model for East and West.*[398]

After the 1989 conference, Robert accompanied Ellerman and others to Eastern Europe to test the waters. They visited Prague, Budapest and Poland, then on to Russia, where they met with some of the young economists that Gorbachev had brought in. The situation looked promising, although in the case of Russia, the rushed and chaotic manner of Gorbachev's resignation and the dissolution of the Soviet Union allowed the oligarchs to pre-empt any chance of establishing even a semblance of an employee-owned sector.

On his return to England, while others watched with fascination the unfolding of events that led to the fall of the Berlin Wall that November, Robert was lobbying for some level of government assistance for JOL to expand its professional and advisory services into Eastern Europe. The Thatcher Government was already thinking along similar lines, with a focus on Poland, which Margaret Thatcher had visited in 1988 and which seemed to be leading the breakaway from the communist grip. By mid-1989 the Thatcher Government was promising to set up a fund of £50 million,

---

[397] *Jobs and Fairness*, pp 25–26.

[398] Published by Unwin Hyman Ltd (Winchester Mass. and London, 1990).

to be known as the 'Know How Fund', to finance British administrative, business, educational, legal, media and political consultants in Poland.

In the autumn of that year, it was agreed that a further £25 million would be allocated for Hungary, a country that had already begun moves to liberalise its economy. The fund for Hungary, like that for Poland, would be spread over five years and become operable from April 1990.[399] Lobbying by Robert Oakeshott almost certainly played a significant role in getting the Know How Fund extended to Hungary, for the announcement came shortly after he returned from a visit to Hungary in September 1989.

Robert had been invited to a trade union conference in Budapest that had been called to discuss privatisation. It was a particularly exciting time for Robert, bearing in mind his previous visit to Hungary, for this was the month the Hungarian Government removed the electric fence along its border with Austria and allowed East Germans to move freely through Hungary, into Austria and on to West Germany – the first step in the events that were to lead to the fall of the Berlin Wall two months later.

It was at the Budapest conference in September that Robert met two representatives of the free-standing trade union of the Herend Porcelain Manufactory and learned about that unique company.

* * *

The Porcelain Manufactory had been founded in 1826 in the village of Herend in the hills to the north of Lake Balaton, and from the 1840s it was manufacturing highly-decorated, fine-quality porcelain aimed at the top end of the market. Its reputation was established when it sold a dinner service to Queen Victoria at the Great Exhibition of 1851. That reputation survived the state-owned communist era, despite briefly aiming at a middle-range market in the 1940s and 1950s, when it made busts of Stalin.

Robert visited the Herend Porcelain Manufactory soon after the Budapest conference. He could see Herend would be 'a good fit' for an

---

[399] Keith Hamilton, *The Know How Fund. The early years* (Foreign & Commonwealth Office, 1997), p 7.

employee buyout. It was a high value-added business, dependent upon its skilled workforce of about 1,500, almost two-thirds of whom were women. It was not dominated by capital but by its labour force, who were not just craftswomen and craftsmen but were exceptionally skilled artists – painters, potters and mould makers. It was this that particularly attracted Robert.[400] And the fact that the employees formed a major part of the Herend village community would have put Robert in mind of Mondragón.

Shortly after the Budapest conference, Robert was invited to visit the Herend Porcelain Manufactory, where he met Laszlo Szesztay who had been with the company since 1985. Szesztay had spent his teenage years in America, where his father had worked in engineering, and he had some background in cooperatives. He was to become a senior executive on a new management team that was in the process of being installed. Robert was extremely impressed by what he saw in Herend, especially the high level of skill of the vast majority of the workforce, and the fact that all the creative work was done by hand, a point emphasised by the use of the word 'manufactory'.

After a tour of the manufactory, Robert was invited to address the directors, management and workers, with Laszlo Szesztay acting as his interpreter. At first there was some suspicion that Robert might be promoting something akin to Tito's Yugoslav model of limited worker participation, which they rejected as another form of state socialism. Robert thus had a delicate path to tread, but with consummate skill he empathised with their perceptions and while asserting the dangers of corporate capitalism, he explained that through employee ownership the workers themselves would be the capitalist owners, with democratic control over their own business.[401]

Fortunately in Budapest there was Dr Janos Lukacs, a sociologist who had studied employee ownership in the United States for several months in 1988. Thus, while Lukacs approached influential contacts in Budapest with a view to getting Employee Stock Ownership Plan (ESOP) legislation

---

[400] *Jobs and Fairness*, pp 332–33, 342.

[401] Laszlo Szesztay, interview, 11 March 2021.

*The Hungarian study tour to England, spring 1991, with Robert (second from right),
Laszlo Szesztay (far right of picture) and two members of the Hungarian Parliament,
Dr Gyula Teller (second from left) and (fifth from left) Dr Pal Becker.
(By kind permission of Laszlo Szesztay)*

through the Hungarian Parliament, Robert arranged for a number of
Hungarians to visit Britain and see for themselves examples of successful
employee-owned businesses.

Laszlo Szesztay and a couple of his Herend colleagues attended the
Merton College conference in January 1991; and a week's study in England
for selected Hungarian government officials and politicians, put forward
by Dr Lukacs that April, helped consolidate support for an employee
buyout at Herend.[402] It also consolidated the personal friendship between
Robert and Laszlo Szesztay.

---

[402] *Jobs and Fairness*, p 344.

The Hungarian Parliament passed ESOP legislation in June 1992, enabling the company to set up an ESOP Trust which negotiated a very favourable deal with the State Property Agency. The employees got 75 per cent of the shares (25 per cent in the ESOP Trust and 50 per cent for the individual employees), with the state holding the remaining 25 per cent. Payment to the State Property Agency was completed two years later.[403]

Robert believed Herend's very fair distribution of shares and democratic decision-making reflected the strength, in an economic sense, of the highly skilled workforce. He regarded the Herend Porcelain Manufactory as one of the great examples of a successful employee buyout, for it established long-term stability and profitability, and through the 1990s he invited Laszlo Szesztay to speak in international fora about the Herend story.

In recognition of Robert's contribution to Herend's success and the close relationship between JOL and the Porcelain Manufactory, the VIth International Employee Ownership Conference was held at a hotel on the shores of Lake Balaton in January 1997. Thecla Mallinson, Tatiana's daughter, was Robert's PA at the time and did the organising from the London end.[404] There was a good international turnout for the conference, particularly memorable for the very cold weather and a day's visit to Herend. This was followed in May by a display of Herend porcelain at the Peter Jones department store in London SW1, the original store of the John Lewis Partnership. There was a special invitation to a demonstration of porcelain painting on 27 May, with drinks and light refreshments, during which Laszlo Szesztay presented Robert with a finely worked Herend porcelain plate, on the back of which was written,

Presented to Job Ownership Limited
with special thanks to Mr Robert Oakeshott,
to commemorate our 7 years of friendship and to express
our gratitude for all your help

---

[403] *Jobs and Fairness*, pp 345–351.
[404] Thecla Mallinson, interview, 7 July 2021.

The porcelain plate presented to Robert and JOL by
the Herend Porcelain Manufactory, 27 May 1997.
(By kind permission of Veronica Oakeshott)

* * *

Robert had been thrilled by David Ellerman's concept that employee ownership and industrial democracy were virtually an 'inalienable right'; through that critical post-communist period from 1989 onwards, he travelled widely through Central and Eastern Europe, including Slovenia, Hungary, Romania and Bulgaria. He visited businesses large and small and spoke with officials, academics and business personnel as he promoted the practical benefits of employee ownership, while always being careful to warn of the potential pitfalls and explain that a management buyout was not genuine employee ownership. Among those whom he met on numerous occasions in these years was Aleksandra Mrčela, a young academic in Ljubljana and a key figure in the spread of employee ownership in Slovenia. She acknowledged Robert's contribution to her own understanding of the issues, through his theoretical knowledge and empirical evidence, and a deep understanding of the Mondragón model.

All eyes on Robert, at a conference in Skopje, Macedonia, 1992.
(By kind permission of David Wheatcroft)

He spent time understanding the specifics of the Slovenian economy and shaped his advice accordingly.[405] David Erdal recalls working with Robert in Slovenia 'helping a dozen companies privatised initially into majority employee ownership, and saw him work that magic again and again, as often as possible over red wine'.[406]

Robert invited individuals and delegations to his Merton College conferences to discuss employee ownership with a wide international audience and to view examples of successful employee-owned businesses in Britain. He also organised further visits to Mondragón. In return he was invited to numerous meetings and conferences in Central and Eastern Europe, where his contributions were always appreciated. At these times he enjoyed the pace and companionship of travelling by train, so much more personal and civilised than flying, and if colleagues were not already close friends, with Robert's warm, humorous and gregarious personality they soon became so.

---

[405] Aleksandra Mrčela, interview, 18 January 2021.

[406] David Erdal, 'Robert Oakeshott: Renewing the Memory, hero and friend' (unpublished typescript for Employee Ownership Association lecture 2019).

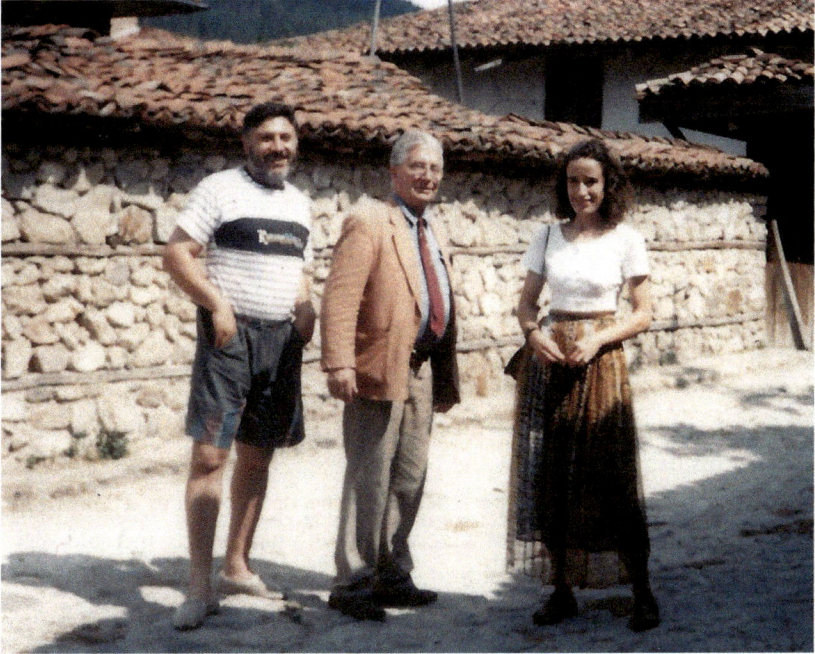

Robert with Eugenie and Fanny Kostourkov, Bulgaria, 1991.
(From Robert Oakeshott's papers, by kind permission of the Oakeshott family)

Fanny and Eugenie Kostourkov of Bulgaria, for instance, were among those who attended the 1991 Merton conference, and they invited Robert to Bulgaria to advise on which businesses might be suitable for conversion to employee ownership. It was the beginning of an enduring friendship between Robert and the Kostourkovs, for whom Robert organised two or three study visits to the UK and one to the United States.

In 1991, on the first of Robert's many visits to Bulgaria, courtesy of the Know-How Fund, he took David Wheatcroft with him for a trade union perspective, although as David recalls, Robert did all the talking.[407] As a result of Robert's advice and professional support, one of the numerous

---

[407] David Wheatcroft, interview, 24 November 2020.

businesses to go private under Bulgaria's new ESOP legislation was a winery, a maker of good-quality Bulgarian red wine. It was a project close to Robert's heart and he invested a sizeable sum of his own money in it, accepting as surety a cellar of its finest red wine. His friend, the banker Jesse Norman, son-in-law of Tom Bingham and future MP and Financial Secretary to the Treasury, advised Robert against investing too heavily in the vineyard,

> … advice he typically and wisely ignored. Robert knew what the right thing to do was.[408]

Eugenie Kostourkov became chairman of the board of the newly-converted, employee-owned winery and Robert worked closely with him for the four or five years that the project lasted, offering advice from his considerable international experience and expertise, as well as establishing a good export market. The red wine was aged in oak barrels and sold very well in Sainsbury's supermarket under the label 'Noble Oak'. It was known jokingly in Bulgaria as 'Noble Oakeshott',[409] and Robert returned the compliment by purchasing large quantities of the wine. It was the wine of choice served at dinners on his *Financial Times* tablecloths.

As often happens with supermarkets and specialist providers, however, the winery grew dependent on the Sainsbury contract. They struggled to meet the quantity that a mass-market outlet like Sainsbury's required and the supermarket withdrew its order. At the same time, Eugenie discovered that his most senior manager had been stealing from the firm. Feeling dispirited and let down, for the whole point of employee ownership was a change of mentality away from greed and the individual, Eugenie left the company and it failed to survive.[410]

The ultimate failure of the wine cooperative did not in any way diminish Robert's love of Bulgaria, with its rich archaeological history, its museum in Sophia and its fishing villages on the Black Sea coast. He revisited the

---

[408] Jesse Norman, interview, 19 February 2021.

[409] Eugenie Kostourkov, interview, 15 February 2021.

[410] Eugenie Kostourkov, interview, 15 February 2021.

country many times, and on one occasion took his nephew Jasper Gaunt, his wife and a friend, a gesture so typical of Robert's generosity.[411]

Despite leading the world in conventional and corporate capitalism, America had a strong tradition of cooperative working. It was healthy ground for employee ownership, and Robert visited the United States on numerous occasions on various consultancies regarding employee or trade union buyouts. Mike Tiller, his friend and colleague from Botswana, was then working with the World Bank in Washington DC. He recalled their paths crossing quite regularly. Suddenly, in 1990, all these new countries – the Czech Republic, Poland, Russia – were joining the World Bank and wanting help in transferring state enterprises into the private sector. Mike remembers meeting Robert and exchanging notes:

> Someone in Prague said we were on opposite sides of the fence, I sustaining the private sector, Robert with employee ownership, but we considered ourselves partners.[412]

---

[411] Jasper Gaunt, interview, 17 December 2020.
[412] Mike Tiller, interview, 12 November 2020.

CHAPTER 19

New Pathways

The deaths in 1987 of two of the most important and influential men in Robert Oakeshott's life opened new avenues of intellectual thought and opportunities for action that he pursued in parallel with employee ownership. His favourite uncle, Sir Penderel Moon, died on 2 June, and his father, Sir Walter Oakeshott, on 13 October.

Penderel Moon had always been close to his elder sister Noel and had paid particular attention to the younger of her twin sons. Aside from sending Robert money 'for travel' in his youth, he had paid for Robert's membership of The Skinners' Company, one of the Livery Companies of the City of London, when he learned that Sir Walter, who had been Master of The Skinners' Company, had paid Evelyn's membership but could not at the time afford to pay for both sons. Skinners' was a convivial and influential fraternity, useful for some of Robert's networking, and he enjoyed treating friends and colleagues to dinner there.

Robert was a huge admirer of his uncle's work and publications concerning India, his critiques of the colonial system and his development work in the Third World, in Zambia and elsewhere. Indeed, his uncle had been a considerable influence in the evolution of Robert's liberal ideals. In 'retirement' Penderel Moon had continued his research and publications relating to India, which he considered should have been allowed its independence long before 1947. Shortly before his death he had completed his manuscript for *The British Conquest and Dominion of India*, which encapsulated much of his previous publications. His nephews, especially Robert and Aunt Emilie's son, William Clarke, ensured that it was published posthumously, to critical acclaim.[413]

---

[413] Sir Penderel Moon, *The British Conquest and Dominion of India* (India Research Press, New Delhi; and Duckworth, London, 1989).

After various specific bequests to those who had worked for him, Penderel's Will left the residue of his considerable estate to his nephews, a quarter each to Robert and Evelyn and an eighth each to his four other nephews, the sons of his younger sisters. As his niece Rose Gaunt has pointed out, Penderel Moon was 'old-fashioned' and considered that his nieces did not need financial support, for that was the responsibility of their husbands.[414]

Robert and William Clarke agreed that their Uncle Pendy should be memorialised with a new edition of his best-known, and perhaps his most important work, *Divide and Quit*, his own eye-witness account from the Punjab of the communal slaughter that accompanied the Partition of India, and his attempts to prevent it and restore order.[415] The book had been published in 1961 and was long out of print.[416] The one controversial part of Moon's account was his estimation of the total number of casualties, which he put at somewhat less than 200,000, a figure that some writers, politicians and popular media claimed was a gross underestimate.

Robert, in defence of his uncle, felt that a new edition should include a new, considered estimate of the numbers involved, and by way of pre-university summer employment, he set one of his nieces the task of conducting some preliminary research in the British Library's Oriental and India Office Collections. It was useful cash and an exciting project for her – Robert was always keen to expose his nephews and nieces, and the children of his friends, to new (adult) experiences – but the research was too cursory to come up with anything conclusive. Robert liked to dig his heels in, but finally he was overruled. It was pointed out that *Divide and Quit* was a contemporary eye-witness account, not a book of academic research, and should be allowed to stand on its own. Instead, they got the BBC's legendary India Correspondent Mark Tully to write an introduction, putting Moon and the book in historical perspective, and the renowned Indian historian Tapan Raychaudhuri wrote an Afterword, 'Re-reading

---

[414] Rose Gaunt, interview, 7 October 2020.

[415] William Clarke, interview, 11 January 2021.

[416] Penderel Moon, *Divide and Quit* (Chatto & Windus, London, 1961).

Divide and Quit. William Clarke took on much of the organising and obtaining permissions for the photographs, which had not featured in the original. Mary Clemmy was also involved. William's work included a trip to Delhi;[417] and the book was published in India in 1997, in time for the 50th anniversary of Partition.[418]

Despite the success of the re-publication of the book, however, Robert would not leave the casualties issue alone and was prepared to use some of his Uncle Pendy inheritance to fund a research project involving several scholars. In 1998 he and William Clarke put the idea to Professor Francis Robinson of Royal Holloway, University of London, a specialist in South Asian history, and he put them in touch with Ian Talbot at Coventry University.[419] After much discussion it was decided the best way forward would be to fund a scholarship for an MA in Third World Studies at Coventry University. Robert advertised it in the press and after an informal interview Pippa Virdee, with an undergraduate dissertation on India and Pakistan, was selected from several applicants. Her proposal was for an oral history of Partition, viewed from both sides, and she pointed out her fluency in spoken and written Punjabi, as well as Hindi and Urdu.

Pippa Virdee has remained forever grateful to Robert, who gave her an opportunity that changed her life, leading as it did to a fellowship, a PhD, and a life in academe. She found him 'incredibly eccentric', but very supportive: his interests resonated with hers, and Robert and William wanted a view from the grassroots.[420]

* * *

Despite his declining health, Sir Walter Oakeshott had remained active in his final years and made a point of visiting his wide range of friends

---

[417] William Clarke, interview, 11 January 2021.

[418] Penderel Moon, *Divide and Quit: An Eyewitness Account of the Partition of India* (Oxford India Paperbacks, New Delhi, 1997). A British edition was later published as part of a four-book compilation, *The Partition Omnibus* (Oxford India Paperbacks, Oxford, 2002).

[419] Ian Talbot, interview, 23 March 2021.

[420] Pippa Virdee, interview, 12 March 2021.

while he was still able to. Robert often visited from London, spending an occasional week at a time when he could. By the beginning of October 1987 it was clear the end was near, and Walter retired to bed under the care of his sister Maggie. The four siblings, Helena and Rose, Robert and Evelyn, gathered at the Old Schoolhouse and in the early hours of Tuesday 13 October, their father lapsed into a coma and died, just a month short of his eighty-fourth birthday.[421]

Following the funeral and memorial service, the family decided to produce a memorial edition of an anthology of contemplative verse and prose, which Walter had had published in 1950 when he was Headmaster of Winchester. Entitled *The Sword of the Spirit*, its origins lay in the wartime years when he was High Master of St Paul's during the school's fairly chaotic wartime evacuation to the countryside. At morning school assembly, rather than focus on traditional prayers, he would read a piece of poetry or prose that he felt would prompt the boys to think and contemplate beyond the information that they learned during the school day. It was an intellectual and eclectic selection, from the Psalms and St Paul to Francis Drake, with Milton, George Herbert and Gerald Manley Hopkins in the mix. With a jacket design by Walter's elder daughter Helena Wakefield, the memorial edition was published by the charitable Friends of Winchester College, to whom the family assigned the copyright and any profits that might accrue.[422]

As with Uncle Pendy, however, the Oakeshott children felt their father deserved greater public recognition beyond his teaching and headmasterships, especially for his historical, literary and artistic work, and the *Men Without Work* report. In 1992 they commissioned John Dancy to write his biography. Robert was much involved in the project and brought in Rose's son Jasper to help track down various sources of evidence. This took Robert to South Africa, both for this project and for his own family interest. He went to Lydenburg, where his father had been born, hoping to track down details about his grandfather's work and death there, and perhaps contact his

---

[421] Dancy, *Walter Oakeshott*, pp 323–324.

[422] Foreword to the Memorial Edition, *The Sword of the Spirit: a meditative and devotional anthology* (The Friends of Winchester College, 1991).

grandmother's Fraser family. Robert and Evelyn went there together again in 1995, the year their father's biography was published.[423]

* * *

While all this memorial publishing was going on, Robert decided he would retire from the directorship of Job Ownership Limited when he reached the age of 65 in 1998; and he felt duty bound to put his knowledge and experience on record, to pass on to his successors. It would be his *magnum opus*, his passing gift to the cause of employee ownership, involving a comprehensive discussion of its theoretical background and rationale, followed by a series of more than twenty detailed case studies of employee-owned businesses from the UK, the US, France, Germany, Italy, Spain and Hungary. He had had personal involvement in most of them and was not afraid to illustrate and discuss the small minority of failures alongside the majority of successes. He worked on the book through the late 1990s and it was finally published in 2000.[424] He dedicated the book to Anne and Willie Charlton, 'for their friendship and support over many years', and to Margaret Elliott, 'for her friendship and support over nearly as many years and for her stunning leadership of employee-owned ventures'.

There was considerable concern within the movement when Robert retired from direct involvement in JOL in 1998. To all practical purposes Robert *was* JOL, and despite it being the leading thinktank, facilitator and promoter of employee ownership in Britain and abroad, it seemed impossible to imagine JOL without Robert. But he had left it in safe hands. David Erdal succeeded him as Executive Director, with James Cornford still as Chairman. The John Lewis Partnership provided the essential financial backing that kept JOL alive during this critical period, with important support also from Tullis Russell, Scott Bader, Unity Trust and the Baxi Partnership, each of whom was represented by a director on the board.[425]

---

[423] John Dancy, *Walter Oakeshott. A Diversity of Gifts* (Michael Russell, Norwich, 1995).

[424] Robert Oakeshott, *Jobs and Fairness. The Logic and Experience of Employee Ownership* (Michael Russell, Norwich, 2000).

[425] Andrew Gunn, email communication, 27 September 2022.

Ironically, Robert's stepping aside was potentially an opportunity for JOL to adapt to a changing world. Andrew Gunn of Scott Bader took over the chairmanship of JOL on James Cornford's retirement in 2002. David Erdal stepped down as Director of JOL and with Ann Tyler holding the fort for a while, Gunn realised a clear business plan was needed before the appointment of a new Executive Director. Patrick Burns, a consultant who had written on industrial democracy and was committed to employee ownership, was brought into the discussion.

Employee ownership was on the rise, but the CBI was not interested in the sector. There was no regular forum at which employee-owned companies could regularly meet, share experiences and ideas, and speak with the power of a representative body. Patrick Burns drafted a strategy that would lead to the conversion of JOL into a membership organisation. The plan received the unanimous support of the JOL board and, after advertisement and interview, Patrick Burns was appointed the new Executive Director.

Although Robert remained on the board during this transition period, he seldom attended meetings. It was under Patrick Burns' leadership

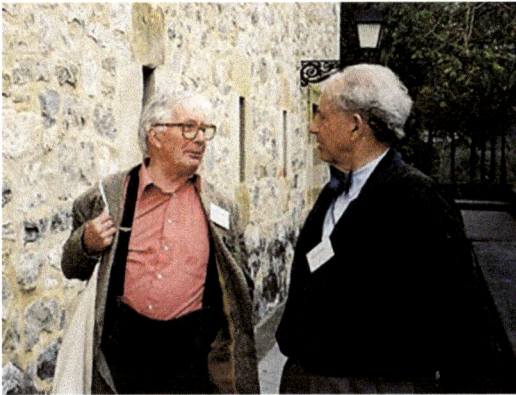

Despite stepping aside from running JOL in 1998, Robert retained an active interest in promoting employee ownership, here at Mondragón with an Australian academic in 2002.
(By kind permission of David Wheatcroft)

that JOL became the representative body for the Employee Ownership sector in 2004. Robert was appointed Founder President, though he had dropped out of involvement by then. JOL re-formed itself as the Employee Ownership Association (EOA) in 2007. From there it grew from strength to strength, the provisions of the Finance Act of 2014 opening the way for employee ownership to become a recognised sector of the British economy; and from under 30 members in 2005 the EOA had in excess of 500 members by 2021.[426]

* * *

Robert was not a man ever to stand still and at the time of his retirement from JOL he set up a charity called 'Art Leisure Enterprises'. It began trading in January 2000 as 'Make Your Mark: A Ceramic Painting and BYO Café' in the Clifton district of Bristol. He may have been inspired by his sister Helena, who was an artist, and her husband, who was a potter in the Isles of Scilly. Make Your Mark provided a wide range of bare ceramics – plates, mugs and other items – which, for a small fee, people could decorate for themselves or as unique gifts, with their own choice of colours and designs. There were books and staff to consult, and Make Your Mark did the glazing. Robert saw it as a benefit for people whose working lives involved high levels of stress. He funded the operation himself, purchasing the leasehold on 97 Whiteladies Road, and raising a loan of £30,000 from the Unity Trust Bank for working capital. In his customary manner, he brought in his friends, in this case Quentin and Rowena Seddon, to serve alongside him as directors. Robert had originally hoped that Make Your Mark would become an employee-owned business, but it never really took off and after a couple of years it had to close.[427]

* * *

---

[426] Interviews: David Erdal (2 December 2020), Patrick Burns (15 December 2020), Andrew Gunn (24 November 2020); and https://employeeownership.co.uk/about-the-employee-ownership-association/about-our-founder-robert-oakeshott/ – [accessed 2 March 2022].

[427] Quentin Seddon, interview, 21 January 2021; numerous documents in a folder in *Oakeshott Papers*.

Robert's main focus following his retirement from JOL was his charitable work, much of which he had already been engaged in through the 1990s. He was not somebody who simply wrote a cheque for a good cause. It was in his very nature to become involved. If he was inspired by an idea that he felt could really make a difference, even if it was only in embryo, he would do everything in his power to help it come to fruition.

In 1991 he met up with an old friend from Zambia, Richard Jolly, who was now Acting Executive Director of UNICEF and had been knighted 'for services to international development'. Such was the range of Robert's friends. They fell into conversation about Africa, the result of which was their joint conclusion that girls' education was the neglected solution to sustainable development in rural Africa. Robert made inquiries and heard that there was a woman who was doing some work with girls' education in Zimbabwe. He tracked her down in early 1992: her name was Ann Cotton and she lived near Cambridge.

Having taught and worked with girls excluded from mainstream education in South London, Ann Cotton developed an interest in women's human rights and girls' education. In 1991 she went to Zimbabwe to do a study under the umbrella of Womankind Worldwide on why so few girls attended school in rural Africa. The standard literature insisted it was a cultural issue, but Ann found quite the opposite: rural women and their daughters were very keen on education. The problem was the circularity of poverty. It was only with education that they could escape poverty, and yet they could not afford to go to school, which, even if the tuition was free, always involved some fees for food, uniforms or other necessities. Ann knew that with education they would have access to good paid employment, and they would not be so vulnerable if they went into town for work. Furthermore, they would be more in control of their own fertility and less vulnerable to HIV/AIDS, by then a serious pandemic in the region.[428] Furthermore, among the other good consequences of girls' education are the benefits for agriculture. In many countries women do the farming as well as the housework and an ability to read and understand the

---

[428] Ann Cotton, interview, 15 January 2021.

instructions on a packet of seeds, a bag of fertiliser or a bottle of medicine for animals, as well as for humans, brings enormous benefits.

Ann was determined to do something about this, but she knew nothing about forming a charity; besides the support and connections of her husband, she was short of allies; and she had no real experience of Africa. Then, out of the blue, she had a phone call from this extraordinary-sounding man. He was very keen on girls' education in rural Africa, and he wanted to come and talk to her about Zimbabwe. At first, she thought it was a hoax, with his very upper-class accent, and 'What, What!' at the end of sentences. But in those days 'even potential allies were not to be dismissed lightly', and she met him off the London train the next day.

From his voice on the phone, Ann imagined she would be meeting a tall, distinguished, rather old-fashioned-looking gentleman. And yet when Robert came through the barrier, she instantly knew it was him. They went to The Green Man pub in Grantchester and talked for three hours. They clicked immediately, despite being from different generations, and Ann's Welsh origins contrasting with Robert's English background. They were both 'unconventional' and very into education. There was a meeting of minds in the way they both thought about poverty. Ann had looked at the conventional model of white-dominated charities in Africa and wanted something different: run as far as possible by and for the African women who were the beneficiaries. Robert agreed. He was very knowledgeable about charities and was prepared to back her all the way.

He contacted Lady Jane Willoughby and she was happy to have a hand in the project. She organised a fund-raising event at her house in London, and there Ann began to be introduced to Robert's large circle of friends. The endorsement of Robert and his network was a huge boost for Ann, and through them she was able to build her own community and support system. She found Robert's friends, 'a great quirky group of people, English eccentric and unconventional in every sense', but warm, generous and very supportive.[429]

Ann persuaded Robert to join the charity's initial board and 'we shaped

---

[429] Ann Cotton, interview, 15 January 2021.

the organisation's growth around my kitchen table'.[430] Lucy Lake was hired to run the office and the charity, CAMFED (Campaign for Female Education), was registered in 1993. That year it paid for 32 girls to go to secondary school in Zimbabwe. Thereafter, the number increased year on year and the charity expanded into Ghana, Zambia, Malawi and Tanzania. Robert was a great sounding-board for Ann – she could bounce ideas off him, and they did not always agree. When Ann suggested an alumni association for the mutual support of their school graduates, Robert felt this was social and not part of their remit, but Ann brought it to the board and pushed and pushed it until Robert gave way. Some years later, after the CAMFED Association (CAMA) had proved its worth in becoming a major peer support and leadership network for African women,[431] Robert admitted to Ann, 'I've never been so happy to be proved wrong'.[432]

* * *

Another major charity to which Robert contributed much was concerned with the welfare of inmates in the English prison system. The germ of the idea had come from Lady Anne Tree, an eccentric aristocrat and daughter of the Duke of Devonshire. She had been a prison visitor for thirty years from 1949, first at Holloway prison for women and then at Wandsworth. She had been struck by the wasted lives of long-term prisoners and felt they should be taught to do skilled work that could be sold at a good price. This would not only provide them with some money to save for their release, or to support their family; it would also enhance their sense of self-worth. She herself had been to the Royal School of Needlework and had always done needlepoint at home. She found the repetitive work very meditative. Her mother-in-law, Nancy Lancaster, owned the upmarket interior design shop Colefax & Fowler, which could provide a marketing outlet for their work. And with generous help from the Royal School of Needlework,

---

[430] *Oakeshott Papers*, Ann Cotton, proposal for a 'Robert Oakeshott Memorial Scholarship'.

[431] https://camfed.org/what-we-do/how-we-operate/camfed-association/ – [accessed 3 October 2021].

[432] Ann Cotton, interview, 15 January 2021.

a group of lifers made two wonderful carpets. ... One was a copy of an old Russian carpet of African heads and the other a design by Tom Parr of Colefax & Fowler. Each went for £10,000, one to the Head of the television station CBS and the other to the head of Ford cars, both in New York.[433]

It had taken more than five years of meticulous work in very difficult conditions, and yet Home Office prison regulations prevented the women inmates who had done the work from receiving even one penny of the money. This was in the 1980s and the Conservative Government considered payment for work in prison cells would be tantamount to rewarding prisoners for their crimes. Despite being from a family of enormously high standing and with links to the Judiciary and to Parliament, Lady Anne could not obtain the necessary permission for her charity. She did not understand how to lobby, terrier-like, in the House of Commons and she hated bureaucracy.[434] In frustration, she told one minister, 'It is shits like you who would let this country down!'[435] Fearing she might have gone too far, she was on the point of giving up when her daughter Isabella, who had earlier worked for Robert in the JOL office, introduced her to Robert Oakeshott. Suddenly, everything seemed possible. She had an energetic and enthusiastic ally, with a reputation for getting things done. And as she willingly acknowledged, it was Robert who got the show on the road.

He approached Anthony Gater in typical Robert fashion, 'You have nothing to do. Become a trustee.'[436] The three met at Lady Anne's house off the King's Road and decided to call the charity 'Fine Cell Work (FCW)', with the work being for men as well as women. But one essential ingredient was permission for the inmates to be properly paid for their work. Where Lady Anne felt no one was listening, Robert, as he had at

---

[433] Lady Anne Tree's Foreword in *FCW Newsletter*, August 2005, copy in a folder marked FCW in *Oakeshott Papers*.

[434] Isabella Tree, interview, 15 December 2020.

[435] Quoted in her obituary by Peter Stanford in *The Guardian*, 20 August 2010.

[436] Anthony Gater, interview, 14 October 2020.

Balliol, was happy to keep running at the wall.[437] Finally, after further years of Robert's terrier-like lobbying, Angela Rumbold, Minister of State at the Home Office, invited them to a meeting and gave them the go-ahead. Prisoners would now be allowed to profit from their cell work, up to a maximum of £500 a year.[438]

Robert got a lawyer to perform the legal work and register the charity, and in due course he got a senior civil servant to persuade the Governor of Bristol Prison to allow them in on a trial basis. Lady Anne and Robert each seeded the charity with £2,000 and with this behind them, they got started in 1997.[439]

Katy Emck was employed as Director – initially part-time, working from home. Katy, who had experience of prison work in America, first met Lady Anne and Robert at the JOL office near Victoria Station. According to Isabella, who had introduced her friend Katy to her mother and to Robert, the three of them together made that extraordinary business work: Robert the idealist, Lady Anne a bit more pragmatic, and Katy held it all together.[440] Robert had initially struck Katy as 'a slightly fusty intellectual philanthropist, dishevelled, but incredibly nice with an energetic spirit'. As she recalls, her employment was very informal:

> Both Robert and Lady Anne were the least bureaucratic people you could ever imagine – free spirit people, visionaries both. But not organised people. So FCW was very informal, natural, even amateurish, but very sincere. Robert gave me a tutorial on how to make a business plan, and one of my many jobs at that point was always to ensure there was wine at board meetings, at least for the first 10 years while Robert was an active board member.
>
> Robert didn't impose himself. It was very much Lady Anne's charity. What he did was support me and Lady Anne. Through lunches, he introduced me to many people. The informality suited me fine and left me

---

[437] Charlie Burrell, interview, 4 January 2021.

[438] Katy Emck, interview, 16 November 2020.

[439] Lady Anne Tree, *FCW Newsletter*, August 2005.

[440] Isabella Tree, interview, 15 December 2020.

free to bring the thing to life. He never criticised or tried to rein me in – I was pleased, and it started to work.[441]

Experts in needlepoint and some of the top names in the fashion industry volunteered their services to design the work and tutor the inmates, whom Robert affectionately referred to as 'the lads', and 'the lasses'. Initially they focussed on embroidering cushions and the quality of their work received high praise in the fashion press. The prison service, too, appreciated its therapeutic value and Wormwood Scrubs and other prisons began to open their doors to the charity. As one inmate, Simon, explained:

> … [FCW] has given me something to channel my frustration into. It's therapeutic because it's repetitive. It puts you into a zone and you just focus and everything else fades away. All you see is the needle.[442]

About three years into the work, when it was still on a very small scale, Lady Anne's son-in-law Charlie Burrell, who had been brought onto the FCW board, proposed having a high-profile reception and auction of 100 celebrity-designed embroidered cushions at his family estate, Knepp Castle in West Sussex, with Isabella ('Izzy') and Charlie footing the bill. The design of each cushion would be the face of some well-known celebrity, or an image submitted by them. People such as Mick Jagger, Jerry Hall, David Bailey, Ralph Fiennes and Emma Thompson sent their own designs, while Home Secretary Jack Straw sent a photo of his face. Friends of the Tree, Burrell and Oakeshott families and various celebrities were invited and Tim Wonnacott of Sotheby's, who lived nearby, was auctioneer.[443] The cushions fetched high prices, with Anthony Gater recalling,

> It was noticeable that as the bidding died down, a lone voice continued bidding – and Robert ended up with more cushions than he could possibly need.[444]

---

[441] Katy Emck, interview, 16 November 2020.

[442] *FCW Newsletter*, 2005.

[443] Isabella Tree, interview, 15 December 2020; Charlie Burrell, interview, 4 January 2021.

[444] Anthony Gater, interview, 14 October 2020.

Before the auction, FCW had about £5,000 in the bank; after it, £30,000.[445] The auction really helped FCW to take off. Some of their work was later displayed in an exhibition at the Victoria and Albert Museum, and the charity is still thriving.

* * *

One further charity in which Robert was directly involved was 'More Transplants Please (MTP)', aimed in particular at kidney transplants, for whom there were never enough donors in Britain. It grew out of a meeting at Robert's flat in 2005, with Stephen Cadney, Maggie Harris and Ann and Chris Seddon. Robert had been impressed by Rafael Matesanz' 'Spanish Model', which was based upon assumed consent and had led through the 1990s to a continuous improvement in post-mortem organ donation in Spain.[446] There was some difficulty in registering MTP as a charity, as they wanted a change in the law and that was declared to be political, but in 2007 Chris Seddon sent a copy of Matesanz and Miranda's book on the Spanish Model to the Charity Commission and with months the charity was registered.[447]

[445] Katy Emck, interview, 16 November 2020.

[446] Rafael Matesanz, 'A decade of continuous improvement in cadaveric organ donation: the Spanish Model', *Nefrologia*, Vol. XXI, Supplemento 5, 2001.

[447] R. Matesanz and B. Miranda (eds), *Organ Donation for Transplantation: The Spanish Model* (Anla Medica, Madrid, 1996).

CHAPTER 20

Robert Oakeshott – Memories

Robert appears to have had just one real regret in his life and that was his failure to marry – his marriage to Kate Shuckburgh was too short to count. He would have loved to have had a partner with whom to share the highs and lows of his extraordinary life. Above all, he would have loved to have had children of his own and been able to give them the love and one-to-one educative attention he felt he did not get in his own childhood. They would certainly have had an unusual and unpredictable life.

Robert was fortunate, however, in the love and affection of his friends and his siblings who invited him to be godfather to their children. It was a privilege that Robert treasured. He did his best to remember birthdays and would slip £10 notes or book tokens into birthday and Christmas cards. Evelyn's daughter Isabel recalls the occasion Robert visited them in

Robert enjoying the company of his goddaughter Julia,
with her mother Caroline Cox-Johnson.
(By kind permission of Caroline Cox-Johnson)

Scotland, soon after they had moved to Edinburgh. She was about six and godfather Uncle Robert took her to a pet shop. Without a thought in the world beyond the desire to make her happy, he told her she could chose whatever pet she liked. He certainly succeeded in making her happy, as she chose a little black kitten. Her parents had not been consulted and they would have responsibility for the adult cat for years, but they took it in their stride. That was Robert.[448] On another occasion he wrote to Isabel's sisters Anstice and Veronica telling them, 'I had a dream it was your birthday', but not being sure, he sent them both watches.

When he was home from Africa in the 1960s and early 1970s, he liked to visit his sister Helena and her husband Humphrey Wakefield for Christmas in the Isles of Scilly. The children loved his visits, their overriding impression being his warmth and humour, his eyes always twinkling as though life were a great joke. He would arrive with no luggage, no spare clothes, just a brief-case full of papers, a cooked ham and a bottle of whisky. The children were thrilled by his eccentricity. He was fascinating to be around, with his sellotaped glasses all askew. He spoke in what his niece Cynthia could only describe as 'extraordinary Edwardian English' and the children would snigger as he punctuated his sentences with '… What! What!' But they loved the way he treated them as though they were adults, and he took them out to a real adult lunch at the Castle Restaurant, somewhere very upmarket where they had never been before.[449] The youngest of the Wakefield children, Neville, did not really know Robert until after he came back from Africa, but he recalls how exciting it was to have a reputedly eccentric uncle in Africa, somewhere so far beyond the limited horizons of the Isles of Scilly. And when Uncle Robert arrived for a visit, he more than lived up to expectations. As Anstice and Veronica recall, 'he took us all seriously, like adults … respecting us as individuals, and leaving us empowered'.[450]

---

[448] Isabel Oakeshott, interview, 5 April 2021.

[449] Lalage Wakefield, interview, 26 November 2020; Cynthia Rickman, interview, 10 January 2021; Neville Wakefield, interview, 28 November 2020.

[450] Anstice Oakeshott, interview, 24 April 2021; Veronica Oakeshott, interview, 9 October 2020.

Rose's daughter Helena recalls family gatherings for Christmas in the Isles of Scilly when Robert would assume the role of organiser of games, which included teaching the children 'crazy bridge', his favourite card game. Later, after Noel had died, there were several big family Christmases at the Old Schoolhouse in Eynsham, with Robert 'holding court with Aunt Emilie, and their spirited arguments about farming in the Cotswolds'. Later still, in about 2000, when Helena was a single mother with three children, Robert invited them to Bristol and spent a day with the children painting pottery in his Make Your Mark café.[451]

At his Lichen Court flat in Finsbury Park Robert used to hold an annual Christmas carol party, open house for all his friends. Those who had been away, out of the country, perhaps for years, always knew they could just turn up and friendships were rejuvenated. He particularly loved to throw parties for his nephews, nieces and godchildren and, later, for the next generation too. This might be his annual children's Christmas party, which included all the children of the neighbourhood.[452] He had an over-the-top, circus approach to children's parties, the priority being for the children to have fun, and the more unusual and memorable fun, the better. He would lay on a conjurer, who could produce a real white rabbit out of a hat, and he would organise 'indoor fireworks', which buzzed, fizzed and threw sparks around the room.

Besides having fun with the children, he was keen on helping young people setting out into the adult world. It was an education in itself being a niece, nephew or godchild of Robert Oakeshott.

When his niece Cynthia, up from the Isles of Scilly, went to music college in London, he invited her round on numerous occasions to dinner at his Lloyd Baker Street flat. There would be high-powered guests with their high-powered conversation, but Robert always made her feel included, as she sat and listened and absorbed it all. When Rose's daughter Helena was only about twelve, Robert had taken her to dinner with Jo Grimond and others, where for the first time she saw real debate going

---

[451] Helena Gaunt, interview, 4 January 2021.

[452] Neves Pereira, interview, 8 November 2021.

on. She sat there enthralled, soaking it all up. Robert never talked down to anybody, whatever their age, class or colour.[453]

Following the death in February 1997 of his great friend Antony Martin, Robert paid close attention to his son Nat, doing his best to be something of a substitute father for him. When Nat was about seventeen, Robert tried to interest him in going to Oxford and invited him to a large dinner at Balliol to meet some of the dons. Included in the party was another of his godchildren, Rose's son Jasper, who had just applied to Oxford.[454] Meanwhile, Robert found tasks for Nat to do, including going to the British Newspaper Library, then at Colindale in North London, to research *The Times* for the Great Exhibition of 1851, to see if there was any mention of the sale of the Herend porcelain dinner service to Queen Victoria. It was not information Robert needed for his work, but he thought Nat might find it interesting and the research would be useful experience. He always paid for these sorts of educative tasks, which was a big deal for a teenager just leaving school. He would invite Nat round to his flat for lunch to meet interesting people such as Sir Samuel Brittan, economics columnist for the *Financial Times*, Mark Tully, the BBC's India Correspondent, or Lawrence Cockcroft, who had worked on African rural development and was co-founder of Transparency International, dedicated to the fight against global corruption.[455]

He employed Thecla Mallinson, Tatiana's daughter, part-time after leaving university. She worked with him in the JOL office, by then near Victoria station. She had no experience, but she learned a lot – office management and accounts. He took her to business meetings with the John Lewis Partnership and others, where she could have felt very young and out of her depth, but in Robert's company she felt at ease as his Personal Assistant.[456] Thecla's school friend Marina Johnston took over from her as Robert's PA, and despite the generational difference, found him 'an unusually congenial friend'. Robert would hammer away on his old Amstrad, two-

---

[453] Helena Gaunt, interview, 4 January 2021.

[454] Jasper Gaunt, interview, 17 December 2020.

[455] Nat Martin, interview, 22 December 2020.

[456] Thecla Mallinson, interview, 7 July 2021.

finger typing, very fast, and would only break for lunch, usually a take-in soup or salad; or if there was something to celebrate, it would be round the corner to Chimes, an old-fashioned restaurant in Pimlico, for some 'no-nonsense' English cooking, with red wine. Then straight back to work.[457]

* * *

Robert's inheritance from his Uncle Pendy enabled him, in about 1990, to double the size of his flat by buying the other top floor flat across the landing, effectively combining the two flats into one, giving him now four bedrooms together with a huge living room. He had three long, low bookshelves filled with a large number of books, some of them review copies from *The Economist, The Spectator* or the *Financial Times.* The collection reflected his wide range of interests – Cuba, cooperatives, history, economics, public policy, Marxism and Alice in Wonderland.

Even before the enlargement of the flat, Robert's place was always somewhere for friends in need, children of friends, and even friends of friends to 'crash', and the extension across the landing meant there was more room for more visitors, with some people staying for months. When he heard that his Slovenian colleague and friend Aleksandra Mrčela was coming to London as a visiting researcher at the London School of Economics, he offered his hospitality, and she, her husband and their two small children stayed in his flat for a year.[458]

On another occasion he hosted a group of African trade unionists and laid on a party for them, inviting Marie Little down to play her radical contemporary folk music – it became in essence a mini folk festival, much to the delight of his African guests. If Robert wanted to lay on a party, he would often invite Marie to come and play, and she, who was very fond of him, was always pleased to respond to his call.

Robert was a very social animal who liked nothing better than good company, conversation and plenty of red wine. Through his final decade, the 2000s, lunches and dinners at Robert's flat were regular occurrences,

---

[457] Marina Johnston, interview, 20 March 2021.

[458] Aleksandra Mrčela, interview, 18 January 2021.

featuring the *FT* tablecloth and a variety of stock dishes that went beyond his early penchant for fish pie. Roast leg of lamb was a particular favourite, with perhaps salmon pâté to start, but also more humble dishes such as corned beef or liver and bacon. He would put the roast in the oven, but then expect his female guests to take charge of the rest of the meal. Robert provided the wine, plenty of it, and of course the stimulating conversation. He chose his guests carefully, according to his own ideas of who they would like to meet and have dinner with. And he would enjoy seeing how the combination and conversation sparkled. If he felt the sparkle was a little lacking, he would throw out some controversial topic that was bound to lead to contrary opinions. And if the conversation lagged, there was always something to read from the *FT* tablecloth that would set them off again.

Andrew Gunn thought Robert's flat was,

> … more like an undergraduate pad – lots of very interesting books, and rickety furniture – lovable, no pretence. On one occasion Tom Holzinger turned up with his two sons for a meal, and there was a woman friend (don't remember who) who had probably made the fish pie. Anyway, at the end of the meal the topic of conversation got onto the legacy of Stalin, I don't know – seems most improbable in the 21st century, but that was Robert, always questioning. There ensued quite a heated discussion for about a quarter of an hour between Robert and Tom about the legacy of Stalin, while the other four of us just listened. Typical of Robert, having a meal with friends always got into interesting discussions, and at this 21st century lunch Stalin cropped up.[459]

And his niece Veronica remembers from his later years,

> … Lunch with Robert was a weird juxtaposition – high powered discussion and plain fun. We had to make sure Robert was near to the table not to drop anything. He needed a bit of management. It could be quite chaotic, with Robert not worried about dropping food – his mind was on higher things. His trousers held up with string, it was always possible they would fall down.[460]

---

[459] Andrew Gunn, interview, 24 November 2020.

[460] Veronica Oakeshott, interview, 20 October 2020.

Much as Robert's family and friends appreciated his sociability, humour and general good company, he could be very irritating, insisting on trivial details of arrangements, which others were making on his behalf, or taking an uncompromising stance on some point of argument. Although he made an effort to be inclusive, he could be quite intimidating – 'he assumed you had as good a knowledge of the world as he himself: "What's your view of the real outcome of the Franco-Prussian War?"'[461]

The vicar of his local church in Stoke Newington was always somewhat daunted on receiving a phone call from Robert asking for a visit, which happened quite often in Robert's declining years. The vicar felt some great trepidation because some topic of discussion with which he was unfamiliar would always take place – a new book, or social policy – and he felt he ought to be able to keep up. Robert's mind was very alert, despite his progressive illness.[462]

He had a very clear relationship with Christianity. He accepted the different denominations as a product of history. What particularly attracted him to the High Anglican Church were the hymns and the historicism of its ceremonial and atmosphere, especially in its elegant old churches, and from this he drew his spirituality. He regularly attended the old church in Stoke Newington, putting £10 in the collection box, but he could not take in all the more mystical precepts of Church belief. He was happy to do a reading for the Sunday service, but he would not read for Easter as he could not be doing with the idea of the Resurrection. He firmly believed in the teachings of Jesus, what he called his 'social policy'. This was the essence of his Christianity.[463]

* * *

Through the late 2000s Robert's personal lifestyle, his smoking and

---

[461] Veronica Oakeshott, interview, 20 October 2020.

[462] Andrew Gunn, interview, 24 November 2020, quoting from the vicar's address at Robert's funeral.

[463] David Wheatcroft, interview, 24 November 2020; and Andrew Gunn, interview, 24 November 2020.

Evelyn and Robert at their '150 Not Out' party, 26 July 2008.
(By kind permission of the Oakeshott family)

drinking and lack of exercise began to take its toll. He had lived his life as he had wanted, and he never complained about the consequences. In the mid-2000s he and Evelyn had both been diagnosed with prostate cancer. Evelyn, who loved the outdoors and kept physically fit, responded well to treatment, whereas Robert had a hard time with the treatment and its side effects.

In 2008 the family threw a joint 75th birthday party at Charlotte's family home of Stonesfield Manor near Woodstock. The party was hosted to celebrate the twins' – Cargs' and Rods' – achievement of '150 Not Out'. It was a great party with a marquee in the garden and family and friends from far and wide. The physical contrast between the twins was striking, with Evelyn looking as though he was in his sixties and Robert as though he was in his eighties.

For some years Robert had chaired the Lichen Court residents' committee and he was well-known and well-liked in his local community. He did not venture far from home. The butcher cashed his cheques and saved him the best pieces of lamb's liver. His local church clubbed together to buy him a new jumper, assuming his scruffiness was through poverty, whereas in fact, thanks to Uncle Pendy, he was really quite wealthy.[464] Neves Pereira, who worked for Rose who lived nearby, came in to clean his flat. She saw him as a very humble but happy man, with never a complaint despite his infirmities. In cold weather he would be sitting with no socks because he could not bend down to put them on. But his door was always open, with a big welcome for any family, friends or neighbours who might drop by. And then he fell, badly, backwards down the stairs, and it became clear that the end could not be that far away. But he was determined to carry on living in his flat.

Mike Tiller, his wife and younger daughter made their last international trip to London to see him:

> We spent a couple of weeks with him, still in his flat, perfectly compos mentis, though not mobile. He could shuffle around but no longer go up or down stairs.
>
> We spent most evenings inviting round someone like Alison Kirton whom we'd both known in Botswana. I'd go to the local grocer; my wife and daughter would cook, and we'd have long chats in the evenings. All day during the day, he'd reminisce and chat. Still mentally very sharp, he would sharply correct me whenever I mis-remembered. He clearly knew his time was limited and it was as though he was downloading his life. For me that was very important in coming to terms with his passing.[465]

In the summer of 2010 Robert had a stroke and ended up in hospital. The stroke was relatively minor, but in hospital he had a fall and a second stroke, more severe this time. It was clear he could no longer live on his own and the family found him a place in a care home near Hammersmith, West London.

He was partially paralysed, his vision was affected and he was in considerable pain, especially in his back. It took a while before he was receiving proper painkillers and medication for his cancer. Charlotte set

[464] Veronica Oakeshott, interview, 10 October 2020.
[465] Mike Tiller, interview, 12 November 2020.

up a hardback notebook for his visitors – of whom there were many – to record their visit and observations about Robert. With visits recorded virtually every day from mid-August, sometimes several visits in one day, it is a unique record of his final nine months. With his eyesight poor, and his phenomenal powers of concentration now largely gone, he could no longer read, but he had his radio for news and soothing music, and visitors brought in audio books, cold drinks and treats like ice-cream or smoked salmon.

His condition varied from day to day, and he was only able to concentrate on brief 'conversations'. He was perked up mostly by reminiscences, especially from visiting friends from his years in Africa or Sunderlandia. He enjoyed a Christmas carol party in late December, but by May 2011 he was clearly fading. It was arranged that Marie Little would come down to visit. She brought her guitar and at a small gathering round his bed she played some of his favourite songs, with Robert managing to join in with some of the words. 'She's quite lovely, isn't she!', he confided to Charlotte.

There were plans for another party for the twins' birthday in July; but it was not to be. By mid-June he was barely conscious. When Veronica and her husband Mark – of whom Robert had observed, 'a wonderful old chap' – came to tell him they were going to Kenya, working for Fairtrade, she was pleased to observe 'a little sense of a smile'. Knowing she would not see him again she was reassured and could depart in the knowledge that her Uncle Robert approved.[466] Shortly afterwards, on 21 June 2011, Robert Oakeshott died.

* * *

His local church was packed for the funeral, and likewise for the memorial service at Balliol College Chapel in December 2011. Charles Keen, who read the memorial sermon, highlighted the difficulty of doing justice to the theme of Robert Oakeshott's life:

On the one hand, you had the hilarious jokes and escapades which characterised his life among his friends. On the other, but by no means in

[466] Veronica Oakeshott, interview, 20 October 2020.

conflict with the jokes and fun, was his dedication to good causes and the remarkable list of his achievements.

… He was, I would say, a virtuoso talker. He was a very serious thinker too, but, as he discoursed on serious issues, jokes and frivolity would be woven into the fabric, and the effect was spell-binding and enormous fun. It was that combination of fun and penetrating discourse that made us all love his company so much. He enhanced all our lives, just with his company and wit and warm-heartedness.[467]

Robert Oakeshott was not only a great thinker and enormous fun; he was also a great doer. He knew he was a man of privilege, and this must partly have been what spurred him to help others less fortunate than himself. But he was never a top-down philanthropist. He worked *with* people, getting his hands – and his clothes – grubby in the process. He had the kind of 'moral magnetism' that drew his friends, and perfect strangers, to support, with their time and/or finance, whatever project he was working on. With his charm, charisma and humour, he was a difficult man to refuse.

In terms of his legacy, both the founders of Fine Cell Work and CAMFED – Lady Anne Tree and Ann Cotton respectively – were happy to admit that it was Robert who got their charities off the ground, and without his energy, know-how and determination, these would never have been able, not only to start, but to go on to become the great successes that they are today. Robert had a particular affinity for CAMFED, taking him back as it did to the roots of many of his life's inspirations in Zambia, Zimbabwe and Botswana. 'Of all the "good causes" with which I am associated', he wrote to Johnny Grimond in 1997, 'that of girls' education in sub-Saharan Africa is, with only one possible exception, the venture that I value most highly'.[468]

His greatest legacy, however, must be his achievements in the field of cooperative production; what he saw as an alternative model to untamed corporate capitalism on the one hand, and the bureaucratic stifling of initiative in nationalised industry on the other.

---

[467] Charles Keen, 'In Memoriam, a Sermon: Robert Oakeshott', 3 December 2011.

[468] *JJ Grimond Papers*, RO to Johnny Grimond, 6 November 1997.

Robert did not 'invent' employee ownership. Various forms of cooperative ventures had been around since at least the Fenwick Weavers of 1761, and the John Lewis Partnership had updated the concept from 1929. But it was Robert Oakeshott, inspired by van Rensburg in Botswana, who had the courage and initiative to put this 'Third World development idea' into practice in England. In doing so, he led a new movement from the 1970s that was focussed on profitable businesses, which countered the capitalist norms and proved that employee ownership could be a practical and growing sector of the current world. To his critics who pointed out that his Sunderlandia cooperative had to be wound up after six years, Robert enjoyed countering that most new capitalist enterprises fail to last six years, but nobody suggests on those grounds that the capitalist system is invalid.

Sunderlandia proved it could be done. Lessons learned there, although never all admitted by Robert – 'I choose not to examine those internal mirrors too closely'[469] – sent him back to the drawing board and which, backed by the resoundingly successful model of Mondragón and much theoretical research, led to the founding of Job Ownership Limited. Thereafter, two decades in the cause of industrial democracy and justice and fairness at work put employee ownership on the business map of the United Kingdom and the Western world. Today's Employee Ownership Association (EOA) is Robert Oakeshott's legacy, a point recognised by the EOA's annual Robert Oakeshott Memorial Lecture, addressed in its first year in 2013 by Nick Clegg, Deputy Prime Minister and leader of the Liberal Democratic Party, the successor to Jo Grimond's Liberal Party. The Finance Act of the following year placed employee ownership in the mainstream.

In 1999, shortly after he officially retired from Job Ownership Limited, some of his closest friends had laid on a dinner at Balliol College in honour of Robert, the one among them who had achieved the most since their time together in Oxford. Maurice Keen booked the Hall while Lady Jane Willoughby de Eresby, Francis and Maureen Nichols and Willie and Anne Charlton did the planning and sent out the invitations. It meant a lot to

[469] Lawrence Cockcroft, interview, 11 February 2021.

Robert to receive such high regard from his friends and peers, not least for the fact that the after-dinner speech was delivered by none other than Tom Bingham, who had risen to the height of Lord Chief Justice.[470]

One striking factor in the life of Robert Oakeshott is that, in his own country, he never received public recognition for his work as a philanthropic social reformer of some considerable note, as recognised by his numerous obituaries: in *The Times, The Guardian, The Economist, The Daily Telegraph,* and *Co-operative News.* Several of those whom he mentored and with whom he worked received OBEs. Pratap Chitnis of the Joseph Rowntree Social Services Trust was made a peer, though he claimed he did not know what for, to which Robert responded, 'never mind why, it's the coronet that counts'. Robert was far too modest to have dreamed he deserved an honour, but he would have loved the opportunity to wear ermine, especially as a member of The Skinners' Company. And with his wide-ranging intellect, he would have added much quality and humour to debates. Perhaps he was too independent-minded, or the powers that be feared he might turn up at the palace in a scruffy old jumper; but as photographs in this book illustrate, Robert was quite capable of dressing suitably smartly if he believed the occasion warranted it. Sadly, it may have been the more mundane reason that the Liberal members of the Lords and Commons, who owed him so much for promoting their cause of a 'third' economic model, simply neglected to put him forward for an honour.

It has been suggested that Robert set his personal appearances as a kind of test to weed out superficial people. And as David Erdal has recalled, 'for those who passed test, knowing Robert was one of life's huge privileges. … People always smile when they think back to Robert: he was a true original, and a wonderful inspiration to hundreds of people'.[471]

The loyalty, love and respect of his multitude of friends, and his numerous obituaries, show that he succeeded in his life's purpose, the pursuit of 'the Good'.

---

[470] *Oakeshott Papers,* copy of the invitation: 'Dinner in Honour of Robert Oakeshott'.

[471] *Oakeshott Papers,* David Erdal, 'Robert Oakeshott: Renewing the memory, hero and friend' (unpublished typescript for Employee Ownership Association lecture, 2019).

Index

Index